THE

EVERYTHING

ONLINE BUSINESS BOOK

Use the Internet to build your business

Rob Liflander

Adams Media Corporation
Holbrook, Massachusetts

M000234836

Acknowledgments

Thanks to the best editor and the best wife in the world. Luckily for me, Pam Liflander is one and the same. To Bridget Mintz Testa, thanks for contributing several case studies, article passages, and both general and specific advice. Also much thanks to my family: my children Gabrielle and Cameron, my siblings Julie and Mark, and my mother Leslie. To my step-father Ralph, thanks for all your mentoring and support. And finally, to all the Internet pioneers I have worked with, thank you. Every site I develop turns out to be a fantastic ride.

For my father, Bernard William Liflander

Published by
Adams Media Corporation
260 Center Street, Holbrook, MA 02343. U.S.A.
www.adamsmedia.com

ISBN: 1-58062-320-4

Printed in the United States of America.

J I H G F E D C B

Library of Congress Cataloging-in-Publication Data
Liflander, Rob.
The everything online business book / by Rob Liflander.
    p.   cm.
ISBN 1-58062-320-4
1. Electronic commerce. 2. Electronic mail systems.
3. Internet (Computer network) 4. World Wide Web. I. Title.
HF5548.32.L53 2000
658.8'4—dc21   00-027194

This publication is designed to provide accurate and authoritative information with regard to the subject matter covered. It is sold with the understanding that the publisher is not engaged in rendering legal, accounting, or other professional advice. If legal advice or other expert assistance is required, the services of a competent professional person should be sought.
—From a *Declaration of Principles* jointly adopted by a Committee of the American Bar Association and a Committee of Publishers and Associations

Illustrations by Barry Littmann.

This book is available at quantity discounts for bulk purchases.
For information, call 1-800-872-5627.

Visit our home page at http://www.businesstown.com

Contents

Introduction

So, you're ready to do business online. Welcome! In this book I will help you get there. Whether you are starting a brand new company on the Internet or building a Web site to showcase and supplement your current business, this book is for you. In this book I will take you through the necessary steps for planning, building, marketing, and running your online business.

There are as many reasons for building a Web site as there are businesses on the Internet. For most people, the primary goal of a Web site is an increase in sales and more effective marketing. There are a wide range of other reasons for constructing Web sites including building customer service, furthering employee relations, and even increasing internal production efficiency. These are all admirable goals but go beyond the scope of this book. In this book I will focus primarily on the sales and marketing of your online business.

I have written this book for a broad cross-section of people, from those with little or no experience in doing business online to those who have been online for years. Whether your budget is large or small, I believe this book can be useful for the online business principles I espouse. If followed, these principles are a sure recipe for success. They include:

1. *Devise and follow a set of specific strategic objectives.* The more focused the development effort, the more likely you will achieve your goals.
2. *Organize and design your Web site from your customer's perspective.* Your customer is the one who will be navigating your Web site. Build it with his needs and perceptions in mind.
3. *Make direct analogies to real world, people-to-people business relationships.* Remember, the Web is just another tool by which to do business.
4. *Provide specific calls to action that prompt interaction by your customers.* If you do not ask, you'll never receive.

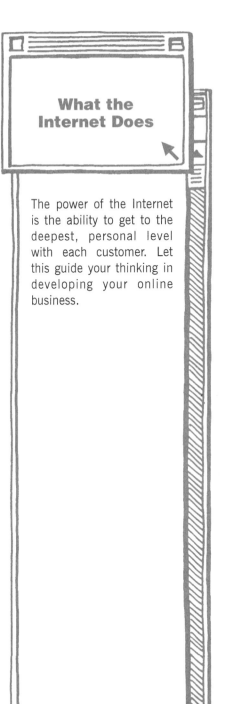

What the Internet Does

The power of the Internet is the ability to get to the deepest, personal level with each customer. Let this guide your thinking in developing your online business.

5. *Tailor your Web site and your marketing to a well-defined audience.* Laser-guided rifle shots work best in Web merchandising, not shotgun approaches.

6. *Build a robust and scalable technical platform.* Plan for an avalanche of success.

7. *Employ constant enhancements and periodic over-hauls.* Never let yourself be satisfied; constantly learn from your customers. You want your customers to keep coming back to your Web site. Keep your content fresh, and update the Web site regularly with new features and services.

People always ask me, "How much does it cost to build a Web site?" The answer, of course, is it depends. It depends on the size, complexity, and quality of the Web site. It depends on who you hire and how professional they are.

People often compare the cost of a Web site to the cost of an automobile—you can buy a Honda for $15,000, a BMW for $50,000, or a Rolls-Royce for $150,000 (you can also buy a 1986 Yugo for $625!). This is narrow-minded and naive thinking. A much more realistic analogy is to compare the cost of a Web site to the cost of trans-portation. You could also buy a bicycle for $300, a small plane for $500,000, or a corporate jet for $4 million. There is literally that much variation. The only question is where do you want to go? Do you want your Web site to utilize the latest technology? Do you want to have pictures and interactive biographies of your entire staff? Or are you looking for a simple online presence that will direct people to your store? Your individual needs and wants will dictate how much your Web site will cost to build and maintain.

The market for hiring a professional Web site developer also runs the gamut from cheap to pricey. At the low end of the market, you can hire someone to build your Web site for less than $5,000— and I can promise you that it will be poorly designed, unscalable, and break down at the worst possible time. Frankly, the ease of constructing Web sites on the Internet has attracted a lot of people with no experience or aptitude whatsoever.

At the top end, large Web site development firms such as Agency.com, U.S. Web, and IBM typically build corporate Web sites for $1 million and much more. The sites they build usually include industrial strength databases, multiple cutting-edge technologies, and hundreds or thousands of pages. If you need or want the resources and reputation of firms like these, then a large Web development firm is for you. Like a Ferrari or a Lear jet, if you happen to have $1 million burning a hole in your pocket, then these large Web site development firms are worth every penny.

Medium and smaller-sized development firms often match the quality of their larger counterparts at significantly lower costs. The key to hiring a smaller firm is to check their references carefully and make sure your contract explicitly defines the work they will do. Include everything you can think of in the deliverables section of the contract—you will be happy you did.

As with a car or any mode of transportation, you get what you pay for. If you are truly content with a Yugo for $625, then do not expect it to be able to run at 120 mph! If you are looking for good quality and reliability, then spend the extra money and hire a quality Web development company with a good reputation.

But to start out putting your business online, you do not need to hire a development firm. With the tips and software illustrated in this book and a good knowledge of HTML, you can build your own small, functional Web site that will attract customers and increase sales.

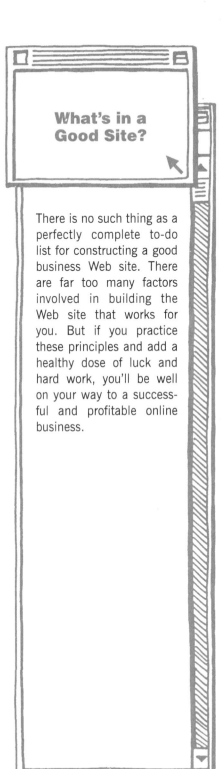

What's in a Good Site?

There is no such thing as a perfectly complete to-do list for constructing a good business Web site. There are far too many factors involved in building the Web site that works for you. But if you practice these principles and add a healthy dose of luck and hard work, you'll be well on your way to a successful and profitable online business.

PART ONE

INTERNET BUSINESS ESSENTIALS

Address http://chapter_one.com ▼ **Link**

Why Your Business Should Be Online

In commerce, sellers can be one of three types: a **retailer**, a **wholesaler** (also called a distributor), or a **manufacturer**. Retailers sell directly to the end consumer. Kmart is an example of a retailer. But where does Kmart get their products from? They get them from the distributor, who sells products to them at a discount. Kmart then marks up the products and resells them to the consumer. Manufacturers build and sell the products that wholesalers distribute to retailers.

The Future of Business

The whole world is going online. At the end of 1998 there were 10 million Web sites in the United States, 3 million of which were companies and small businesses. Despite the proliferation of personal home pages, academic institutions, and sites for every interest and hobby, the rapid acceptance of the World Wide Web by consumers has opened a floodgate of opportunity in electronic commerce. Seventy percent of Fortune 1000 companies are doing business online; 25 percent of small businesses. The future of business is clear. The revolution will *not* be televised. The battle for the future of business will be fought on the Internet.

In boardrooms, small offices, basements, and, yes, garages across the country, executives and entrepreneurs are taking their business to the Internet. More to the point, they are *meeting their customers* on the Internet, as well as their partners, suppliers, and employees. In fact, doing business online penetrates every aspect of a company. The nature of Internet technology drives this development. It is simply a way to electronically deliver, obtain, and share information with other human beings. The Web at its core is a medium of communication.

The power of the Web lies in three fundamental features:

1. The Web is global
2. The Web is a powerful information source
3. The Web is interactive

First, the Web is a global phenomenon. It was developed from the ground up to be an open standard, accessible by any kind of computer or operating system. Built around this standard are the servers and browsers that connect businesses with consumers. This open technology has also allowed the Internet to grow globally, encompassing every country and language into the World Wide Web.

Second, the Web is a powerful information source for both consumers and businesses. Consumers easily gain access to rich information about products and services, comparing offerings from many different companies in real time. Need product literature or information on warranty services? A great Web site can provide this type of information instantaneously, without the need for a customer service operator.

Third, the Web is interactive. The true nature of the Internet, and the basis of its power, is in the ability to conduct a dialogue with the consumer. Their input can affect not only what they see on the Web site, but the real operations of your company. This integration becomes a partnership whereby buyer and seller work together for their mutual benefit.

Until 1994 the Internet was the sole domain of the academic world, computer programmers, and UNIX experts. Once user-friendly browsers hit the market, providing an easy way for the average computer user to get online, the Internet demographic started to change. By the end of 1994, commercial Web sites had outgrown academic ones. Since 1994, that trend has continued exponentially. Users and commercial Web sites have literally exploded onto the Internet. It took radio nearly forty years before it reached 50 million users. Television took only about twelve years to do the same thing. But in less than five years, the Internet has expanded to include over 50 million users, and this incredible growth trend is expected to continue according to the U.S. Department of Commerce.

Several of the largest Internet research firms predicted the 1999 holiday shopping season to result in close to 10 billion dollars in online sales. That's a jump of nearly 100 percent over the 1998 holiday season, the first season that online ordering and e-commerce really burst onto the scene.

Even the advertising industry for the 1999 holiday season focused on e-commerce. Many sites timed their launch to coincide with this busiest of shopping periods, and you cannot turn on a television without running into a commercial for Amazon.com, BN.com, Drugstore.com, or several dozen other online-only retailers that gear up for holiday shoppers.

Advertising revenues have long been an indicator of good financial growth. How much money an industry spends on advertising is often dictated by the growth of the market and the health of the companies within that industry. According to the Internet

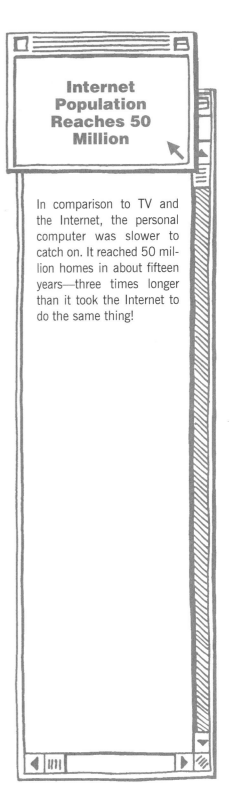

Internet Population Reaches 50 Million

In comparison to TV and the Internet, the personal computer was slower to catch on. It reached 50 million homes in about fifteen years—three times longer than it took the Internet to do the same thing!

Where Is the Internet Heading?

Forrester Research forecasts that by 2003 the Internet economy will equal about 9.4 percent of the total world economy. International Data Corporation forecasts that by the end of 2001 the Internet economy will total $1 trillion, and by the end of 2003 it will total more than $2.8 trillion!

Advertising Bureau, online advertising revenues grew from about $900 million in 1997 to $1.9 billion in 1998. That's more than double the amount spent in the prior year and an 800 percent increase over 1996! In 1998 online advertising even exceeded outdoor advertising, long a popular way to market businesses. Outdoor advertising revenues topped $1.5 billion in 1998, about standard for that industry.

Companies are investing a lot of time, money, and marketing efforts on the Internet to target the e-commerce consumer. Many Internet experts maintain that every business should have a presence on the Web. This is largely a personal decision, but throughout this book we will take you through some of the different types of Web sites your company can build and some of the responsibilities and opportunities for growth in e-commerce. The decision of whether to put your business online should be made only after you are sure you can commit the time and resources to its development and nurturing. The Net is a growing marketplace and, if handled right, your Web site can do more than tell people where you are and how to reach you.

Top Five Reasons to Build a Web Site

There are many factors to think about *before* deciding to invest the time, effort, and money into establishing a business presence on the World Wide Web. And your Web site is just that—an investment. As with any other investment, it may work out well for you and your business. But it also may not, costing more to develop and implement than you will ever make back. Here are the top five reasons to develop a Web site for your business.

1. Establish a Presence

Estimating the number of people on the World Wide Web is nearly impossible. But Internet growth is exponential, doubling at fantastic rates. Current estimates place the number of Web users between 200 and 240 million. That means there are nearly 240 million potential customers using the Web for their shopping and information gathering needs.

The demographics of a typical Web user are perfect for an online business. Web users are typically either college-educated or in college. Higher education has always been used as an excellent indicator of potential earnings. You want to sell to customers who have the disposable income to spend, and Web users, by and large, do. One of the biggest reasons companies establish Web sites is to get their name in front of these high-potential customers.

Not all of these Web users live in the United States. Opening a traditional business in other countries can be confusing, time consuming, and difficult. Regulations vary from country to country, sometimes even from province to province. Setting up a presence on the Web gives the international community access to the products and services your company offers, and does so during their hours of business. To keep your company open on London time would not only increase your overhead but cost you a lot of money in employee overtime. Your online storefront is available to anyone, anytime, anywhere in the world, and it is always working for you.

2. Improve Customer Service

In recent years, a lot of attention has been given to the service a company provides. More and more, customers are looking beyond just low prices or excellent stock to the feeling they get from the company they are doing business with. Are the salespeople courteous and helpful? Are questions answered in a timely manner and handled professionally? Many customers will even pay more in a store where they feel they are treated right. Good customer service leads to repeat customers, and repeat customers can be a large portion of a company's business. A company Web site can help build relationships that will help satisfy your customer's desire for efficient, effective customer service.

There are many ways to enhance your customer service by using a Web site. The first, and probably most obvious, is to

Integrating Your Customers into the Business Cycle

Customers like to feel like they are a part of the transaction. Online businesses can be frightening, and customers want to keep track of the process. For instance, Federal Express found that the biggest concern customers had with its service was making sure that their documents and packages arrived at the destination on time. By integrating package tracking into its Web site, FedEx was able to make a lot of information available to customers and involve them better in the cycle of doing business. Customers felt more comfortable with sending packages with FedEx, and with that increased comfort level came increased consumer satisfaction!

make your business information available whenever the customer may need it. From hours of operation to current items in stock, a Web site will allow your customers to find just the information they need, whenever they need it, even if your bricks-and-mortar business is closed for the day. The fact that customers on the Web can shop in many different and nontraditional ways has led many small businesses into developing storefronts on the Web. The ability to build an order over the course of a few days and the opportunity to specially configure products and build complicated custom orders are all reasons to take your business online. There is an added benefit to having this information online. Think how much of your staff's time is spent answering the same question over and over again, day in and day out. With a presence on the Web, your staff can answer customers' questions and direct them to your Web site for further information. After a while, your customers will know to go to your Web site to get the information they need and save your staff the time and energy of answering the same repetitious questions all day, every day.

Having a Web site also makes it easy for your customers to send you feedback on anything from their latest purchase to the look of your last marketing campaign. Customers are more likely to rifle off an e-mail or fill out an online response form than to sit and take the time to write and mail a letter. It is the directness and immediacy of online communications that makes it perfect for consumer feedback. Feedback makes your customers feel good about your company, especially if your reply is prompt, but it allows you to better gauge the effectiveness of your advertising efforts and your existing customer service.

It is the twenty-four-hour nature of the Web that makes a site attractive for customer service. Your site will serve your clients or customers at their convenience, which is the hallmark of good customer service. A happy customer is a repeat customer.

3. Foster Employee Relations

Does your business employ a sales staff that works all over the country or around the world? The World Wide Web makes it easy for your employees to stay in touch with the home office, without tying up home office resources. With a laptop and a telephone connection to the Internet, employees in far-flung locations can access their files and have all the information they need to complete their deals.

Even if you are a local business with employees who work on site, your business Web site is a valuable resource. With a secure employee section, you can post work schedules and newsletters. You can even offer downloadable insurance information and forms that let employees change their company health care, investment, and tax choices at their own convenience.

Your Web site is also an excellent way to recruit the best and brightest employees from all over the country. More and more highly qualified candidates are using the Web to drum up job leads and apply for positions. The Web is an especially popular resource for candidates looking to relocate to a new city. By posting your job openings on the Web, and even accepting resumes via e-mail, you expand the pool of talent you have to choose from.

4. Reduce Costs

A penny you have not spent is a penny you do not need to earn back. If a business handles its foray into e-commerce well, the Web can lower costs in many different areas. Businesses that have implemented Internet-based solutions have seen lower costs in printing, postage, order taking, market research, and in customer service while seeing the amount of items purchased in a single transaction increase. Recent studies conclude that online orders can be as much as four percent more profitable than orders placed over the phone via a catalog. Your business Web site can also help save you money on labor costs by making information available to your customers without taking up a lot of your staff's precious time.

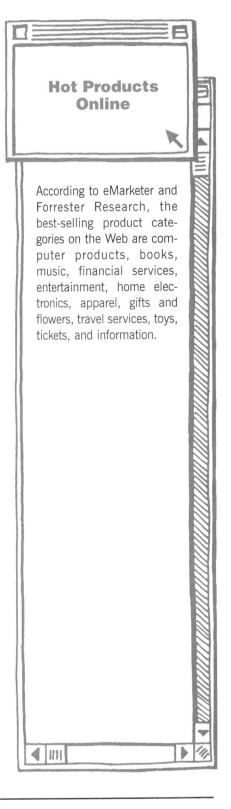

Hot Products Online

According to eMarketer and Forrester Research, the best-selling product categories on the Web are computer products, books, music, financial services, entertainment, home electronics, apparel, gifts and flowers, travel services, toys, tickets, and information.

More Reasons to Be on the Web

There are more than five reasons to be on the Web. You can also put your business on the Web to help you test market new products. It is very expensive to roll out a new product to your line or add a service in the bricks-and-mortar world. With a presence on the Web, you can market a new product or service at a fraction of the cost of doing it offline. Give new products and services a spin on the Web to see how they do before you integrate them into your bricks-and-mortar business.

Businesses are also going online so that they can offer more products to the customer than they could ever fit in an ordinary catalog or in a traditional brick-and-mortar store. For example, Amazon.com has more than three million book titles available for purchase. It would be prohibitively expensive for a business to fit that many books into a store, much less a catalog.

5. Increase Sales

Of course, the number one reason for building a business Web site is to sell your products and services! Because of personalization features (which we'll explain later) and some of the higher technology database applications, Web businesses can offer suggestions of related items that a customer might enjoy. In the past, this task fell to salespeople, who are often too busy or not trained correctly to offer this kind of personal service. When handled electronically, this kind of suggestive selling can result in increased ordering.

Besides just the increased sales you can achieve from online orders, increasing your customer's level of satisfaction is one of the biggest keys to providing effective and excellent customer service.

Take a look at our first case study and see how Electronic Systems uses its Web site, not to sell but as a tool in the sales process.

However, the benefits to the manufacturer in this situation may seem a little more difficult to grasp. A lot of the benefit to the OEM comes from the speed of the transaction. Because of the immediacy of the Web, the equipment manufacturer can take advantage of directing the customer to one of its sellers when he is at the highest level of interest in the product and making a transaction. The customer likes being directed to a dealer that the manufacturer has confidence in, and the manufacturer gets added sales by not losing the customer to competitors that make the purchase process easier and more immediate.

Case Study: Electronic Systems

At Electronic Systems, a network integration and management services company in Virginia Beach, Virginia, the Web site has gone beyond basic. Says sales manager Glenn Webb: "The Web site is one of our key tools for helping customers understand all the offerings we have. This is one of our biggest challenges because we have such a large line of products and services."

Indeed, Electronic Systems has an extensive list of offerings. From a start as a local area network (LAN) integrator in the early 1980s, the company now operates as an Internet service provider (ISP), a developer of e-commerce-enabled Web sites, the largest provider of computer-related training courses in southeast Virginia, a seller of network-related products and, of course, an integrator and manager of network systems.

The Web site is used as the first point of contact for many customers, going beyond information to customer recruitment. Requests for training and Net services are made via a set of online forms. Though initially Electronic Systems only received one or two requests per month, Webb says 25 to 30 requests per month began coming in after about 6 months. Furthermore, he says, "Every month there is a 20 percent to 50 percent increase in requests for training and Internet services." Webb says the company plans to streamline the request process by going to a single form that customers can reach from several different locations on the site.

Electronic Systems has also designed and deployed two e-commerce offerings on its Web site, both of which function as major points-of-sale. The first is a set of specialized product ordering forms for major customers, designed according to those customers' specifications. Those major customers use the forms internally to order directly from Electronic Systems, and the orders are output at Electronic Systems' Web site. The second offering is an online catalog featuring tens of thousands of products from various distributors, which customers can order through Electronic Systems. Essentially, the catalog is a front-end to their suppliers' products. "It's designed for purchasing and management information system departments, but end users can use it, too," says Webb.

One particularly lucrative feature of Electronic Systems' Web site is its function as a sales channel for major OEMs.

Most dealers and distributors link to OEM Web sites as a matter of course. But what's important for increasing the dealers' and distributors' bottom lines is whether those original equipment manufacturer sites refer customers back to them—and how quickly they do so. In Electronic Systems' case, a number of OEMs link back to the Web site, including Citrix, Tektronix, Adtran, Hewlett-Packard, Compaq, and Microsoft. Webb says that Electronic Systems gets four to five dozen leads each month from these link-back referrals.

Citrix's leads are of especially high quality, probably due to the fact that the company's "thin-client" servers are especially hot sellers right now. "The links are part of the reseller/marketing agreement. If you're an upper-line dealer or VAR, the vendors support you on your Web site, including Web links," says Webb. Having this kind of support is beneficial to both the original equipment manufacturer and to the dealer. For the dealer or value-added reseller, the benefits are obvious. They get important leads, and it allows the smaller company to leverage the size and scope of the larger company's Web site to provide a much stronger overall Web presence than the dealer could achieve alone. Using Xerox as an example, customers who want to purchase Xerox products are going to look for the Xerox Web site, not necessarily the Web site of the company that sells the Xerox products to the consumer. This enables the smaller dealer to take advantage of the power and presence of the Xerox site for giving product information and specs, while the final purchase comes through their company.

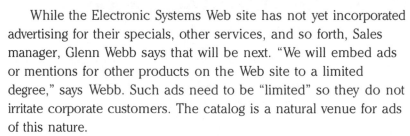

An OEM is an **original equipment manufacturer**. Xerox is an example of an OEM, manufacturing document management products such as printers and copiers. The office supply store that sells Xerox machines is a reseller, or sometimes a VAR, a **value-added reseller**. If your company deals in products as a VAR or has OEM suppliers, look into link exchange programs offered by the manufacturer. It may help you increase traffic to your Web site

While the Electronic Systems Web site has not yet incorporated advertising for their specials, other services, and so forth, Sales manager, Glenn Webb says that will be next. "We will embed ads or mentions for other products on the Web site to a limited degree," says Webb. Such ads need to be "limited" so they do not irritate corporate customers. The catalog is a natural venue for ads of this nature.

"The catalog is a marketing and sales tool," says Webb. "There are many places where services, rental, supplies, etc., can be advertised."

The online marketing is thoroughly integrated with offline initiatives. "All of our marketing campaigns in the future will point to the catalog and target our e-commerce capabilities," says Webb. "We will spend some marketing efforts and all print, radio, and TV campaigns will point to the site. Everyone can buy online via a secure site. We will have specialized business-to-business e-commerce. That's how we integrate these together."

Electronic Systems's Web site is more than a source of information. It is a basic business tool. "It's more beneficial every month as we offer more ways to do business with customers over the Net," says Webb. "Customers want to communicate this way—more and more of them each month."

WORKSHEET

Take some time to answer these questions for your business. Write down the answers and give some thought to them as you read on.

Why do you think your business should go online?

_____

_____

_____

_____

_____

_____

_____

What aspects of your business do you think would best be served by creating a Web site?

_____

_____

_____

_____

_____

_____

_____

What has kept you from developing a Web presence for your business until now?

_____

_____

_____

_____

_____

_____

_____

Add items to Cart
 Ratings & Reviews
 Compare Prices
Find Products
 Buy Now!

Address http://chapter_two.com **Link**

Commerce Versus E-Commerce

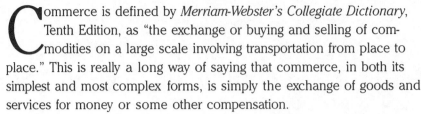

Bartering, or the exchange of goods and services for other goods and services of an equal value, is also a method of commerce and can even be done over the Internet! Companies exchange their services for product and price considerations all the time!

Commerce is defined by *Merriam-Webster's Collegiate Dictionary*, Tenth Edition, as "the exchange or buying and selling of commodities on a large scale involving transportation from place to place." This is really a long way of saying that commerce, in both its simplest and most complex forms, is simply the exchange of goods and services for money or some other compensation.

Every time you buy something at your local mall or the neighborhood grocery store you are participating in commerce from the buyer's side. If you own your own business, you participate in commerce from the seller's side. Commerce can be divided into four roles: the buyer, the seller, the distributor and the producer. The inherent nature of commerce is that buyers want to buy, sellers want to sell, distributors want to distribute, and producers create the products that are eventually sold to buyers.

The Definition of E-Commerce

So what does e-commerce mean anyway? E-commerce is the pre-eminent buzzword of the online business revolution. It captures the excitement and focus of this fast emerging market. But it is more than a slogan or glib party line. At its core it embodies a concept for doing business online.

Electronic commerce is the paperless exchange of business information using electronic data interchange (EDI), e-mail, electronic bulletin boards, fax transmissions, and electronic funds transfer. It refers to Internet shopping, online stock and bond transactions, the downloading and selling of "soft merchandise" (software, documents, graphics, music, etc.), and business-to-business transactions.

The concept of e-commerce is all about using the Internet to do business *better and faster*. It is about giving customers controlled access to your computer systems and letting people serve themselves. It is about committing your company to a serious online effort and integrating your Web site with the heart of your business. If you do that, you will see results!

The Internet's role in business can be compared to that of the telephone. It is a way for people to communicate with each other. It is also a way for a consumer to communicate with a company's computer systems without human intervention. In fact, the Internet is a

communication medium like the many others we use in business every day.

Think of the ways you communicate with people in business. The best way is face to face. Body language, tone of voice, and facial expressions all help you understand what the other person is trying to say. When you cannot meet face to face, you may use any of a number of different means to communicate: a telephone, a fax machine, Federal Express, the U.S. Postal Service, or maybe even a messenger service. These are all ways to deliver or receive information, authorization, even shipments of goods and merchandise.

The Internet is a reasonable alternative to all of those means of communication. Any place and any way that your business communicates with its customers, you should think about how you could have done it online. That is the power of e-commerce.

Can't meet face to face? Send an e-mail with an attached photograph. When it comes time to pay for merchandise, use a secured server to pay by credit card, or even digital cash! The opportunities and situations in which online business is possible are limitless.

Components of an Internet Business

Every era of business yields new strategies and new ways of doing business. With the advent of radio and television came the first mass-market advertising. Now, the Internet has so radically changed business that the rules for corporate strategy that held for the last 50 years (since the dawn of television) have begun to crumble.

There are some literal elements of commerce that are necessary for any transactions to take place, which are as true for regular bricks-and-mortar commerce as they are for e-commerce. First, whether you are doing business online or in the real world, you have to have a product to sell or a service to offer. Then, you must have a place from which to do business. In the traditional world of commerce this can be a physical store or, in a more figurative sense, a catalog or phone number. In the world of e-commerce the place from which you do business is your Web site.

Most businesses already exist in the bricks-and-mortar world of commerce. Adding a Web site is a means to enhance their business. For Internet startups, the Web site is the only place that they do business.

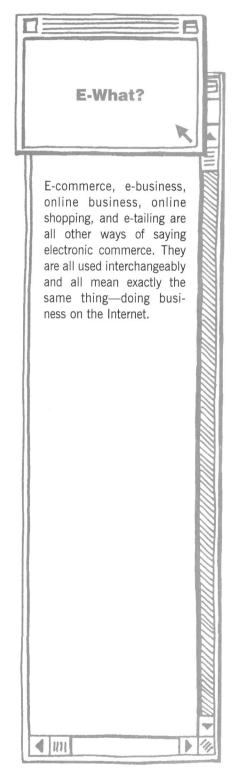

E-What?

E-commerce, e-business, online business, online shopping, and e-tailing are all other ways of saying electronic commerce. They are all used interchangeably and all mean exactly the same thing—doing business on the Internet.

Lou Gerstner Knows

Someone once asked Lou Gerstner, the CEO of IBM, about the future of IBM in the Internet business. He turned and responded, "The Internet is not a separate business, it is business itself." This concept of e-commerce as a tool for all businesses, not a business unto itself, is essential for understanding how e-commerce can make your own business larger and more profitable.

In both regular commerce and e-commerce you need to find a way to attract customers to your place of business. This is embodied by your marketing strategy, and everything from advertising to word of mouth fits into this category.

In order to do business, you also need a way to take orders and process payment. In a retail store there are no orders. Customers simply find the products they want, get in a line at the register, and pay the cashier. In e-commerce, orders have to be placed and items shipped. Orders are usually handled through interactive, online forms. Money is another issue easily handled in traditional commerce. Customers in a retail store pay by check, cash, or credit or debit cards. Online customers cannot pay by cash or check, only through electronic means. Also, there are issues of security that surround online payment that do not come into play in the traditional bricks-and-mortar world. E-commerce transactions have to take place through secure electronic connections and special merchant accounts for accepting payment.

Once payment is collected, delivery of the product must take place. Fulfillment in traditional stores is as easy as putting the item in a bag and handing it over to the customer. Fulfillment in the world of e-commerce is more difficult, requiring shipping and transportation similar to catalog and mail order businesses. For businesses that integrate e-commerce into their existing business plan, fulfillment is as easy as hiring an extra employee to ship online orders. In Internet startup businesses, fulfillment must often be outsourced to a facility that can handle order processing and shipping in a more timely and professional manner.

New Rules of E-Commerce

Both e-commerce and traditional commercial transactions require a way to accept returns in the case of broken, or otherwise unsatisfactory products. Both need to handle warranty claims if they are a part of selling the product. In traditional commerce, customers just bring back a product for a refund if they do not like it, or bring it back to the store for warranty repairs.

Since there is no "store" in the e-commerce process shipping arrangements must be made for accepting returns and handling

Five Ways to Bring the
Global Internet to a Local Level

The World Wide Web is a global marketplace. Your site will be visited by hundreds of people from all over the world. That's great if you have a store, product, or service that people from all over the world will want. But what if you are just a local bricks-and-mortar store interested in increasing your local customer service and local sales? How do you target your site to take advantage of the Web in a more local fashion? Here are five ways to take the global and make it as local as your corner store.

1. Make your Web site do more than just offer product information. Let your customers make repair appointments or review their service agreements on your Web site. Not only does this give your customer a great opportunity to get the information they want, when they want it, but it frees up your staff, too.

2. Partner with some noncompeting local vendors to sponsor promotions on local Web sites. Most local newspapers have a site already. Get a few other business and contact them about running a special contest or other promotion.

3. Look for advertising opportunities on heavily trafficked local Web sites. Newspapers, radio stations, local cable TV channels, even chambers of commerce have sites that specifically relate to the interests of people in and around your area. People have a real investment in what's happening in their backyard. Spend your advertising dollars where these locals are going to look for their information.

4. There is a great deal of power in numbers. Band together with other dealers or industry associations to multiply your advertising dollars through cooperative advertising purchases. Through cooperative advertising, smart ads are developed that can determine the nearest dealer to the customer through address or phone information. By pooling your money, advertising can be purchased on sites that would otherwise have been prohibitively expensive for the small business.

5. Buy banner ad space in local sections on major portal sites. Microsoft's Sidewalk and Yahoo! have information on local towns and cities. Purchase space here, where your local customer is most likely to see it.

E-Commerce Rules

Shift the power of the business relationship to your customer.

Personalize each customer's experience on the Web.

Eliminate all hurdles and barriers to the final transaction.

The goals of speed and time saving should impact every aspect of your Web business—from contents to design technology.

warranty service. Often the company that has taken over fulfillment for an Internet business will also handle returns.

Finally, customer service and support is a necessary part of doing business, both in the real world and online. Customer service in the bricks-and-mortar world often takes place in person or over the phone, whereas online customer service must be handled through more indirect means via e-mail or other online means.

E-commerce has changed a lot of the ways that companies do business. But the e-commerce revolution has also made *new* rules necessary. This is not surprising. As with all new eras, advances in technology have forced businesses to evolve, creating new ways of doing business and new rules for conducting business.

E-Commerce Rule #1: Empowerment

The first new rule is that the customer should be in charge of his experience, which is just a re-emphasis of the most tried-and-true business strategy throughout history: The customer is always right. But there is a very useful twist to this old axiom. Self-service by your customers will help your business by reducing your cost of operations. When you let customers serve themselves from your Web site, you do not need to employ as many sales and customer service representatives. Better yet, your sales and service representatives can focus on the more important aspects of their work.

The side benefit is that your customers will feel more in control of their relationship with your company. Customers will value the opportunity to help themselves. Customers will feel like they are in better control of their experience with you, and they feel grateful to you for giving them this power.

E-Commerce Rule #2: Personalization

Information and personalization are the key empowering attributes of a marketing business strategy on the Internet. The more customer intelligence you can build into your Web site, the better you'll be able to personalize it for specific customers.

Personalization on the Web is achieved in one of two ways: either placing a *cookie* in the user's cookie file or requiring them to log in to your Web site every time they visit.

Cookies That Are not Fattening!

A cookie is a piece of information sent by a Web server (the Web site) to a Web browser (the customer) that the Web browser is expected to save and send back to the Web server whenever the browser goes back to that site. Cookies can contain any information you choose to include, such as login information, user preferences, items of interest, and other tidbits that help customize the user's experience on a Web site.

There are countless advantages to personalizing a Web site. Besides the good feeling it gives your customers, customers can tailor your information to meet their needs. They can see prior orders without having to go through a lengthy process. They can check on the latest prices for items they've placed on their shopping list. Personalization helps induce customers to return to your site because it provides the specific information *they* need with greater speed and ease.

The concept of personalization is at the core of many financial services Web sites. For instance, when you store a personal investment portfolio with a brokerage site on the Web, that information is directly linked to your account. Your portfolio information is saved in a database, and when you return to the Web site and login with a username and password the information is automatically retrieved.

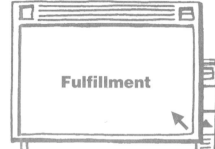

E-Commerce Rule #3: Directness

Dell Computers is one of the most successful online businesses in the world. Their success is embodied in their motto: "Be Direct."

Being direct means getting from point A to point B without taking any detours or stopping for any road blocks. Being direct online means connecting your customers to the information and tools that they need most, by passing or eliminating superfluous questions and extraneous hurdles. The goal is to get your customer to the decision to buy as quickly and efficiently as possible.

Fulfillment

There are full-service businesses that will handle all your online fulfillment needs for a fee. Many of these have front-end services that will take orders from your customers and a back-end warehouse that will fill and ship orders. Some of these full-service fulfillment companies will even help you market your products, providing real-world catalogs or direct mail support!

AN E-COMMERCE CHECKLIST

In order to do business on the Web (or anywhere really) you need to control these nine business issues:

- ❑ *A product (of course).* Choose a product whose attributes or purchasing process are well-suited to selling on the internet.

- ❑ *A place to sell the product (your Web site).* A well-designed Web site is the most important factor in online business success.

- ❑ *A way to get people to come to your Web site.* This includes advertising and marketing efforts, both online and in the traditional media.

- ❑ *A way to accept orders.* This can be an online form of some sort or even an online form that then prompts a phone call.

- ❑ *A way to accept money.* You can set up a merchant account to handle credit card payments through your bank, or you can use more traditional billing techniques either online or through the U.S. Postal Service.

- ❑ *A fulfillment facility to ship products to customers.* If you ship products regularly, this is already in place, otherwise, this can be outsourced to a subcontractor. If you are selling software or information, a download mechanism can be added to your site, eliminating the need to physically ship anything at all!

- ❑ *A way to accept returns.* Luckily, the U.S. Postal Service can help you with this.

- ❑ *A way to handle warranty claims if necessary.*

- ❑ *A way to provide customer service.* Make sure your customers can contact you whether by e-mail, phone, or traditional mail.

E-Commerce Rule #4: Speed

If time is the enemy of opportunity, then speed is the partner of success! People use the Internet for many different reasons, but the reason most often cited by consumers is "saving time." Telephone companies knew the importance of "saving time" for the consumer. The Yellow Pages directories were marketed as time-saving devices. Remember—"Let Your Fingers Do the Walking."

Well, the Web is marketed as a way for consumers to save time by not only finding places to shop, but actually doing the shopping right on their computer once they get there.

The rule of speed for online business impacts many areas, including:

- Clear and logical Web site design so consumers can find what they want quickly and easily
- Small file sizes for photos and graphics so Web pages download faster
- Powerful hardware and high speed reliable Internet connections for your Web server

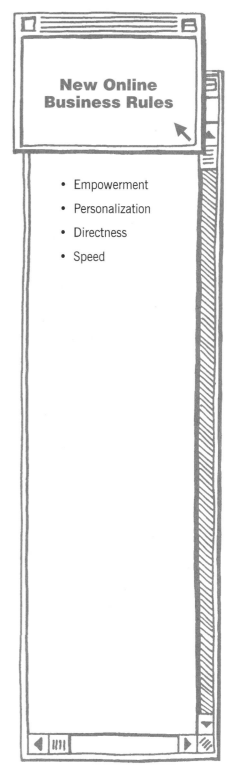

New Online Business Rules

- Empowerment
- Personalization
- Directness
- Speed

Types of Products and Services that Sell on the Web

Now that you know the rules for conducting business online, how do you know if you have the right kind of product? The type of product often dictates how you offer it for sale. It will also often dictate how you design a Web site to maximize that product's exposure.

There are many different types of products that are available for sale on the Web, and they are primarily divided into five categories. Where your product fits in those categories determines not only how your customers will shop for the product, but how you should present it to maximize sales.

Gifts and Impulse Products

These are products you often do not know you wanted until you saw them. Trinkets, music boxes, and small gift items are all examples of this kind of purchase. Customers look to buy little items like this by wandering around until they see what they like. If you are selling gift or impulse products, you want to design a site that is fun to browse through. Think of a curio or antique shop where items are on display. That is the kind of atmosphere you want to create on your Web site if you are going to be able to sell products. The medium will be largely visual, and the navigation must be creative and freeform, allowing a customer to browse or go virtual window shopping. Gift items can be sold on the Web, but it takes a specific approach to doing so, which does not make them the ideal products to sell. These products sell well if presented properly.

Commodity Products

Commodity products are those products where presentation does not mean much. You know what a book looks like. You know what a videotape looks like. The actual appearance of the item does not matter as much as the *price*, *selection*, and *availability*. People rarely need to see a book jacket to know if that is the book they want to read. They will want a synopsis of the book, who wrote it, and maybe even a list of other books that author has written. Commodity products sell wonderfully on the Web, as evidenced by sites like Amazon.com and CDNow.com. These sites are built around solid searching capabilities because most people heading to those sites know they want a CD or a book by a particular artist or author. Whereas gift sites are more graphically based, commodity sites are more text based, relying on description and product attributes.

Price is critical to commodity sites as customers are likely to comparison shop. But beyond price and availability, customers also want added value where they shop. Things like more convenience, personalized customer service, and enhanced searching will draw customers to your site even if you do not have the absolute lowest price.

Considered Purchase Products

It is rare to find anyone willing to go out and purchase a new car the same day they decide they want one. Purchasing an automobile requires a lot of thought, which puts it in the category of considered purchase products. Any expensive product that comes in various models with different options and pricing can require customers to take a serious step back and think carefully about their purchase before buying.

"Calls to Action"

You also will want to find a way to add value to your service to attract customers to you and away from your competitors. It is not enough to deliver services on time and within a budget. Every business does that. Your business has to give something more to customers, not only to get them to do business with you but to entice them to take that extra step.

You should consider adding anything that will ease the purchase process for your customer. Can they schedule carpet cleaning online? Choose the menu they want you to prepare? These are all value-added services that make your site more attractive and more convenient for your customers.

Make sure you make the call to action as easy for the customer as possible. It is already difficult enough for customers to take that additional step; do not make it any harder for them. Be absolutely explicit about what that next step is asking from the customer. Do you want your customers to contact you by phone? Do you prefer to get their information via e-mail? Decide what the call to action will be and then make sure there is no question in your customers' mind about what it is they have to do.

If it's a phone call, plaster the number all over the site. Do not make your customer have to search for it. If you would rather them e-mail you, make sure you do the same with the e-mail address.

Just because you do not have a product that fits into one of the five categories does not mean you cannot have a presence on the Web, and it does not mean that your Web presence cannot result in an increase in your bottom line. But selling a service instead of a product does mean you have to use careful consideration in what you will expect from your Web site and your customer and how you intend to best translate that onto the Web. Remember, the lack of personal contact is a big drawback to doing business on the Web. This impact is not felt as strongly in a product-oriented business where the customer can see what they are getting, but it is a big hurdle to an online service-oriented business. However, with a little creative thought and a strong feeling of what your customers will value in your image and your service, you can build a successful Web site that will positively impact your bottom line.

There are a lot of factors to consider when building a Web site offering considered purchase products for sale, but the most important one is going to be information. In order to best make up their mind about the products they want, your customers will need to know all about the product. What colors does it come in? What options can they get? What do those options do? The more information you give your customers the more likely they are to make the best decision for them, and the more likely they are to value the services your site offers. A good example of sites that sell considered purchase products are automobile manufacturers and dealerships. They make a point to not only show you pictures of the vehicles they have in stock but all the available options and gizmos that you can order. Customers compare prices between dealerships and even between different manufacturers, coming to a decision based on a complex mix of all the information. Oftentimes the decision on where they finally end up buying their vehicle will rest on which site provided the best information with the least hassle.

Configurable Products

Configurable products are much like considered purchase products, differing only in the fact that they focus on all the options available. Computers are great examples of configurable products. The basic components are much the same across the board, but how they are put together determines the final product. Computer companies like Gateway, Dell, and Compaq have made a real name for themselves in developing sites that specialize in customized products.

Sites that sell configurable products are developed much the same as those that sell considered purchase products. If you have a configurable product, you want to make sure to give your customers all the information they need to make their decision. Configurable products can be confusing for laypeople, computers especially so. The best computer sales sites demystify hardware and software options, letting the customer feel at ease about building a computer and making difficult configuration decisions on their own.

Products Sold by Category

There are a lot of products that can be sold online that do not really fit into any one category. Things you would find at a drugstore fit perfectly into this category. That does not mean they cannot be sold online though. Drugstore.com is a great example of a site that sells products by category.

The key to any kind of category-based Web site is organization. The categories and subcategories must be organized so that a customer can find exactly the kind of vitamin or deodorant he or she wants. In most cases customers already know what toothpaste they want or what kind of paper clips they need. Finding them quickly and easily is key. They do not need to see a detailed picture of the item or get a long detailed description on the benefits of the product. They want to see what it costs and maybe compare that cost against a few other brands in the category, so the index and the category/subcategory/sub-subcategory structure must be well designed, easy to navigate, and very intuitive.

When deciding whether to put your business online, you need to figure out what is right for your company and your products, not necessarily what is going to be the easiest to build. Take a good look at your products and the needs your customers have when shopping for those products, too.

Service Businesses

What do you do if you do not have a product to sell? What if you clean carpets or are a personal chef? These are services, not products. There is no tangible item that can be shipped at the click of a mouse. What do you do then? Should you abandon all hopes of building a Web site for your business?

Certainly not!

Just because you have a service to sell instead of a product does not mean you should ignore the Web as a means to build your business. You merely need to look at the Web in a different way and approach the creation and planning of your Web site in a more specific manner.

Most businesses that sell services can have a presence online. Often they list things like location of the business, costs for services, and other informational items that help customers find the business and make sense of the services they provide. A company that cleans carpets would put information on its site regarding cleaning options available and how much it costs to clean different carpet sizes. In most

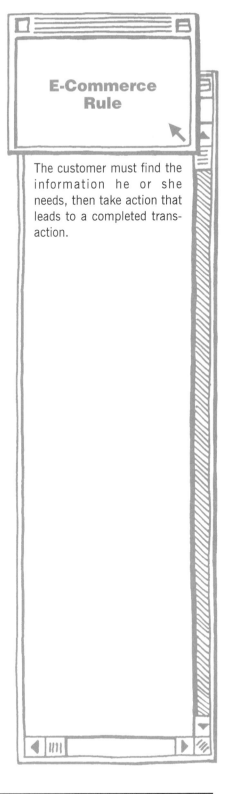

E-Commerce Rule

The customer must find the information he or she needs, then take action that leads to a completed transaction.

cases, a further call to action is required to close a deal. The call to action is usually a phone call or an e-mail inquiry, which forces the customer to take an extra step to purchase the service required. Whenever there is an extra step, you run the risk of losing the customer to a competitor.

Selling services online is a difficult thing to do. While you are deciding whether to go online, you are saddled with the additional responsibility of finding a way to make your service something more substantial, something more like a product. You have to find a way to convince your customer not only that you have a service worth purchasing but that it is worth the time to send an e-mail or pick up the telephone to call you. That is not an easy task.

Brand Image

One of the ways to make your service tangible in the minds of consumers is to brand that service—create a brand image for your company that your customers will want to buy into.

Using the Web to Speed Up the Sales Cycle

Some businesses do not sell anything at all online. They use their Web site to collect leads and enhance the functioning of the sales cycle. Businesses like this are often corporations that specialize in business-to-business sales and consulting. They do not actually sell anything on their Web site, so like the smaller service-oriented businesses they have to construct their Web site carefully. Companies like this can be large or small, but the thing they have in common are a more in-depth sales cycle than exists in product-oriented sales, or even the service-oriented sales noted above.

The sales cycle can vary greatly across industries, but it can be roughly boiled down to a few basic parts. The first part of the sales cycle is the qualification of a sales lead. Many leads can come in but only some of them will be ready and willing to buy. The first step in the sales cycle is to determine which of these leads are qualified leads, based on a variety of factors that change from industry to industry.

Once the lead is qualified, the potential customer must be approached, and this is the second part of the cycle. Setting up an appointment, sending or e-mailing sales literature, and phone contact are all ways to approach the qualified lead.

After the initial approach and meeting, a review occurs in which your sales staff reviews the business methods and needs of

Case Study: Deal-a-Day
An Online Success Blossoms

After thirty years in traditional retail, dealing mostly in moderate- to better-quality women's clothing, Ed Mufson decided to open his own retail operation. He was quite far along in the process when one of his major financial backers told him that retail stores were history and he did not want to get into that business.

Mufson was astounded. "Someone at a party said I should go on the Internet. I did not even know how to turn my computer on." But he spent the next several months researching, learning, exploring marketing options, and, incidentally, learning how to turn on his computer among other things.

In February of 1998, Mufson opened Deal-A-Day, a Web site where you can buy good quality, name-brand clothing at steeply discounted prices. "My business," says Mufson, "is deal oriented. We carry small to moderate quantities at good prices and we sell out. We carry 72 to 300 pieces in a deal. As we grow, we'll carry more. We have hundreds of different deals on the site right now, so there are thousands and thousands of garments." Mufson has a 4,000 square foot warehouse outside of Boston for storage of the garments. Everything is shipped out from that location.

Mufson has done absolutely no off-line marketing of any kind. His sole marketing technique has been to rent Rosalind Resnick's e-mail lists every week for three to four months. "It's worked out great," Mufson says. "We've become a poster boy for opt-in e-mail. We send out about 10,000 e-mails a week and get between 800 and 1,000 responses. That's a high number and they are very highly qualified. These are people who shop online. We'll get 400 to 500 who sign up for the contests and about 50 orders from those." Through this technique, Mufson has built up a customer base of about 11,000, which is growing by about 75 to 100 people per day! These are voluntarily signed up members of the Deal-A-Day Preferred Customer Club, which offers special deals of various kinds.

Not only is his customer base growing, but so is his order size. From an average of about $20 when he started in February 1998, his orders were averaging about $52 by September of that year. Ninety-five percent of his orders are over the Web, but he also offers fax and phone ordering. Shipments are made from the warehouse on the same or next day and they offer a no-questions-asked return policy.

Mufson believes the Web is the future for retailing. He advises that anyone who wants to follow his model should do a lot of homework and research. "It's very easy to open up a cheap Web site," he says. "But a $500 Web site looks like it! The Web is littered with mediocre, home-movie type sites." Mufson used professional photographers and professional models for the catalog on his site.

"Everyone told me not to do this," he says, " and I'm proving them wrong every day." He sure did! Deal-A-Day was recently purchased by CyberShop International, Inc. CyberShop is a publicly traded online merchant, and the Deal-A-Day site was folded in to their larger retail superstore.

Deal-A-Day is a great example of a company that adjusted its business rules to take advantage of the Web! The investor who pulled his backing truly believed in the Web, and with an open mind Mr. Mufson decided to try that route. Deal-A-Day is a great example of how successful Web sites get started. A little innovation and an open mind toward the Internet and the new ways of doing business it creates are all it takes.

Consumer Purchasing Cycle

Every time you buy a product or service, you go through a purchasing cycle. The initial spark of recognition that you need or want something sets into motion a complex process whereby you evaluate your needs, research your options, convince yourself of the solution, and finally make the purchase. Whether this happens over a period of seconds or months, we all go through this process every time we purchase something. Your customers will also go through this process when presented with the opportunity to purchase items via your Web site.

Understanding the consumer purchasing cycle is critical to designing your Web site with the right "push" and "pull" marketing techniques. Web surfers are hungry for information, of course. But they are also hungry to do more than surf. Especially in the ever changing world nowadays, surfers inherently want to accomplish their goals, to check off items on their shopping list as quickly and efficiently as possible. That is one of the main reasons why e-commerce appeals to so many people.

the lead. Next, your sales staff presents the product to the lead, which usually takes the form of a formal proposal in a meeting or via a written proposal.

Once the customer is satisfied and has decided his or her course of action, the deal is closed and the sales cycle ends.

The biggest enemy to the sales cycle is time. Every step takes time, from the point where a lead is deemed qualified to the point at which the deal is finally closed. At any step during the process the customer can choose to terminate the relationship and move on, either to a competitor or simply because the products or services you are offering are no longer needed.

The best time to get a customer to buy is as close to the moment of qualification as possible, right after the customer decides that he or she wants something. In a product-oriented business this means taking advantage of customers' impulse buys, and the Web does that very well. But in the larger corporate, service-oriented businesses the sales cycle is longer, posing more of a risk to closing the deal.

When the time comes to decide whether to put a large service-oriented business on the Web, the issues that need to be considered are far different. Not only must you add value and clarify the call to action, as in a small service-oriented business, but you also have to determine how your Web site can best speed up this sales cycle, cutting the time from the initial qualification to the final closing. For example, by using your Web site to deliver proposals, either through a secured area or electronic transmission of documents, you shorten the time it takes the customer to review your proposal. Even approaching the customer electronically (via e-mail) cuts down on the time from qualification to closing and keeps your customer interested in your service or product.

The goal of building a business Web site should be applying the Internet and all its benefits to your business in every way you can. Just because you are not selling a commodity or impulse product does not mean you should not have a presence on the World Wide Web. Through careful thought and planning you can create a Web presence for your business that will enhance your goals and your bottom line in hundreds of ways.

Address http://chapter_three.com Link

Know Your Online Customers

J ust throwing a Web site together and slapping it online is not going to guarantee your success. You need to give serious thought to your business image online and what you want your Web site to do for your customers. To do that you need to decide who your customers are. Knowing how your customers do business with you, their likes and dislikes, even their level of technical sophistication will help you determine what you want your Web site to do.

Demographics: Who Are Your Customers and Why Does It Matter?

Whatever your plans are for your Web site, the most important issue is your audience. Knowing who your audience is, what they know (and do not know), and what they want to accomplish is critical to a successful e-commerce Web site. After all, you do not want to create a site appropriate for motorcyclers when your product is more suitable for garden lovers! There is a general demographic profile of Internet users, but you must also keep in mind that your audience is unique. There is a place on the Web for businesses selling motorcycle parts as well as businesses selling potted hydrangeas.

I cannot tell you who your audience is. There is nobody who knows your customers better than you! Since you know who your customers are and what they like, building a Web site that is appealing and useful to them should be easy. Knowing their level of technical sophistication, the product or service issues they are most concerned with, and even their sense of humor will all help you build the best Web site possible. You can determine some of the more qualitative aspects of your audience based on demographic trends. After all, senior citizens are less likely to be Web savvy than your average college student. But again, only you know your audience. If your products are designed specifically for the techo-savvy senior, then the qualitative aspects of the demographic group mean nothing to you. There are no easy answers; The best advice is to rely on your common sense.

DEFINITION PLEASE

Demographics refer to the statistical data of a population, especially those statistics that show average age, income, education and other related facts.

But we can still help. Let's start with the stereotypical profile of an Internet user. By and large, an Internet user is young, male, single, well-educated, and prosperous. That may describe a lot of people on the Net, but the Net is also changing! In fact, a cross-section of people on the Internet is starting to look a lot like a cross-section of the United States. From soccer moms in North Carolina to teenage girls in Ohio to grandfathers in Florida, everyone is getting on the Internet.

According to eMarketer, in 1999 nearly 81 million people between the ages of 35 and 54 were online in the United States. People in this age category represent 39 percent of the population but 43 percent of online users. There were 64 million Internet users between the ages of 18 and 34 in the same year. This demographic represents 32 percent of the greater population but almost 40 percent of the online population. The 55 and over population is underrepresented on the Internet. Only 58 million people in this demographic are Net users, representing 16 percent of the online population, even though people 55 and over represent 28 percent of the general population.

By looking at these facts, you can see that your typical Net user is between the ages of 18 and 54, which also means that these are the people most likely to shop online as well. But look at your customers. What age group do they fall into? Are you marketing to senior citizens or teenagers? The age group that most makes use of your products and services will determine not only how you build your site but the type of site you start off with.

It is also important to consider the gender of your customers. According to eMarketer, women make up approximately 51 percent of the world's population, yet in 1998 they only made up 44 percent of Internet users. In 1999 that number grew to 46 percent, and in the year 2000 it is expected to rise to 49 percent. Women are not expected to reach population parity until the year 2002 when it is anticipated they will make up 51 percent of the Internet population.

The changing attitudes of Internet users is almost as important as *who* is online. According to a recent study questioning people on their attitudes towards e-commerce and online transactions, 40 percent of those surveyed said they had made a purchase online

Women as an Internet Trend

More and more women are getting online, but it is unclear if they are getting on because of the new boom in women-oriented sites or if the Web sites are booming because more and more women are getting online. Sites like iVillage, Women.com, and Oxygen.com are specially designed for the growing population of women Internet users.

within the last three months or were planning to make a purchase online within the next three months. This compares to 1997 in which only 15 percent of respondents were similarly inclined toward online shopping.

The total amount of money spent worldwide online is staggering. In 1998, $37.6 billion worldwide were spent online. In 1999 that number was expected to more than double to $98.4 billion. After that, growth is expected to rise exponentially, reaching $197.2 billion in the year 2000 and more than $700 billion in 2002! Of that number, in 1998 $28.2 billion was spent by United States citizens. In 1999, the amount spent by Americans was expected to reach $71 billion, topping out at $400 billion in 2002, the last year for which statistics were forecast.

There are a lot of reasons people are more comfortable doing business online now than they were just a few years ago. Improvements in the technology that make e-commerce transactions secure have laid to rest many of the fears that consumers had about entering their credit card numbers on the Web. Web site design and technology have also improved, which has helped companies build sites that are more user-friendly, informative, entertaining, and interactive.

Also, as commercial Web sites have gained experience in e-commerce over the last several years, they have begun to offer consumers more of what they want. This learning process was unavoidable as Web businesspeople learned the ins and outs of electronic commerce. Many retailing tactics work great in a store or over the phone yet fail online. Unfortunately, for the early Internet businessmen, the only way to find out that these tactics were not Net appropriate was to try them and watch them fail. But one of the great things about e-Commerce is that you can experiment with different tactics and strategies from one day to the next.

While demographics of Internet users should be important to you in determining what you want your site to accomplish, all the statistics in the world will not help you if you lose sight of who your audience is.

The demographics of Internet users are even more important if you're starting up a Web-only business from scratch. In that situation, Web users are your *entire* audience. But Web-only startups have an advantage that multi-medium businesses do not: the opportunity to build a business without the capital required in traditional businesses. You do not have to purchase a storefront in a mall or other well-traveled area. Your employee needs are minimized, so there are no hefty social security taxes or insurance premiums to deal with. You just build your site, and you're ready to take orders online.

Age is one of the primary demographic variables on the Internet. Although many more people over 40 are getting access to the Net, the majority of Internet users fall into the 18 to 40 age range. This fact has spawned many of the current trends in Internet business product categories, for example, online music, online software stores, and online books.

Technology products, to no one's surprise, are also one of the most popular categories of electronic commerce. This is at least partly due to the proclivities of the people running technology businesses and the dizzyingly fast pace of computer technology. But it also points to a self-evident demographic trend of online users: the average online user likes technology and new products.

But how can you use all this information? Once you understand your customers and really put yourself in their shoes, you can build the Web site of their dreams.

It is important to build the site from the eyes of your customers. Like any advertising for your business, you want it to be appealing, informative, and, most of all, memorable. Take your customers into account when you design your Web site. Think about what they like and what they will look for in your company. If you design a site that they will like, they are sure to come back.

You can survey your customers to find out all kinds of information. Distribute surveys through catalogs, direct mail, faxes, and phone calls. Talk to those people you do business with and ask them if they have Web access. Ask them if they are interested in getting to you on the Web. Find out how they view commerce on the Internet before you make the decision to build a site.

Internet-only Startup Businesses

Internet-only startups are businesses that have no real world bricks-and-mortar facility. You can only do business with these companies via the Web. Wingspan Bank is an example of just such an Internet startup business. Wingspan was founded from the beginning as a Web-only bank that offers lower expenses and higher interest rates to banking customers. They can do this because they have low overhead costs. There is no building facility or high employment costs associated with tellers and managers. As a business, Wingspan Bank appeals to both Web users who are technology leaders and early adopters of technology.

In fact, we can break down the general population of consumers into different categories based on their interest in and willingness to use new technology in their daily lives. This is a key factor in consumers' likelihood for using your Web site.

Types of Internet Consumers

- High-tech focused leaders—must always have the latest and greatest technology tools and are willing to pay for it. High-tech leaders are typically executives who are very valuable customers because they provide plenty of word-of-mouth advertising—if you give them good service. Make sure to provide faultless service to this group.
- Early adopters—obtain and use technology methods and products before most of the general population. Early adopters are usually employed in the software industry or other computer industries. They are likely to have the latest and greatest computers available, and are willing to experiment with technology. Online businesses with customers in this group can afford to pull out all the stops in developing a Web site with the late technologies and whiz-bang software.
- Mainstream users—wait until technology and business processes are tried and tested. Mainstream users are hard to pin down because they represent the broadest section of the market. Sites for this group usually emphasize price competition and freebies to attract and retain customers.
- Laggards—are resistant to new technology and new methods of commerce. Laggards are the most difficult online group to market to because they are so resistant to new technology. The best approach for marketing to this group is to keep everything as simple as possible, and create very specific calls to action to accomplish the goals of your site.

Important Issues to Web Shoppers

- Security—How secure is your site? What encryption technology do you use?
- Reliability—Are orders ever lost? Are questions answered promptly? Do you deliver on your promises?
- Reputation—What do other consumers say about your online business in chat rooms or newsgroups?
- Price—The primary reasons people cite for shopping online are price-saving and time-saving.
- Service—The real reason people will come back to your site is convenience and super service.

Shopping List

✔ **Security**

✔ **Reliability**

✔ **Reputation**

✔ **Price**

✔ **Service**

Business Practices and Online Goals

Determining what you want your Web site to do is not easy or cut and dry. Of course, you probably want to sell products online. After all, that is probably the reason you picked up this book in the first place. But have you given thought to the other things you can do online?

When the time comes to figure out what you want your Web site to accomplish for your business, you need to think about all aspects of your business plan. How do you do business with customers now, and how do you expect to do business with them online?

No Web solution is going to do everything. There is no such thing as being all things to all customers. Does your business rely on personal communication? Real, interpersonal communication is difficult to achieve on the Net, so if your business practices depend on it, you will have to build your site to approximate the personal feeling your company usually presents.

Does your business rely on fast order processing? The Internet is perfect for quick business transactions, but if this is how you do business, you must develop your Web site and your expectations of it to make the most of your business practices.

Strategic Goals and Objectives

Since keeping your customers satisfied will result in sales almost every time, your Web site's goals and objectives should reflect the experience you want for your customers. Think about the people that you do business with. Think about the conversations you have with them. What information do they request from you before they make a purchasing decision? What questions do they have after they have bought your product?

The best way to think about Web site objectives is to contemplate a typical day in your business. Who do you talk to? How do you use the fax machine? How do you generate new customer leads? How do you meet with your customers? Do you use the mail, UPS, or other delivery and courier services? What information from the customer do you find absolutely critical to helping you

Reduce Your Costs

Did you know that you can reduce your costs by putting your business online? Correspondence handled via electronic means such as e-mail is less expensive than the paper and postage type. If you are not figuring the costs of paper, postage, and printing into your business practices, you should be. Give thought to other areas you can reduce costs online!

close the sale? The answers to these questions will help you devise a solid list of goals and objectives for your Web site.

Your objectives should be as specific and as measurable as possible. To generate objectives that are both specific and measurable you must think in quantitative terms. Things like the number of times that customers access your database, download a product specification sheet, or send an inquiry to customer service are all specific and measurable.

Core Constituencies

The foundation of a good Web business strategy lies in a deep understanding of the people you do business with and *how* you do business with them. There are your customers, of course. But you also need to think about suppliers, business partners, employees, and even investors. These people are your *core constituencies*.

Core constituencies can be defined as your prototypical customers. Core constituencies are the group or groups of people that you want to please most with your Web site. But do not make the mistake of assuming that your customers are the only people that make up the core constituency. If you own a golf pro shop, the people who supply your products can also be a core constituency you want to address on your site. Think of ways your Web site can make it easier for you to do business not only with your customers but with your vendors and other business partners as well.

Great business Web sites, and ones that are successful, treat each user that enters as a real, valued customer on the other end of the line. This does not happen by accident. A great Web site takes planning and dedication.

Case Study:
Greenwich Capital Markets

Greenwich Capital Markets (GCM) is an investment bank specializing in the trading of fixed income and collateralized securities for institutional clients and their own accounts. Their beginning on the Web was rather scattered. By the spring of 1998, Greenwich Capital Markets had no real Web presence, just a hodge-podge of internal, employee-only Web pages. These employee-developed pages were implemented by various departments with little or no interactivity between them. Greenwich Capital Markets decided to hire Solvent Media, a Web development firm, to help them consolidate their Web strategy and build a unified Web presence for their company. Solvent Media was presented with the task of creating an overall unified strategy for the Web site as well as the design and execution.

Solvent Media began by analyzing how Greenwich Capital Markets did their business. They looked carefully at not only the bank's business practices and cycles but who they did business with and the cycles of those firms. Through this careful analysis Solvent Media and Greenwich Capital Markets came up with three primary goals for the Web site. They wanted to use it to improve client interaction, recruit employee candidates, and facilitate the flow of information among their own employees.

Once Greenwich Capital Markets had determined what they wanted their Web site to accomplish, they then had to determine the best ways to meet those goals. Solvent Media began a series of interviews with key employees at GCM to discover all the nuances of how they did business. Because the Web is an interactive media, Solvent paid particularly close attention to how communication between employees and clients was handled. Solvent also engaged in a document analysis, looking at reports, documents, and information that passed between GCM and its clients during the course of business. In order to find ways to meet their goals, GCM and Solvent Media first had to figure out how the company did business and how that business could be made more effective and more efficient by putting them on the Web. This phase of development was called the research and investigation phase.

Once the research and investigation phase was completed, Solvent Media developed a flow chart and functional specification of the Web site. This laid out for the decision-makers at the bank just what the Web site would look like and how it would work. As designed, the new Greenwich Capital Markets Web site would allow analysts and salesmen to share financial statistics and analysis between clients and employees more easily and efficiently. The new site would also allow potential employees to easily find overview information on Greenwich Capital Markets and what it was like to work there.

Once the flow chart and functional specifications were modified and approved, design mockups were prepared and transformed into storyboards giving a step-by-step tour of the proposed Web site. After another set of modifications and approvals by the decision-makers at Greenwich Capital Markets, the site was programmed by Solvent Media.

The design of the site was created to brand the bank in a certain way. As a financial services institution, Greenwich Capital Markets wanted the "look and feel" of their site to be artistic and aesthetically pleasing yet well-organized and professional. They wanted customers to get a solid and comfortable feel from the Web site, giving the customer confidence in the bank as a lasting, safe place to put his or her money.

Some technological aspects were added to the site to ease the functionality and operations of the site. CGI (common gateway interface) programs were created to allow access to several dozen constantly updated reports and financial statistics generated by GCM analysts. There was also a way for college and MBA students to upload their resume to reach the requisite individuals at Greenwich Capital Markets human resources department.

Web sites should never be static, and GCM took that concept to heart. Since its initial launch, Greenwich Capital Markets has upgraded their site, expanding its focus and revamping the content. The new site launch contains more information and was upscaled to serve more people. The Web site was constructed so that Greenwich Capital Markets could easily add on to the site as technology expands without having to worry if the existing site would integrate with ease.

You can see from this case study that Greenwich Capital Markets spent a lot of time carefully considering their audience and how they wanted them to interact with the Web site. They included employees in that audience, and with the help of a quality development firm, made a site that works well for their particular business needs. You should give the same kind of depth of consideration when defining your audience.

WORKSHEET

1. What are the demographics of your customers?

2. What features do you think your customers will want to see on your Web site?

3. What business practices do you have that are unique to your business, product, or service?

4. List at least three ways you think you can use the Web to help you with these unique business practices.

PART TWO

PLANNING AND BUILDING YOUR BUSINESS WEB SITE

Add items to Cart | **Ratings & Reviews** | **Compare Prices** | **Find Products** | **Buy Now!**

Address http://chapter_four.com **Link**

What Kind of Site Do You Need?

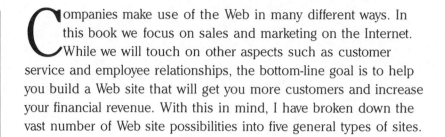

Companies make use of the Web in many different ways. In this book we focus on sales and marketing on the Internet. While we will touch on other aspects such as customer service and employee relationships, the bottom-line goal is to help you build a Web site that will get you more customers and increase your financial revenue. With this in mind, I have broken down the vast number of Web site possibilities into five general types of sites.

- Business card sites
- Brochure sites
- Sales presentation sites
- Online stores
- Interactive e-commerce sites

Online Business Card

For some businesses, all you need is to let people know where you are, what you do, how to reach you, or that your Web site is under construction and will be coming soon. This is the concept behind the online business card.

An online business card does not need to be lacking in content or be unattractive, however. It should be well-designed and informative. Remember, it is a home base for your domain name and represents your business. You want it to do so in the best possible way!

The online business card Web site is a contact central for you and your business. Any information about you or your company that people may need should be on this page. This includes standard contact information but can also include specific information that customers, colleagues, or vendors may require. You might include your federal tax ID number or the phone number at your hotel while you are away on business.

The online business card is perfect for small businesses. If you own a small local card and gift shop, you can use an online business card to list your address, hours of operation, phone number, and even mention some of the products you carry.

The **online business card** has everything you would normally find on a business card, and more. This is great for small businesses who merely want a place for their customers to find them on the Web.

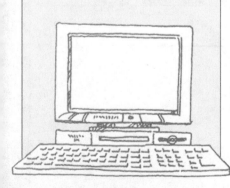

The online business card can include the following information:

- Your name
- Company name
- Address
- Phone number
- Fax number
- E-mail address
- Cellular phone number
- Pager number

The advantages of an online business card are speed and simplicity. There's no need for a long planning process, complicated hardware or software, or expensive development.

ONLINE BUSINESS CARD EXAMPLE: LOUISA HARDWARE

Online Brochure

The next level of sophistication in Web sites is the online brochure. Just like a paper brochure, the online brochure is a sales piece showcasing your products or services. It is your chance to play up what is great and unique about your company. It is also your face on the Internet available twenty-four hours a day, seven days a week.

Building an Online Business Card

With the simple HTML tutorial in this book, you can construct an online business card with practically no expense. Most Internet service providers will give you a small amount of server space free with your dial-up connection, so this is a great way to get your business online quickly and inexpensively.

Building an Online Brochure

Online brochures are the next level in technological advancement. If you were going to publish an online brochure yourself, you would probably have to purchase some additional space from your ISP and utilize one of the software tools we talk about later in this book. Higher end catalogs require some database technology that can be too advanced for Web site development software, so if your catalog is going to have any depth to it or require searching you may want to consult a developer.

The online brochure requires planning, graphic design, copy writing, and a moderate level of technical expertise. Anyone with average intelligence and a willingness to learn new technology can create a successful online brochure. But you may also want to consider hiring out for one or more aspects of this Web site.

ONLINE BROCHURE EXAMPLE: AUDI USA

People use online brochures in a variety of ways to support their sales efforts. Whether your company is product- or service-oriented, you can use the Web to define and describe your offerings to customers. As a salesman, you can steer potential customers to your Web site *before* you meet with them or leave behind your Web address after the meeting. Demonstrating your company Web site *during* a meeting can transform a boring meeting into an exciting and effective dialogue.

For small businesses, such as our local card and gift shop, an online brochure is the ideal solution. The online brochure allows you to showcase special products for holidays and seasons.

Online Sales Presentation

Nothing is more important than *impact* when you are making a business presentation. You dress your best, gather all of your materials, and prepare for every question. Let's face it: you usually only get one chance with a prospective customer.

An online presentation helps you make an impact with potential customers. The multimedia capabilities of the Web offer exciting graphics, audio, and video. You can tap great databases, or even reference other sites on the Web. Because the Web is such a visual medium, showing customers the benefits of your product is easy.

There are exciting technologies to help make your online presentation successful. Flash, JavaScript, ActiveX, Windows Media Technologies, RealAudio and RealVideo, as well as plain old animated gifs bring sound and action to the Net. But multimedia pyrotechnics are only half the story. ASP, CGI, and a litany of interactive tools can help you pull your customer into the heart of your Web site to show off your company at its best.

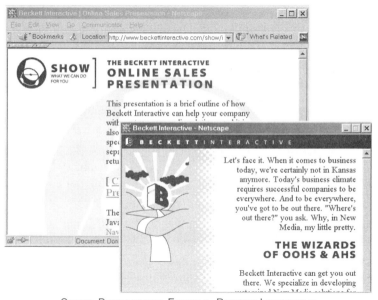

ONLINE PRESENTATION EXAMPLE: BECKETT INTERACTIVE

Creating an Online Presentation

You may be able to host your online presentation with your regular ISP for the additional cost of extra server space. In order to make the presentation shine, you are going to need to use some additional technology. While basic presentations can be created with the Web site creation software we talk about later in this book, for presentations with greater depth you should definitely consult a professional Web developer.

Online Store

The Internet has been described as the world's largest shopping mall. Anything you could ever imagine is for sale on the Web. From books to baseball cards, groceries to jewelry, mortgages, or insurance—you name it; you can find it on the Web.

Traditional bricks-and-mortar businesses such as Barnes & Noble and Internet-only businesses such as CDNow.com (which sells music online) have realized what direct marketers have known for decades: If you present people with an opportunity to buy your product, they will take you up on that offer a good part of the time.

ONLINE STORE EXAMPLE: AMAZON.COM

While it is true that large direct marketers with the finances and back-end infrastructure to support high-volume sales have a leg up on smaller competitors, the Internet goes a long way toward leveling the playing field. With the Internet, there is no need to pay for high-priced storefronts or a customer service call center to compete with the big companies.

Grassroots marketing and strong promotion can bring small companies as far as they want to go on the Web. There are tremendous opportunities in affiliate marketing, viral marketing, link exchange services, newsgroups, mailing lists, industry directories, and direct e-mail campaigns to help bring in new business.

If you want your online store to shine, you really should not try any high-end functions yourself. For low-end stores, feel free to use one of the terrific services we mention later. But for anything more advanced, call in the professionals.

Database technology, while not essential for an online catalog, is the preferred method for building an online store. Scalability in the number of customers you can service at one time, the number of products you can offer, and the services available on your Web site depend on using a robust database system. We will cover the various hardware and software options in later chapters.

Case Study: OfficeWare

OfficeWare, in Cincinnati, Ohio, specializes in every form of document output and uses its Web site primarily as a point of presence—a place where end-users can get information about the company and its products. "The site exemplifies our corporate image," says Bilyana Mundisev, OfficeWare's marketing manager. "It's classy, simple, not fancy, not a 'screaming' Web site." This is an example of a business using its Web site as more of an online business card than a way of doing business.

As an information source, OfficeWare's Web site is important to the company's marketing strategy. "All our letterhead, cards, and promotional material have the Web site on them," says Mundisev. The site does have a section where end-users can order supplies, thus functioning as a point of sale, and that section offers several avenues where the end-user can make contact with Office Ware.

While some leads come through the Web site, Mundisev says that the company is currently focusing its marketing efforts on a purchased, targeted prospect list. However, all those prospects will be pointed back to the Web site for information. In addition, since the company has eliminated all print and radio advertising to focus on the targeted leads, "The Web page will be the only thing out there for anyone else to see," says Mundisev. Because OfficeWare is not attempting to generate leads anywhere but through that targeted list, its online customer service becomes all important.

Mundisev explains that OfficeWare has chosen not to use its Web site as a point of sale for equipment because the company wants to establish a relationship with customers through real interaction rather than just making a sale. It is very difficult to establish a personal relationship with customers that order through a Web site, so rather than push their products online, OfficeWare has made the focal point of their business relationship a "Docutivity" study, which is a free needs analysis OfficeWare performs for its customers.

"It's the study we're selling, not the product," says Mundisev. "If we set up sales on our Web site, it would have a different effect. So it's not a point of sale, it's a point of contact." By offering something that customers want online through its Web site, OfficeWare creates the contacts it needs. They use traditional, personal methods to turn those contacts into sales.

The OfficeWare site is a good example of an online sales presentation. OfficeWare uses the site to build awareness of their products, generate leads, and generally show off the company to potential customers.

Building an Online Store

Now you are getting into some major heavy-duty Web sites. In the software tools section of this book we talk about some programs and online services to help you build an online storefront. It is unlikely your ISP will be able to host your site unless it specifically offers business hosting services. You'll pay a premium for the extra storage space on the Web server and for the maintenance and upgrading of the site.

Interactive E-Commerce

The ultimate power of the Internet is captured by interactive e-commerce. Integrating every aspect of your business into the Web can transform your company into a powerhouse capable of competing with anyone, anywhere in the world. If you take a hard look at your business operations you'll surely see opportunities where the Internet can help you reach more and more people faster and more easily. This is the promise of e-commerce in the new millenium.

An interactive e-commerce Web presence can also revitalize the *way* you do business. Customers can instantly search product databases to get the latest prices and updates. They can input their requirements to create customized solutions that are designed and built for their unique needs. And with the click of a mouse they can make a direct purchase using a credit card or account number.

There are several technologies that work together to power an e-commerce Web site. Databases and dynamic Web page generation allow for the *personalization* of Web pages for every visitor. Security systems allow for the private transmission of sensitive information like credit card numbers and passwords. Credit card authentication and authorization software allow the e-commerce transaction to be completed successfully.

INTERACTIVE E-COMMERCE SITE EXAMPLE: DELL COMPUTER

Successful Internet businesses base their entire operations around databases that are co-owned by themselves and their customers. Customers can become equal stakeholders who help your business by contributing critical information and keeping their own records up-to-date. All this occurs with the proper security and data precautions in place, ensuring the integrity and safety of your business information.

Your customers will truly appreciate the efforts you make with a sophisticated and service-oriented Web site. As they find useful capabilities on your Web site, they will invest more and more time using it to do business with you. Once that process is started, your Web site will become an invaluable tool for your customers, and then they're hooked! They will be dedicated customers. Amazon.com has succeeded in precisely the same way: building great business relationships one customer at a time.

The type of Web site you need depends on your product, your goals, and your budget. No one can say which is best for you. Think hard about the time and resources you are willing to put into the initial development of your site, as well as its ongoing care and maintenance.

An online business card or sales presentation may be simple enough to put up yourself. The most important aspect of these types of Web sites is getting the basic information up and available on the Web. An online brochure can be more involved, describing in detail your company and its products or services.

Online stores and interactivity e-commerce Web sites are the most exciting forms of businesses on the Internet. They sometimes require expert programming and database capabilities, but there are software services such as Yahoo! Store and Bigstep.com that will provide the back-end systems for these interactive Web sites.

Alternatively, you can choose to hire a professional Web developer to build your site. This will free up your time to focus on the real issues in making your online business successful: namely, the content and services provided by your site.

Building an Interactive E-Commerce Web Site

This is truly what the Internet was meant to be. But along with the bells and whistles that make up interactive e-commerce come some inherent costs. Interactive Web sites are best left to professional developers or programmers if you want them to look the way they should. You should also hire a professional hosting company to house the site, as they have the resources necessary to keep it running smoothly twenty-four hours a day, seven days a week.

WORKSHEET

True or false:

1. An online business card is the simplest type of
   business Web site.   *True*   *False*

2. You must hire a developer to build an online brochure. *True*   *False*

3. Sales presentation sites are only good for large,
   multidivisional corporations.   *True*   *False*

4. There is no way to build an online store besides
   hiring a developer.   *True*   *False*

5. Interactive e-commerce sites require the most amount of
   labor to build and maintain.   *True*   *False*

6. You should spend as little as possible on your Web site. *True*   *False*

7. If you do not have enough money to start an online
   business, you are out of luck.   *True*   *False*

Address http://chapter_five.com **Link**

Planning Your Web Site

Domain Names

The first thing to do when you decide you are going to put your business online is to register a domain name. A domain name is the unique name that identifies a site on the Internet. Amazon.com is a domain name. You want to select and register a name that is descriptive for your business. A good choice is your company name, such as Joesdiner.com. Choosing a name that describes what you do can also be a good choice, such as wesellfish.com. Your domain name should be memorable and descriptive. You want your customers to remember when they sit down at their computer that for quality fish and fish supplies they only need to look as far as wesellfish.com. A domain name can be no more than 26 characters long, including those used to identify the top level domain. The TLD or top level domain, is the .com, .net, .org, etc. that comes after the name you come up with.

Once you decide on the name you are going to register, the next step is the registration process.

In the beginning, domain names were registered by a company called Network Solutions Incorporated. For $70, you could register any domain name for two years. For many years InterNIC (Internet Network Information Center), a cooperative activity between the U.S. government and Network Solutions, was solely responsible for registering and maintaining top level domain names, while the actual registration process was carried out by Network Solutions. But that is all ending. On June 25, 1999, Network Solutions lost the exclusive right to register domain names, and other companies have begun to offer domain registration solutions. Because the Web needs to be structured in an orderly fashion, InterNIC still hands out domain names, but now you can go through several different companies to get them.

It will still cost you the $70 for two years from InterNIC, but on top of that the registration services charge their own fees for everything from processing to site hosting. Look around before choosing a registration service. Do some homework and see what each service offers. They've all added value to their service, but it is that value that determines the final price for registering your domain. You should also check with the company that will be hosting your

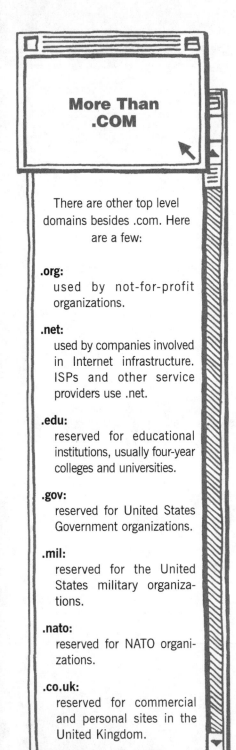

More Than .COM

There are other top level domains besides .com. Here are a few:

.org:
 used by not-for-profit organizations.

.net:
 used by companies involved in Internet infrastructure. ISPs and other service providers use .net.

.edu:
 reserved for educational institutions, usually four-year colleges and universities.

.gov:
 reserved for United States Government organizations.

.mil:
 reserved for the United States military organizations.

.nato:
 reserved for NATO organizations.

.co.uk:
 reserved for commercial and personal sites in the United Kingdom.

site. Some hosting services offer free domain registration if you sign a contract with them.

Once you've registered a domain name, how does a Web browser know where to go when you type in "http://www.wesell-fish.com"? The answer lies in the domain name system established by Network Solutions.

Besides a Web server, every Web site must also run a domain name system (DNS) server. The DNS server essentially translates English domain names into the Internet Protocol (IP) addresses that tell Web browsers where to get Web pages and Web servers where to send those Web pages. You can think of these DNS servers as kind of a huge telephone book. In a traditional telephone book, people are listed alphabetically according to their last name, which lets you look up their telephone number. You then pick up the phone and give them a call. The central DNS database is like the phone book, listing the Web site domain names you typed in and automatically finding the phone number, in this case, the IP address. Your browser acts as the telephone, connecting you to the Web server, who is the person you wanted to call. Thankfully, this all takes far less time than hauling out the big old Yellow Pages.

DNS servers provide the technology that enables the Internet to be the easy, one-click hyperlinking system that it is today. Without it, we would all have to keep a list of every Web site's IP address to get anywhere on the Web. With the DNS system, Web sites can be physically located anywhere on any Web server. Web sites can even change their hosting service (which, since they are changing Web servers, will change their IP address), but they can keep their same domain name. After all, your name stays exactly the same when you move to a new home, right? Just your phone number and address change. It works the same for Web sites.

Planning for Success

Nothing is more important to the success of a Web site than proper planning. It may be difficult to overcome a bad user experience, disorganized information, or pointless content. But if you plan your Web site carefully, the right site will emerge, even if by trial and error.

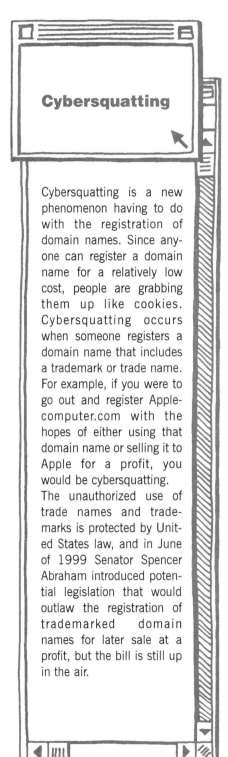

Cybersquatting

Cybersquatting is a new phenomenon having to do with the registration of domain names. Since anyone can register a domain name for a relatively low cost, people are grabbing them up like cookies. Cybersquatting occurs when someone registers a domain name that includes a trademark or trade name. For example, if you were to go out and register Apple-computer.com with the hopes of either using that domain name or selling it to Apple for a profit, you would be cybersquatting. The unauthorized use of trade names and trademarks is protected by United States law, and in June of 1999 Senator Spencer Abraham introduced potential legislation that would outlaw the registration of trademarked domain names for later sale at a profit, but the bill is still up in the air.

Web Site Planning Process

There are four simple steps in the planning process. Follow these and you are on your way to building a great Web site:

1. *Strategy*. Like anything, a failure to plan is a plan to fail.

2. *Functional objectives*. What do you want your Web site to do for you or your customers?

3. *Functional specifications*. Describe your site in plain English. How do you want it to look? How do you want to accomplish your functional objectives?

4. *Production*. Time to construct the Web site. Who will you hire? Can you handle construction and maintenance yourself?

Strategy

Setting a strategy for your online business is the first step to success. A great strategy should succinctly outline the *results* you want your Web site to achieve and the overall means by which it is going to achieve those results. Be as definitive as possible about what success will mean. It is easy to just define your Web site's success as an increase in sales. You may also want to look at other leading indicators. Do you want to generate more high-quality leads of people who use your products? How about reaching a certain percentage of your sales from e-commerce alone, or increasing the average order size? Keep a list of what a successful Web site means to you and your business. Make sure to update it as your expectations change. Explicitly defining success for your Web site will help you design every graphic, write every line, and place every button on the site with those goals in mind.

Results usually describe a target audience and how the Web site is going to make that target audience *feel* or what the Web site is going to make that target audience *do*. For example:

> The site will increase revenue and improve customer loyalty by learning about customers' needs and offering them customized products and solutions they can order quickly and easily.

Notice how there are two goals, one very tangible and the other intangible, followed by a logical plan for achieving those goals. It is important that your strategy clearly defines what your goals are and how you plan on achieving them.

Functional Objectives

A well-defined strategy will yield the next step in the planning process—functional objectives. Functional objectives are important because they are the foundation of your development effort. Functional objectives define and categorize what your Web site will do. The categories you should think about for creating the functional objectives include:

1. *Security.* How will I protect my customers' personal and financial information? How can I make them feel safe and comfortable doing business on my site?

2. *Information to be collected from customers.* Do I want to generate a database of leads from my Web site? Will I need to know specifications of specific products customers are interested in to serve them better?

3. *Information to be delivered to customers.* Besides our address and phone number, what other information will your customers require? Do they need to know your prices? Product specs?

4. *Databases customers can search.* Can some of the information you deliver to your customers be collected in a searchable database?

5. *Photos or graphics customers can see.* Your Web site should be interesting and exciting to visit! Do you have photographs of your facility? The products you provide? Your staff? Let your online customer feel as important as a real face-to-face customer! Give them the ability to see your products, and they will be more likely to buy them.

6. *Transactions customers can make.* Will customers be able to purchase products directly from your Web site?

7. *Ways customers can contact you.* Can customers simply fill out a form to contact you or must they send an e-mail? Can they reach you online or do they have to call or come in?

8. *Ways customers can personalize their experience on your site.* Personalization makes customers feel important and special! How can you make your Web site unique to their needs and desires?

Do you want to generate a database of your products that your customers can use to find what they need? Should that database have pictures along with product information? Once they know what they want, will your customers be able to order products online?

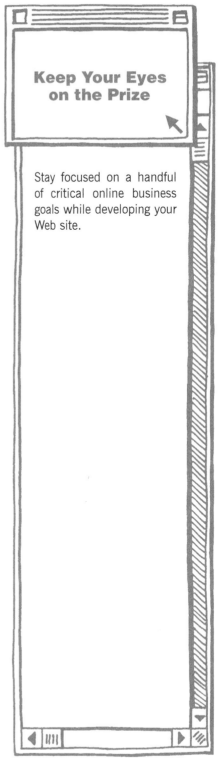

Keep Your Eyes on the Prize

Stay focused on a handful of critical online business goals while developing your Web site.

How will they do that, and how will you make it secure for them? Think about your core constituencies (see Chapter 3) and how to best please them.

Functional Specification

Once you have defined your strategy and functional objectives, the next step is to create a functional specification. A functional specification describes in detail the content and functionality of the Web site. It is the document that will be handed over to the designers and programmers when they begin to build the site. Every page, and every available interactivity on every page, needs to be outlined in detail. In essence, the functional specification is the blueprint for the Web site.

There are many ways to create a functional specification. The first place to start is by taking your functional objectives and building a flow chart of all the pages on your Web site. Start with the home page at the top, then work your way down through the second level (major) sections of the Web site, then through the third level pages, and so on until you have a pyramid-looking structure. This organizational flow chart should have a title and brief description for each page.

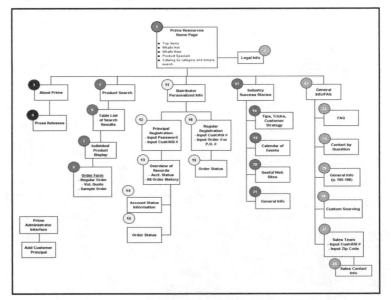

SAMPLE FLOW CHART

Once you have developed a flow chart, the next step is to develop a storyboard. This step is optional, but I have found that it is really helpful in visualizing how every page will look standing alone, as well as in the context of the entire Web site.

The storyboard should have a simple graphical representation of each page on the Web site, along with the content and function of each page. You can lay out the content as you think it will appear on the site, but that is not critical. The point here is to create a detailed road map based on your flow chart and functional specification.

How you build your storyboard is up to you, but I have found that working with a pencil and large-format paper works best. Or you may want to use a single 5 x 7 piece of paper for each Web page and tape them up on a large blank wall. (This can create the effect of a war room, which is kind of fun.) In any case, everything a user can see or do should be noted on each page. Every bit of content, every navigation bar, every *interactive* component on each page should be on the storyboard.

In the end, the functional specification should describe the site in detailed plain English so that you can hand over this blueprint to the people producing the site and they will know exactly what they are being asked to build.

Design Issues

How do you define design? What is it? Is it fine art, the ability to draw beautiful pictures? Is it the way a page is laid out to focus the user's eye on certain material? Is it the way that the entire site is organized in an information architecture? Is it the Web's vaunted *interactivity*, the ability to connect with a customer and make something happen? Well, yes! It is *all of the above*.

There are differences in how all these issues are addressed in Web site design, but each one of them is very important. Each of these design issues must be thought through carefully and completely to call a Web site well designed. If you have a beautiful Web site visually but it is poorly organized, your site can hardly be called well designed.

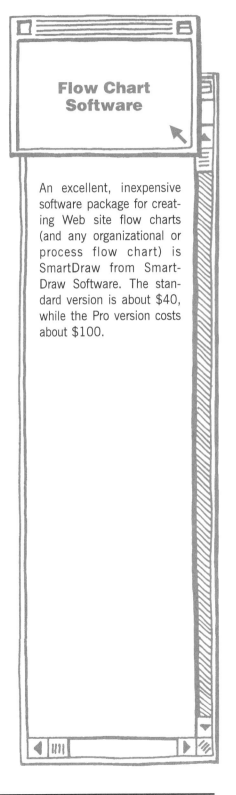

Flow Chart Software

An excellent, inexpensive software package for creating Web site flow charts (and any organizational or process flow chart) is SmartDraw from Smart-Draw Software. The standard version is about $40, while the Pro version costs about $100.

Web Design

Visit any Web site on the Internet and you will instantly be confronted by one of two overwhelming feelings. You will either feel, like Dorothy in the *Wizard of Oz*, that you have landed in a very "good place" or a very "bad place." Though there is such a thing as a simply mediocre Web site, the feelings you get are either good or bad. That feeling is derived from a complex set of emotions and observations that we all experience when we arrive at a new place, no matter how jaded or naive we may be. Rarely do you look around a place and say "Wow, this is really average." Either you like something or you do not. This is more a general reaction to the way something, in this case a Web site, *speaks* to you than any one piece of information. Sure, you may like or dislike the pictures you see or the choices that are presented to you, but chances are you will be reacting primarily to the *overall design* of the site.

Let's face it, looks count in this world. We have all faced that in life, from elementary school to well past college. First impressions are extraordinarily important in our society. And the same goes for the way you present your business in advertising and on the Internet. For many your Web site is going to be the very first impression of your company. If people come to your home page and like what they see, they will be much more likely to explore the rest of the site and in the end make a transaction or give you information you need to make a sale. In the same way you dress to impress for an important business meeting or keep your house neat and clean (a valiant goal for me!) when company is coming over, you must focus on the design of your Web site so that you present the very best impression to everyone who visits your site, not just the first time, but every time. It is the single most imperative factor in the success of your Web site.

This is not to say that design is the only factor in a Web site's success. Of course, there must be useful, updated information, and every interactive tool and application must function well. But remember, if people do not like your site, all the helpful and interesting information in the world will not get them to stay. First impressions can be last impressions, so if you were to choose the first and foremost important factor in people's overall impression and memory of your Web site, there is only one issue to consider: *design.*

Web surfers are renowned for their critical eye with regard to Web site design and their lack of patience with poorly designed and organized Web sites. One study of Internet usage gauged the click habits of typical Web consumers. The study found that as Web consumers surfed the Internet, the average time between mouse clicks was only seven seconds! This means that Web surfers are not only constantly analyzing and critiquing the Web sites they visit, but they are doing it quickly with little regard to the content. After all, how much can you read in seven seconds? Web surfers are looking for something when they click on to a Web site, even if they are not quite sure what that *something* is. And they are constantly making quick decisions about whether the Web page that they have surfed to is worth their time.

Over the first few years of the consumer Internet (1995 through 1997) the state of design for Web sites was, quite frankly, atrocious. There were several reasons for this, and not all of them are entirely fair comparisons. First, Web sites have always been compared to other forms of media. It is an unfair comparison but a bias that is ingrained in our culture. Many people *look* at a computer monitor and *see* a television set. They expect to see vivid, moving pictures and graphics that constantly stimulate and challenge their senses. But in many cases it is nearly impossible to compete with the graphic capability of television. The reason is simple: graphics, and especially moving graphics (video), take vast amounts of information. Large files take incredible amounts of time to download. Also, moving around huge files on the Internet is a very tedious process.

These early Web sites were also subpar because the workforce creating Web sites in the first few years was immature. It is said that babies must crawl before they walk and walk before they run, and the same principle applies to Web development. In its infancy, Web development was a new and untrained vocation. This resulted in people who were hard pressed to find their footing in a new

COLA Principles

When designing a Web page, there are four principles to remember. Think COLA: content, organization, links, and appropriateness.

C = Content:
A site must have good content or it is useless to a visitor.

O = Organization:
A site must be easy to use and logically organized.

L = Links:
A site must hold your attention until it has communicated its message to you.

A = Appropriateness:
A site should not have too many graphics and should provide plain text links. Special features should be functional, not cute. The site should not use hard-to-read colors, backgrounds, or fonts.

medium. Programmers were trying to act like artists and designers, while designers were struggling with the inherent layout difficulties of HTML. Nowadays you can find all kinds of books just like this one that deal in great detail with issues of design and programming. But back when the commercial Internet was just getting started there was no such assistance. People had to learn by trial and error, teaching themselves the intricacies of designing for this new, untested media.

As the general population of Web developers has grown and matured, the standard for Web site design has risen dramatically in the last few years. No Web surfer would stand for one of these original sites in today's world of high-tech, high-impact Web sites. There have been several trends that have greatly improved the state of design on the Internet. For a long time, the design of Web sites was handled by developers who made the transition from print media to online media. Unfortunately, some of the rules considered canon in print do not translate well online. Today there is a new crop of Web designers who have not simply switched over from print design. These new designers have literally grown up with computers and video games. From the earliest Commodore 64 to today's fastest Pentium processors, they have always had a computer in their homes. These new designers have seen the evolution first hand and taken a part in it. It became such a part of their lives that they majored in computer and Web graphic design in college. But most importantly, they have trained their thought processes to work in Web mode.

Design Approaches

Different types of Web sites require different design approaches. If your Web site's content is going to be very text heavy you may want to consider the publishing model. Publishing-type Web sites are similar in design to magazines. They utilize multiple columns of text with many option lists for navigation. They usually utilize software that will allow customers to use keywords to search the entire Web site for specific Web pages that are relevant to their needs.

The online catalog Web site we discussed in Chapter 3 focuses on product searches and display. All the information on your products are kept in databases. The customer does not interface with your database though. The primary interface for the consumer will be either a categorized table of contents or an advanced search utility. In this kind of search, your consumer can specify many search options, not just simple keywords like color or product model. Advanced search utilities allow customers to search with a great degree of specificity. Searches like this go far beyond simple keywords, letting your customers search on items like product specifications, date, file type, even color all at once, producing results that have all or some of the specifications they desire.

Web Page Design Strategy

The design strategy for your Web site covers the overall look of the pages as well as the interaction between the pages. Depending on your target audience and what you are trying to achieve on the site, different amounts of text and graphics, navigation tools, and results boxes will be employed. The trick is to achieve the right balance of elements so that the Web site is easy to use and comfortable for a customer to navigate through.

There are certain elements of design that are universal to all media but are of special concern to developing a Web site. Use this checklist of elements on every Web page to ensure that your site is well-designed and professional.

- navigation and content organization
- page layout and interactivity—excitement and interest
- color
- typography
- imagery—illustration and photography
- proportion—size and spacing

Navigation

A fine overall navigation scheme can make the difference between a good Web site and a great Web site. Getting around the site and finding the information they want and need can be the single most frustrating experience for Web surfers. There is nothing more off-putting then feeling lost in a Web site without the ability to get back to the home page or to find what you want. People like to know where they are, they like to have escape routes available if

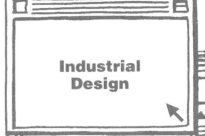

Industrial Design

When evaluating the design of your Web site, you must think in terms of industrial design where, in the very best examples, form follows function. The function of an item is the primary concern and the visual appeal, or form, follows after. When designing your Web site, every design issue must be viewed from the user's perspective. You know your customer best; make sure you tailor your site to what the user sees, feels, and experiences. Give them what they want to experience. Designing a good Web site is truly a matter of ergonomics.

CONTENT

they start to feel lost. Your customers will have no tolerance for sites that are poorly constructed. For this reason, having a solid navigation scheme that is easy to follow is critical.

The navigation scheme is defined by the icons and hyperlinks representing each distinct section of the Web site. The typical method of navigating around the Web site is a *navigation bar* with graphic icons that hyperlink to a content section of the Web site. Always make sure that you supplement icons with small text links for customers who have older browsers that are text-based or whose connection speed may not allow them to download the graphic icons quickly. Text icons are easy to find and allow those with older machines (or those who are just impatient) to quickly move to the section of your Web site they need.

Content organization goes hand-in-hand with the navigation scheme of a Web site. It is defined as a logical grouping of content on your Web site into distinct areas. When thinking about content organization, remember the old adage "Organization will set me free." People like to see things grouped into logical, neat little areas. A flow chart in the shape of a pyramid is the usual method for defining information architecture. A box is used to represent each Web page in the site, starting with the home page at the top. Each of the main sections of the Web site are then laid out underneath the home page in their own separate boxes. The Web site flow chart is built up in this way until you have a schematic organizational chart showing all of the content for the Web site on one piece of paper. That flow chart is what you need to make sure your site is not only easily navigable but that every link and button you place links up with the appropriate page somewhere else. About the only thing worse than having a poorly thought out navigation scheme is having links and buttons that do not go anywhere or result in error messages. The next click your customer will make after hitting his or her back button will be off your site and somewhere else. If you lose your customer, you lose the sale.

By and large, people use the Internet for one of four purposes: to complete transactions, to learn or disseminate information, to provide entertainment, or to communicate with others. Whatever they are using it for, customers usually want to see small amounts of information at a time with explicit instructions on what they should do next. Assume nothing about your customers' product or technology experience. You should always keep the lowest common denominator in mind. If you assume none of your customers know how to use the Internet or your site and create your site with explicit instructions that are not patronizing but informative, all your customers, from the techno-savvy to the Internet beginner, will be able to easily navigate and activate the features of your site. If you develop a Web site that is clear and concise, people will be able to easily find what they need.

The division of content areas on a Web site depend largely on which type of Web site you are building. For instance, if you are building an online brochure, you may organize your content into the following groups:

- About Us
- Products/Services
- Contact Us

In the About Us section, you would have pages that list your company's address, hours, and mission statement. This area can even contain information about your sales staff or pages about your corporate charitable contributions. Under Products/Services, you would have your searchable database of products, pages about how to use products or repair them, even detailed product specifications. Contact Us is fairly self explanatory. On these pages, you could generate forms for your customer to offer feedback, ask you questions, or opt-in to your e-mail reminder service.

However, if you build a full-blown interactive Web site, the organization may be very different:

- About Us
- Products/Services
- Customer Service
- Technical Support
- Project Management Area
- Employee Intranet
- Contact Us

DEFINITION PLEASE

Another common navigation method is the **frame**. A frame is a separate window-within-a-window that stays the same no matter where on the Web site your customer goes. Frames are often found on the left side of the screen and allow for easy navigation to any part of the site from any page on the site. One of the drawbacks to frame-based navigation is that the frame takes space away from the main window of your site. If you are utilizing a graphics or text-intensive site, you are left with a lot less room to devote to your products. Think carefully, or have a talk with your Web developer about the best way to build your navigation system.

Whichever type of Web site you are building, put yourself in your customer's shoes and think about the reasons you would be coming to this Web site. Are you trying to solve a problem? Are you trying to reach someone? Are you there to get more information about the products? The more you understand about the needs and desires of your customers, the better you will be able to create, design, and organize the Web site to fit those needs.

Page Layout and Interactivity

Page layout is an important issue in Web design. Page layout describes the location and interaction between the various content elements on a Web page. In other words, should your graphics be on the left or the right? Should your frame-based navigation be on the left or the bottom? Where should you place your text in relation to the pictures, and how big should it be. When the time comes to confront the issues surrounding page layout, readability and logic are two of your prime concerns. You want your site to be easily read and understood by your customer, and, of course, it should be laid out in as logical a manner as possible. You also want to evoke a specific, desired action from your customer, whether it is to buy your product or provide you with information about him or her. Achieving a complex page layout has traditionally been a difficult task within the constraints of HTML. However, the evolution of Web browsers into the 4.0 versions in 1998 moved page layout ahead with the addition of dynamic HTML (DHTML), cascading style sheets (CSS), and HTML layers.

Your page layout strategy depends strongly on the amount of information on your site. Is your product purely visual? Then a minimalist approach to page layout is best, presenting an uncluttered view of the objects you are trying to sell. Remember, if a Web page has too many graphics they tend to split the focus of the eye. If there is too much to look at on the site, your customer will not look at anything.

Is the site information rich? Do your products or services rely more on description than image? Then a layout more typical of magazines with multiple columns, sidebars, and photos with captions may be more appropriate. Many of the same rules apply to the placement of text as to the placement of graphics. Too much crowded text on a page makes the text very difficult to read. On smaller monitors, lots of cluttered text is practically undecipherable.

Interactivity is the heart of any great Web site. In order to really capture the hearts and minds of your customers, you need to open up your company and let people personalize their experience on your Web site. By allowing people to download customized information from your Web site and upload specific information about themselves, a customer will begin to feel like he is really working with you.

Color

Color can be used to set the atmosphere of your Web site or to distinguish one section from another. You can set the color for many different aspects of a Web page through HTML. HTML allows you to specify different colors for:

- background color
- plain text
- unvisited hyperlinks
- visited hyperlinks
- individual cell backgrounds in tables
- borders in tables
- borders around pictures

Typography

Typography concerns the character fonts in all your headings, logos, call-outs, and sidebars on the Web site. There are literally thousands of different fonts available, with new fonts being created every day. The best practice is to stick with one or two primary fonts for your Web site. Within those two fonts you can vary size, color, and treatment (bold, italics, etc.). If you use too many fonts, your pages will appear overly busy and confusing.

Imagery

Imagery—both illustrations and photography—bring life and a dynamic quality to a Web site. As they say, a picture is worth a

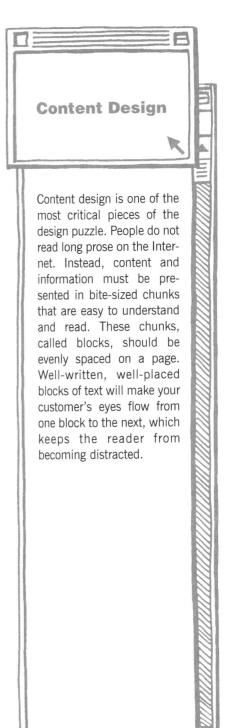

Content Design

Content design is one of the most critical pieces of the design puzzle. People do not read long prose on the Internet. Instead, content and information must be presented in bite-sized chunks that are easy to understand and read. These chunks, called blocks, should be evenly spaced on a page. Well-written, well-placed blocks of text will make your customer's eyes flow from one block to the next, which keeps the reader from becoming distracted.

thousand words. Make sure the content of your images matches up well with the content of your text.

Web sites that rely heavily on illustration have a playful look and feel. Think of the Sunday comics where the illustrations are whimsical and comforting. Web sites that use illustration tend to present a more comfortable posture to customers. Often using humorous elements, illustration Web sites are more casual and well suited to businesses where a strong, trusting relationship with the customer is your goal. Use illustration to give your customers a good "warm-fuzzy" feeling about your company. It will help build a strong customer service-oriented relationship with your customers.

Sharp, high-resolution photography tends to give Web sites a more serious and informative look. Sites that market and sell high-end products such as computers and other electronic equipment benefit greatly from the crisp, distinct style of photo montages combined with interesting headline type—commonly referred to as layered PhotoShop images. Think of the brochure covers for popular electronic items, where lots of clear photographic images combine to create a pleasing look and high-tech feel. Of course, any kind of sharp photography means large files. Care must be taken not to overload the page with too many of these photo montages or you run the risk of having pages that take too long to download or that look too cluttered and busy. Cluttered pages take attention away from your text, and your text will tell the story about your Web site and your product.

The standard image formats for the Web are JPEG (Joint Photographic Experts Group) and GIF (Graphics Interchange Format). JPEGs are best for photos and other images that have fine gradations in color. They can be saved in a choice of resolutions, differing in the tradeoff between quality and file size. GIFs are best for illustrations and other images that have a limited number of solid colors. GIFs also have the added benefit of being able to handle animation (called an animated GIF or GIF89a).

Spacing and proportion are design elements that are often overlooked or forgotten in the Web page design process, mostly because they deal with what is *not* there. But if there is not enough white space on a Web page it can start to look cluttered and be difficult to read. A good trick when using tables to effect a complicated page layout is to make sure that there is plenty of *cell padding*. Cell padding defines the free space in an HTML table that resides between the content and the borders of each cell. Setting cell padding = 6 is a good place to start.

Standard Contents of a Web Page

Every Web page is built up from pieces to create a complete page. These are the raw components of Web page content. As you plan the design of your Web site, the storyboard you use to shape the organization and content of the site will rely on these *content receptacles*. Do not think that each and every page must contain every element listed below.

- HTML title
- page header, navigation bar, and footer
- content
- call-outs, input and output areas

Every page on your Web site should have a page title embedded in the HTML that accurately portrays the location of the page in the scheme of the entire site. It is displayed in your browser's active title bar, above its pull-down menus. In fact, the page title can be a virtual assistant to your navigation menu by denoting the physical location of that particular Web page vis-a-vis the information architecture of the entire site. For example, you can use the following page title in the employee section of your Web site:

Acme Tool Co. | Sales | People | John Smith contact info

This page title helps you ascertain exactly where you are in the Web site—specifically, you are four levels down in the site's flow chart at John Smith's contact page.

The header area is used to create a mast head for the page and also to offer global navigation options either within the Web site or out to the rest of the Internet. The navigation bar holds hyperlinks to the major sections of the site. The footer area is used for general housekeeping information like a copyright symbol, address and phone number information, legal disclaimers, etc.

The best Web design reserves the majority of page real estate for content. After all, people do not come to your site for the navigation

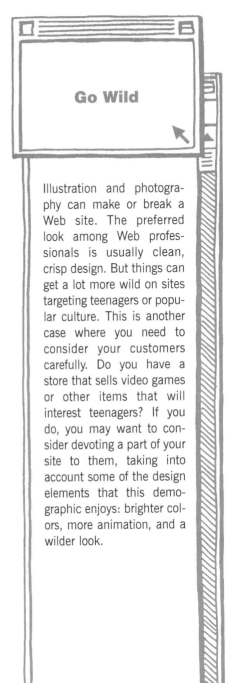

Go Wild

Illustration and photography can make or break a Web site. The preferred look among Web professionals is usually clean, crisp design. But things can get a lot more wild on sites targeting teenagers or popular culture. This is another case where you need to consider your customers carefully. Do you have a store that sells video games or other items that will interest teenagers? If you do, you may want to consider devoting a part of your site to them, taking into account some of the design elements that this demographic enjoys: brighter colors, more animation, and a wilder look.

bar or the copyright information! They come for the substance. It is a good rule of thumb to save at least 75 percent of the space on each page for content. *HTML frames* offer a nice technique for highlighting your site's content. Separating the content frame from the header, navigation, and footer frames creates a "command and control" feeling to the page, which makes the user feel like he is in better control of the site's navigation.

Do not forget about the great opportunities for merchandising your products or your ideas. Call-out boxes are a terrific way to highlight important content. Make them big and bold, with primary colors and large type. The same aggressive design credo should be used with interactive areas of your site. Interactivity is the reason people love the Web—make the interactive bells and whistles a focal point!

 Add items to Cart ★★★ Ratings & Reviews Compare Prices Find Products  Buy Now!

Address | http://chapter_six.com | Link

Building Your Web Site

The Seven Second Rule

The average time between mouse clicks for the typical Web user is only seven seconds. Seven seconds! That means that when a Web surfer visits your site you have less than seven seconds to impress him and keep him on your site. You also have only seven seconds to get your site to your customer's monitor. If it takes too long to download, your customer will find someone else to satisfy his or her needs. That means more business for your competitor.

Here's a secret tip: the face of a beautiful woman (or a handsome man) never hurts! People like looking at beautiful people. If you can find a legitimate reason to put a pretty male or female model on your homepage, do it!

Expertise Required:
Do You Have What It Takes?

Building a great e-commerce Web site is difficult. It requires experience, skill, patience, and planning. In most cases, constructing your Web site is best left to professionals. But if you are intent on doing it yourself, take heart, you can! Or you can outsource part of the job, such as the graphic design.

You need expertise in three basic areas to build a successful business Web site: business (Chapters 1, 2, and 3), design (Chapter 5), and technology (Chapters 7, 8, and 9). These are three very different skill sets. One person can do it all, but it usually works best when these tasks are divided up between individual experts in each area.

The business skills needed to build a great business Web site center around strategic planning, marketing, and operations. We discussed strategy in Chapter 5, but it is worth repeating that having a solid strategy with specific strategic objectives is the first step for any online business. On the marketing side, you need the ability to understand your customers and the ability to communicate well. On the operational side, an understanding of business processes and the flow of information between employees and customers helps build smoothly running Web sites that mesh well with a company's real world operations.

As we learned in Chapter 5, design is probably the most important skill one needs to build a successful Web site. As it often is in real world business, first impressions are all-important in online business.

It is not only graphic design that counts on a well-built Web site but the design of information as well. *Information architecture* is a key concept that describes the way information is laid out on the Web site. Information architecture is defined as the science of figuring out exactly what you want your site to do and the best way to lay it out for your customer. Whole books have been devoted to this area, which is closely related to interface design, also known as human interface design. Like *ergonomic design* in automobiles, interface design's preoccupation is with how people interact with the Web site. What do their eyes see first? What are they most likely to click on? What are they least likely to click on?

Design skills for the Web often crossover with technology and programming skills. Programming is a catchall phrase that covers many areas of expertise in Web site development.

The most basic Web programming is HTML. Professional Web site developers are well versed in HTML and are able to handle the coding of your Web site. While there are many WYSIWYG programs out there that would enable you to design a page yourself, the fact remains that Web pages that support complex design and interactivity can only be handled by someone with a level of programming expertise you will only find in a professional developer.

Until recently, WYSIWYG (what you see is what you get) Web development software programs were slow and finicky. These programs allowed you to simply place graphics or text on your screen and would automatically produce the HTML code for the site you designed. Unfortunately, the HTML code these programs generated was far inferior to what a good human HTML programmer could produce. This has changed somewhat among Web development professionals with the latest versions of Microsoft FrontPage 2000 and Macromedia DreamWeaver 3.0. Of course, many good Web designers still prefer hand-coding their Web pages, but these two programs are so good that they are making more and more converts every day. There are other software packages available, but if you are going to develop your Web site yourself, you will probably want to stick with one of these two WYSIWYG Web development tools. We talk more about these tools in Chapter 9.

Most Web designers have had to learn **HTML (hypertext markup language)** to be successful in their field. Although HTML is really a software programming language, Web designers have had to become proficient in it because it is not just a programming language but the layout language of the Web as well.

Web Programming: CGI, Java, and Plug-ins

Programming for the Web is a very broad subject. Remember, the World Wide Web was originally conceived as a *content receptacle*. Web servers, Web browsers, and all the technology in between were developed to *fit the content*. The Web was also originally conceived as an open platform that would allow software developers to write extensions and interpretations limited only by their imagination.

And extend the Web they did! Plug-ins are a prevalent form of Web technology expansion. A plug-in is a form of software that integrates with a Web browser to display new content types within the browser's window. CGI programs allow a Web site to harness the

resources of many different types of programs on the Web server besides the server software itself. For example, CGI applications (or scripts) can be used to access a database and deliver a customized Web page to a specific user. Any time you see some form of interactivity on a Web page, CGI or a similar technology is at work.

Connecting the front-end design of a Web site, what your user sees and interacts with, to the back-end databases, all that behind-the-scenes stuff, requires networking and database expertise. There are many products, such as Cold Fusion, which can bridge that gap for you. Most sites will need a database expert who also knows how to make the database come alive on the Web site.

Besides HTML and databases, there are a host of other technologies that are supported either directly or indirectly by the major Web browsers. Whether it is audio, video, streaming media, or something else, no single programmer can know it all.

Java (and JavaScript) is a special programming/scripting language developed by Sun Microsystems to help extend the capabilities of a Web browser. The language was specifically designed to write programs that can safely be downloaded to your computer and run without fear of virus infection or other harm to your system. With Java, a programmer can develop an actual software application that can run via the browser and coexist with your Web page. Java programs can be simple animations or mathematical formulas like payment calendars or financial interest generators. Server administration refers to the set up, configuration, and maintenance of the basic software that runs a Web site. Leading Web server software packages include Microsoft Internet Information Server (IIS), Netscape Web server, Apache, and BSDI. They all do basically the same thing and run basically the same way, but you will still want to evaluate which package is right for you. Then you will need to find either a server administrator or a hosting company that offers services you need.

Still think you can handle everything yourself—the planning (strategic planning, marketing, operations), design (page design, information architecture), and technology (HTML programming, plug-ins, CGI, Java, networking, databases, server administration)? Chapters 7, 8, and 9 will help you identify the areas you can handle yourself and enable you to find people with the expertise you need to construct your business Web site.

Costs

Web sites can very greatly in price depending on what you build and who you hire. Many people think of a commercial Web site as a standard format, but nothing can be farther from the truth. In fact, there are so many different elements and technologies that can go into a Web site that costs can vary from a few thousand dollars to a few million dollars. Remember what we said about transportation way back in Chapter 1? The more bells and whistles you build into your Web site, the more it is going to cost you to get it up and running—and keep it running.

Hiring a professional Web development company is the safest way to go for Web sites with complex content or that require high levels of technology. Because they have the experience and capabilities to do the job right, they are invaluable resources. But they are expensive, and if you're reading this book you may be inclined to manage the process yourself.

What Do I Pay a Designer and Programmer?

You want your Web site to reflect the image of your business, so of course you want to hire qualified people. Qualified people cost money. For qualified, skilled professionals you can expect to pay between $50 and $125 per hour for a Web designer and between $75 and $150 per hour for a Web programmer. This does not mean that you can find someone for less (or more); these are the current median salary ranges for skilled, professional Web developers.

A common rule of thumb dictates you should allow five to ten hours per individual Web page for both the design and HTML coding. If you assume $100 per hour for midrange professional Web development, you can expect to pay between $500 and $1,000 per page. That works out to $6,000 to $12,000 for a typical twelve-page online brochure.

But that is just for design and HTML. Add in $4,000 to $6,000 for database development and another $4,000 to $6,000 for strategy and project management. So a typical small company Web site costs between $14,000 and $24,000.

Hosting a Web site is not expensive, but costs increase depending on what technologies and services you

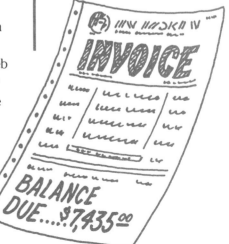

utilize. There are several decisions you have to make. Do you want to use a shared server or a dedicated server? Do you want to purchase an in-house server or pay a Web hosting company to house your site? If you buy your own in-house server should it operate on Windows NT or Unix? Do not forget that you will also pay more for special services like SSL (secure server), SQL database servers, video servers, live chat, etc.

In-house Versus Professional Development

Most companies doing business online for the first time will hire a professional Web development company to build and maintain their site. However, it is also possible to hire full-time employees to create and maintain the Web site. The decision to hire in-house staff depends largely on the amount of control you want to have over the Web site and the level of commitment your business has made to e-commerce over the next few years.

At a minimum, you will want to have a dedicated in-house general manager to oversee the development and running of the site. Having this general manager is absolutely critical because there is no way that an outside consultant can ever know your business as well as someone who works within it every day. Another reason you want a dedicated general manager is that an outside Web developer will need assistance from within your company to procure resources and make essential decisions.

You could also hire individual freelancers in the different areas of expertise and manage the Web development project yourself, but this is not advisable. It is better to hire a team of people who are familiar with each other and dedicated to delivering a finished product, not just individual pieces slapped together.

Remember, if your Web site is a success it will pay for itself time and time again. But if your Web site is put together poorly and does not work, it will be worth less than nothing. It will have taken up your valuable time, squandered valuable capital, and produced nothing but headaches. So do not skimp. And do not take shortcuts. Pay for a quality, professional Web development company and you will see quality, professional results. Do not be afraid to check references. Ask the companies you interview for the URLs to Web sites that they've constructed. There are a lot of quality developers out there, but there are just as many who are not. So choose carefully. You'll be rewarded for your research.

Choosing a Developer

So you have decided to use a professional Web site development firm. Good choice. Now it is time to choose a Web site developer that will work for you. The cost of using a development firm is increasing all the time. Big-name firms that handle companies like Nike and Intel can cost more than $500,000 just for a basic site. Even small shops can charge $10,000 or more.

Before you can choose a development firm you really need to have a grasp of the Net and how it works. Even if you never plan on updating or maintaining your site alone, the only way to know if the money you are spending is justified is to go out and brush up on the basic concepts of the Internet, how it works and what kind of technologies are out there. This book will cover a lot of the very basic concepts but it is wise to hit the Internet and see for yourself. There are several great resources you can find with a simple search engine, such as www.cnet.com and http://howto.yahoo.com.

Once you know what is out there, it is time to figure out what you like and what you do not. Spend some time looking at all different kinds of sites. Check out your competition. Look at Web sites devoted to your core target audience. Look at sites from all ends of the spectrum, from the biggest e-commerce site to the smallest online business card sites. What do you like? Do you like the flashier sites or does a simple Web design idea strike you as more appropriate.

The first thing you need to do is create a legitimate, formal request for proposal (RFP). An RFP is a document that outlines all of the functionality and capability of a Web site. It states the objectives that you will develop with your functional objectives and functional specifications. Once you develop an RFP, you can distribute it to potential developers to solicit proposals. The development of an RFP is an important step. If you do not lay down specific parameters

When you figure out what you like, what your customers would like, and what is most appropriate for your business, use it to generate your **request for proposal** (RFP).

for your Web site, you will receive such wildly disparate proposals that they will be impossible to evaluate against each other. Without outlining your objectives, one company may give you a proposal for a simple online brochure, while another may send you a proposal for a full e-commerce Web site with the most modern bells and whistles. Knowing what is out there and what you want will help you narrow the many proposals you get.

The strategies and objectives you have developed are an excellent starting point for creating your RFP. Another possible route is to hire a consultant to help you write a strategic plan before you hire a Web development company. Oftentimes, Web development firms will offer this service as a course of business. However you choose to do it, the goal of working with a consultant is to sketch out the strategic objectives for your company's online presence and translate that into a road map from which potential vendors can then build an accurate proposal.

Sending out an RFP

How do you decide which firm to send your request for proposal to? A good place to start is to find out what firms designed some of those sites you admired. Occasionally, a development firm will put their logo or other mark on sites they develop, but it never hurts to contact the company, tell them you liked their site (people like to hear this), and ask them what firm designed and built their Web site. Even if a design firm is out of your price range, it might be able to provide resource lists of smaller firms that you may want to submit your RFP to.

You can also try a more traditional approach, hitting the phone book or an industry directory like NetMarketing's Developer Directory to find development firms near you. Because you will be working very closely with whatever firm you choose, geography should play a factor in the decision.

When the time comes to whittle down the available choices to the few firms you will send an RFP, check the sites they've already built. Look for the same level of quality you want to see in your site. If the design is hideous or the site is not functional in any way, move on. There are other fish in the sea, and other developers to choose from.

If you find a firm you like, with sites you like, look into the services they provide. Have they made sites that specialize in serious e-commerce? Do they specialize in business cards or catalogs? Do they have clients whose products are similar to yours. (Remember those product categories we talked about earlier? Have they created Web sites for other considered purchase products? For other impulse and gift products?) Firms tend to be specialists in some areas and lag in others, so look into their experience before making a decision.

Once you've narrowed down the larger list of available firms into a few firms you are interested in doing business with, contact them. Most firms have new-business reps who will accept RFPs. When the proposals come in, you'll probably find firms that come in with high proposals and some with low proposals.

Evaluating Bids

Once you receive the proposals, be careful not to fall into the trap of automatically choosing the lowest bidder. Think about the hidden costs in doing something over if it's done wrong the first time. There is no reason to believe that companies that come in as low bids will be less professional than the others, but can you take the chance? Are you sure this company will do the site correctly?

Some low-ballers are simply young companies that are no longer brand new but are by no means established. These companies need your business so they have something to show. It is a portfolio builder, so they bid low and hope to get the job. If this is the case, there is no reason not to go with a firm like this provided you are aware of some of the complications that can arise.

These newer companies are still learning the ropes so the entire process may take a little longer than it would with a well-established development firm. But because these new firms are anxious to use your Web site as a showpiece and use you as a reference, they will be very concerned about getting everything right the first time and living up to your expectations.

Some bids will probably be higher than the amount you have budgeted for development, but if the firm really wants your business, they may be willing to negotiate with you. If your product is one that is well positioned to take advantage of new technologies and high-end services, in the interest of building a relationship,

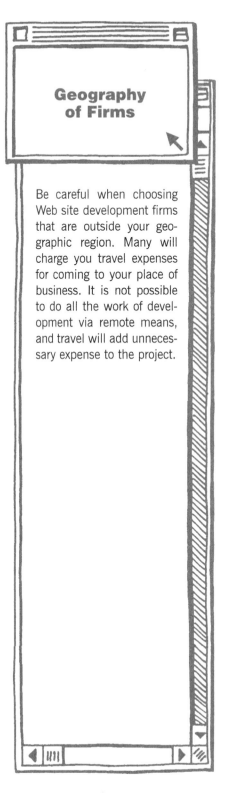

Geography of Firms

Be careful when choosing Web site development firms that are outside your geographic region. Many will charge you travel expenses for coming to your place of business. It is not possible to do all the work of development via remote means, and travel will add unnecessary expense to the project.

many developers may cut you a price break. They do this with the understanding that they will get your business when the time comes to expand the site to take advantage of newer technologies.

If you truly want to use a high-priced developer, remember that nothing will save you more money than being prepared. If you do as much of the planning as possible before you contract a developer, you can cut the final costs involved in the site.

This book can help you with planning your site design, setting up your objectives, and getting everything ready to hand off to a developer. If you have an in-house marketing team, let them write some of the copy. The more you can hand off, the fewer meetings you'll have to arrange (and pay for) and the more money you can save on final development.

Pay very close attention to how your potential Web developer will work with you to develop the site you want and need. Look closely at the sites they've done in the last year and ask them about the specific challenges they faced in those projects. Finally, ask for and thoroughly check at least two client references. Remember, all the research will pay off in the end.

Project Planning

If you expect your Web site development to go smoothly and the final product to be a functional model of all your objectives, you must work closely with whatever Web developer you choose. This involves a very delicate balancing act. You will want to monitor the progress of development closely yet give the developer enough space and free rein to do their thing. After all, they know what to do better than anyone!

One way to achieve this balance is to have a solid functional specification before you start development. If the developers know precisely what it is you want, they will be better able to provide that to you. It's just another example of prior planning paying off when it counts. As we've said before: A failure to plan is a plan to fail.

Planning the steps of your project is as important as creating your strategic plan or your functional specifications. Now it's time to create your project timeline and flow charts. This is one of the critical planning steps involved in building a Web site. Besides creating the big picture, a project plan will help you decide who needs to be hired and the time that should be allotted for each segment of the Web site construction.

Once you have your strategic plan and a set of functional specifications for your Web site, now you need to map out a build plan. Taking this master plan and breaking it into discrete subprojects and then coordinating the team of developers is not easy. It is akin to acting as your own contractor when building a house. You need to take into account all the different factors from the plumbing to the electrical work, even the heat and air conditioning. Then you must hire, coordinate, and direct all the workers who will do their part to complete the house.

The first thing you will want to do is create a project flow chart. Your flow chart should include the following:

1. Overall Web site design and navigation
2. Individual page design and layout
3. HTML production
4. Graphic elements production
5. Database programming
6. Interactivity programming
7. Server set up and configuration
8. Web site beta testing
9. Final site launch

You also want to work with your developer to institute deliverables and milestones that are as specific and detailed as possible. This is the best way to monitor progress on something that for you is extremely abstract. Create a timeline of concrete goals, and make sure your developer sticks to them or gives you a reason why they cannot. This is a superset of the deliverables that you can expect to see as the project progresses:

- strategy
- objectives
- functional specification
- design compositions
- Web site flow chart

- storyboards
- site copy
- database programming
- HTML pages
- beta site
- final site
- marketing plan
- maintenance plan

You will need to determine who on your development team is best suited to handling each part of the project. After all, you would not want to have a plumber wiring your dining room chandelier, would you?

Both your business and the developer you choose should designate a point person or dedicated contact for the Web site development project. Once this is done, all communication on both sides of the project should either go through these point people or be carbon copied to the point people. There are thousands of details that go into a business Web site, and someone on each side must be responsible for picking up potential snags and possible duplication of effort. The only way to a smooth Web site construction project is to have one person on each end know exactly what is going on at all times. Having point people is not only good for spotting problems. Terrific opportunities may arise that can only be recognized by a person who is seeing the entire picture.

Everyone on the development team should start out with a clear vision of the purpose and function of the Web site. For this, professional Web site developers usually prepare what is called a *design platform*. It has nothing to do with graphic design, rather it is more closely related to industrial design. A design platform describes the company, its products, the audience, and the Web site in explanatory terms that make it clear who the Web site is for, what the Web site should look like, and what it should do.

Project Timeline

Now is not the time to get overeager. You should expect to spend at least four to six weeks planning the Web site. After all, anything worth doing right is going to take some time. A hastily designed Web site will look that way. No development should start until everyone's role on the development team is clear. Once you have a project plan in place, development can begin.

The timeline of the Web site completely depends on what you are building. A sixty-story office building would take much longer to build than a three-bedroom house. The same goes for a Web site. There is no standard time allotment for the building of a Web site. However, a good rule of thumb is to allow two months at a minimum for a basic online brochure of eight to ten Web pages. Add in database programming, fancy graphics like Macromedia Shockwave or Flash, e-commerce programming, dynamically generated Web pages, or personalization programming and your time allotment should increase according to this rule: Ask the programmer for his honest assessment of how long that part of the project will take—then multiply by *three* to get a realistic prediction! If it's worth doing, it should be worth doing right. You can save yourself a lot of time and money by building your Web site right the first time, rather than cutting corners and having to take the site offline for redevelopment later.

A medium-size site of 30 to 40 Web pages with online security, a straightforward database, and several interactive features should take between three to four months. Much of the work can be done in parallel by different people on the development team. One person can be working on the graphic design while another works on the copy and a third works on the database development. But as the scope of the project gets more complex, the challenge of project management becomes more difficult. For large Web sites, time should be factored in for putting out fires, retracing steps, and generally organizing and driving the project to completion.

Contracts and Legal Issues

Everybody hates contracts, but they are a necessary part of life. The relationship between a company and its Web developer can be quite complex, and everything needs to be spelled out completely and clearly.

The sooner both parties get to work on the project, the sooner it will be finished. However, do not make the error of succumbing

to the feeling that you must begin development yesterday and finish by tonight. That would be a terrible mistake. It is imperative that both parties agree on and sign the development contract before you start. This will save many headaches (and possibly many thousands of dollars) down the road.

The development contract should lay out exactly what the developer will do during the course of the project. Detail is the goal here. Even if things do not work out exactly as planned, at least you and your developer will have a clear, common understanding of the original plan. Then, when the project takes the inevitable forks in the road, it will be much easier to agree on new courses of action.

The first thing you will need is a confidentiality agreement. The agreement should be completely reciprocal, that is, both parties should use the same care in keeping the other's information confidential. Be wary of confidentiality agreements that seek to limit your rights to deal with other vendors or seek to limit your use of content and applications created by the developer. Your Web site is yours, and should the time come to change developers or maintenance providers there should be no proviso in the contract that keeps you from doing so.

This leads to the question of who owns the elements of the Web site created during the development process: you or the developer? Under the United States Copyright Act of 1976, work that is defined as "work for hire" is owned by the entity paying for that work. This means that any designs or work specific to the Web site will be owned by you.

However, many developers will specifically denote exceptions to the Copyright Act of 1976. They will exclude any "software applications" that are either created during the project, even if they are specifically developed for a particular client. Developers feel that if they create a software application that has any sort of universal application, they are entitled to reuse and resell that software application. This is a legitimate stance by the developer, provided that they grant a perpetual, irrevocable license for you to use that software application in your Web site. This license allows you to always use the software they developed for as long as you want, even if you terminate your agreement with their company. After all, you paid them to develop the software, you should be able to use it! Sometimes, developers also stipulate this clause in their agreement to maintain control over a proprietary software asset they had previously developed for someone else.

Many Web developers have modeled their business processes on the advertising industry. To that end, compensation schedules often reflect the same practices. Most developers will ask for some amount of money before the project begins—a deposit usually at the signing of the contract. Then there is usually a mid-term payment and a final payment upon completion of the project. Actual numbers vary, but it is typical to find a developer asking for one-third payment up front. It is not unheard of to find a developer asking for 50 percent up front.

Financing

Building a successful Web site takes time, effort, and, most of all, money. You get what you pay for, but do not pay for more than you need. Once you have determined your strategy you will need to raise the capital to put the whole plan into effect. If you have the cash to finance your Web site completely by yourself, that's great! Otherwise, you'll have to begin to assess your options for raising the necessary capital.

Getting a bank loan is an ideal solution because you do not have to give up any equity in your business. But the money must be repaid on the bank's schedule, and unsecured lines of credit from commercial banks are difficult to obtain.

There are many sources of equity capital for the Web entrepreneur, each with its own pluses and minuses. Generally, the more professional the investor, and the more expertise that investor brings to the table, the more equity you will need to give up to obtain the investment capital he has to offer.

The easiest and least demanding source of equity capital is usually what is referred to as "friends and family" money. Just as it sounds, funding your Internet business development through a wealthy sister, parent, uncle, or old buddy from college is the easiest route to take. Not only will they probably take a lower percentage of

Meetings and More Meetings

Meetings are a fact of business in today's world; there is no way around them. When you are constructing a Web site, you can expect to have several. As the project progresses, you can expect to have meetings for:

1. Project kickoff to review strategy and objectives for site
2. Design compositions for overall look and feel of site
3. Detailed development and review of information architecture
4. Detailed development and review of functional specifications
5. Reviewing technology platform decisions—hardware and software
6. Creating and instituting marketing plan
7. Copywriting review
8. Beta testing of the Web site
9. Final Web site launch
10. Creation and review of maintenance plan

your business, but their trust in you will go a long way toward convincing them that your Internet business is a good investment.

The next type of investors are called angel investors, but along with the increase in sophistication comes an increased demand on your equity capital. Angel investors are usually wealthy individuals who have an interest either in your industry or in the Internet in general. The term "angel" also implies a certain romantic involvement by the investor. The patience of an angel investor can probably be stretched longer than venture capitalists, but angel investors are still serious people who expect a high return on their initial investment.

Venture capitalists are the most serious and most demanding investors an Internet business can approach. Venture capitalists are professional investors who may see hundreds of business plans a year. Their only business is to invest money in businesses, with the expectation, of course, of a high return on their investment. Of the hundreds of business plans that cross their desks in a year, venture capitalists will probably only take a serious interest in a couple of dozen. They will only make an actual investment in a handful of those cases.

An attractive feature of venture capitalists is that they bring much more than just money to the table. As professional investors, they have extensive experience in taking young companies from birth through prosperous maturity. If your goal is to someday take your business public, venture capitalists are some of the very best people to work with.

Web entrepreneurs can also seek business advice and high-level corporate contacts from their investors. In this realm, venture capitalists are unparalleled. The usually have many contacts in hundreds of different industries, and they can help the young company develop business partnerships and attract the very best employee talent.

The financing options you have available to you are largely based on who you know, your background and qualifications, the strength of your business ideas and plan, and not a little bit of luck. Remember to weigh the pros and cons of different investors carefully. If one investor is much more likely to help you succeed, it is better to have 20 percent of a million dollars than 80 percent of nothing!

Hosting and Maintaining Your Site

Once you have built your site, you need to find a place to host it. Web sites are not located in virtual places. They run on computers. When you visit a Web site on the Internet, your browser software (Netscape Communicator or Microsoft's Internet Explorer) communicates directly with that Web site, which is on a computer(s) running Web server software and a variety of other applications server software products such as database, security, content, and mail servers. In other words, there is a *there* there.

In choosing a place to host your Web site, you will consider two basic options: host it yourself or pay a company that specializes in Web site hosting to do it. It does not matter where you physically host it, because software is available to set up, configure, and maintain your Web site remotely. So even though your site may make its home off the premises, you can make changes from anywhere! There are benefits to both hosting your Web site locally on your premises as well as having a company host it for you. If you decide to host your site locally, you will need to purchase the hardware and connections required to run a server, plus the server itself, and you should probably hire a full-time employee to upgrade, maintain, and work on the equipment and the Web site. For more on Web servers and technology issues, see Chapter 7.

One of the big benefits of having a company host your site is that should a problem arise and a crash occur, the hosting company has a battery of staff members to fix the problem and get your site up and running fast. Sometimes they'll even have it back up before you know there was a problem! Your Web site is your online presence twenty-four hours a day, seven days a week. Your customers expect to be able to find it any time of day or night. If you choose to host your own site and it goes down at 4:00 A.M. on a Sunday morning, who will be there to fix it? It is definitely something to be considered.

Trademarks and Copyright

Trademark and copyright laws provide important protection over the names and designs you use every day in conducting your business. For that reason, you should make sure to include a copyright notice at the bottom of every page on your Web site. You do not want another company stealing your logo or trademarks. Logos and trademarks are the identity by which your company is recognized. Can you imagine if someone else started to use the Microsoft logo? Microsoft protects their logos, and you should, too. Any trademarks or servicemarks your company owns should be prominently displayed on the Web site and protected by a clear copyright notice at the bottom of every page.

What Should I Look for When Making Hosting Decisions?

Building a great Web site gets you nowhere if your customers cannot reach it! If your Web server is down or if it is as slow as molasses, customers will be instantly turned off to your company. So reliability and speed are the two primary issues in Web site hosting.

In most cases you will want to pay a Web hosting company for this service. First of all, by the time you invest enough money to host your Web site reliably and efficiently, you would need to start your own Web hosting service to recoup the costs. Second, the expertise needed to maintain a high-quality Web server and high-speed connectivity to the Internet is not trivial. It is very, very difficult. In short, in 999 cases out of 1,000 there is no question about the best route to take: hire a Web site hosting company.

There are thousands of companies that will host your site. Their services and prices vary significantly, as does their quality. On the low end there are Web hosting companies that charge as little as $19.95 per month for basic hosting services. This type of hosting usually does not include any kind of interactivity, database services, POP3 e-mail services, or high-end multimedia capabilities like RealAudio or RealVideo.

At the other end of the spectrum, high-end Web hosting companies—UUNet, Exodus, MCI, and all of the other major telecommunications companies—offer robust, yet very expensive, Web hosting services. For most businesses, the services are overkill. You just do not need the fail safe, fault tolerant redundant systems and huge data transfer pipes of the high-end Web hosting services.

Shared Versus Dedicated Versus Co-Located Web Servers

A major impact on price and reliability is the type of server where you host your Web site. A single Web site does not necessarily need its own server. Web servers can be set up to handle dozens of Web sites at a time. This type of computer is called a shared server. But if your Web site is hosted on its own computer, with no other Web sites, you are using what is called a dedicated server.

In both the shared and dedicated server options you lease the physical hard disk space on the computer, the software running all of your server applications, and the connection between your server and the rest of the Internet. You also pay for the monitoring and upkeep of network services. Your Web site hosting service will run all the necessary ancillary servers that make sure your specific Web server machine is listed in the domain name system and accessible to the rest of the Internet.

One other option exists for hosting your Web site. In cases where you need or want total control over the technical running of your Web site, it may be necessary to purchase a Web server outright. You can still bring this computer to a Web hosting service and let them handle only its connectivity to the Internet. This is called a co-located server.

Now that you have seen the issues and requirements of building a Web site, you should be prepared to make the decision on how to build your Web site. There are many issues involved in design, technology, marketing, and the law. It is difficult to coordinate all of the content for the site with the technology development and marketing needs. Creating an overall project plan will help you maintain control over this complicated process.

Outsourcing some or all of your Web site development is a critical issue. The experience and know-how required to successfully develop a professional Web site is substantial. You can do it yourself, but it will take a lot of hard work and research. One option is to act as the general contractor for your site and hire the raw talent, such as designers and programmers, to accomplish the technical work. But there are many pitfalls that only the experience of Web site building can help avoid.

Hiring a lawyer experienced in Web site development legal issues is important. Ownership of programming code, copyright and trademark law, and contractual issues as they relate to the vagaries of Web site development all require a subtle hand to deflect potential legal problems. Make sure you have explicitly defined the developer's deliverables and each of your responsibilities in the contract. Pay careful attention to content development and copy writing for the Web site. Also beware of data format and delivery in the creation databases. All this points toward hiring a lawyer to work with you.

If you treat your online business like any other business, creating a business plan and covering all the bases, you will be well on your way toward a successful e-commerce Web site. Take it slow, get advice from experts and friends, and do not forget to have fun building your little corner of the World Wide Web!

Where Do I Go to Host?

Start out by giving your Internet service provider a call. Most major ISPs give you a certain amount of server space free with a business or personal dial-up account. The larger the ISP, the more chance you have of them offering a business services division that will have business hosting capabilities. If you are putting up a small site, you may be able to save the high cost of hosting and do it with your existing ISP.

WORKSHEET

1. Come up with a list of your own functional objectives for your site.

2. What is your budget?

3. What should you include in your RFP?

 Add items to Cart | ★★★ Ratings & Reviews |  Compare Prices | Find Products | Buy Now!

Address | http://chapter_seven.com ▼ | Link

Technology

In order to build a great e-commerce Web site, it is important to understand the basic technology of the World Wide Web. Knowing the breadth and capabilities of Web hardware and software frees your imagination to focus on the business issues as you plan your Web site, rather than the agonizing details of technology. Knowing the capabilities as well as the limitations of Web technology will also help you to choose the most appropriate tools for achieving each particular goal of your online business.

The hardest part of building a Web site is choosing the right hardware and software platforms. A technology platform is the basic technology you use to build the overall Web site or specific section such as the database or the transaction processing system. If you design your Web site on a platform that is too simple, you will end up with a Web site that is overburdened and slow, or that crashes frequently. Remember, you only have seven seconds to make an impression on your customer to get him or her to stay. Do not let that impression be of a server error or an interminable wait for the Web page to download. If you build your Web site too complex, you will end up spending needless money on overcapacity you will never use, wasting more and more money every month on hosting and maintenance services.

The trick to development lies in proper capacity planning, where the result is a robust technical back-end that is efficient for your needs now, yet scalable for the future.

If you are building your Web site yourself, you have a wide range of development tools to choose from. These development tools run the gamut from easy-to-learn, beginner's software products to high-end professional applications. (We will talk more about site development tools in Chapter 8.) A common mistake many people make is assuming that they need to buy the most sophisticated, expensive, and complicated Web development software. People make that mistake in other areas, too. How many people do you know run out and buy the best VCR, or the most state-of-the-art computer, when they'll hardly ever use it? Much like purchasing any appliance, this is the exact opposite of what they should be doing! Most people will only use 20 to 25 percent of a development product's capabilities. Pay attention to the characteristics that you require. For most people constructing the Web site on their own, the most important software characteristics will be ease-of-use and how fast you can get up to speed.

This is where some of the lastest Web development software tools like Microsoft FrontPage 2000 and Dreamweaver 3.0 really shine. They are both easy to use and pack powerful features that let you build rebust, complex Web sites with relative ease.

Internet and Business Technology Background

Where did the Internet come from and how did it become what it is today? While those questions might seem trivial, the answers help today's businesspeople keep the Net in perspective. Knowing how and why the Internet evolved into the robust business platform it is today can help you in developing a Web site that is meaningful and sure-footed with customers.

The Internet originally evolved from a military project sponsored by DARPA (the Defense Advanced Research Projects Agency) in which computers from university research laboratories and Department of Defense scientists were linked together in the late 1960s to assist the military in the development of modern military technology. The intent was to share computing resources among a few mainframe computers, which were scarce at the time.

In the 1970s, this concept was extended to the corporate world as businesses and academic institutions began to connect over phone lines to large mainframes in order to access the processing power of those computers. This practice became known as *time-sharing* because users would actually rent a portion of the mainframe's processing power in specific cycles.

As computer technology made its way to the corporate desktop with the introduction of the IBM PC in 1981, mainframe computers had begun to shrink in complexity and cost. The mini computers (smaller than mainframes but larger than desktop computers) in use at this time from companies such as Digital Equipment Corporation were repositories of information that needed to be accessed by

What Is the Internet Made Of?

The primary physical medium that constitutes the Internet, is optical fiber. OC stands for optical carrier and is based on a standard called OC1. OC1 fibers can carry 51.84 megabits per second. Right now the Internet backbone is mostly running at OC12, 622 megabits per second.

In mid-1998 there were more than 40,000 miles of OC12 capacity fibers in the United States. In 1999, that was upgraded to OC48. By the end of 1999, they anticipate having nearly 270,000 miles of OC48 cable powering the Internet, running at the lower speed of OC12 until router technology catches up with the speed of the backbone. At GTE Internetworking, a spokesman has said that eventually there will be 17,000 miles of optical fibers capable of OC192.

workers at their desktops, so the trend of local area networks (LANs) began to take shape.

The practice of networking many computers together evolved into the primary technology of the Internet: client/server computing. Everything on the Internet is based on client/server computing where a large centralized computer (called the server) holds most of the primary applications and data accessed by users (called clients). Client/server computing allowed the people in charge of corporate computer systems to maintain control over what was delivered to users. Multiple LANs were eventually strung together over great distances into wide area networks (WANs), providing a foundation for the Internet.

Web Servers

The client/server protocol used by Web servers was first developed in Switzerland by Tim Berners-Lee at CERN in 1991. This began the end of the mainframe computer dynasty where terminals were "dumb," that is, they did not really do anything except manipulate the mainframe computer from a remote location.

So the Web is really just a giant network of computers all hooked together. It works like any other computer network, that is, by client computers accessing information from server, or host, computers. All these computers are connected together by a variety of different methods, both wired and wireless, but primarily over good old copper telephone wires.

There is no such thing as cyberspace. Web sites do not just float around and wait for someone to access them from thin air. All Web sites reside on a Web server, somewhere. A Web server can be any type of computer that is running server software and connected to the Internet. Technically, a plain old PC that has a full-time connection to the Internet is a Web server, but most Web servers are specialized computers that run on either Windows NT or the Unix operating system.

Once you have made your decision and your Web server is set up and configured properly, it waits to be contacted by the right client software (Web browser software like Netscape Communicator or Microsoft's Internet Explorer are common examples of client software). The Web browser and the Web server speak to each other through a well-defined language called a *protocol*. The World Wide Web is that protocol.

These two software applications connect with each other by sending messages back and forth. Each message or request that the browser sends to the server contains a *header*, with information about who it is and where it is coming from. More importantly, it also contains a set of instructions requesting a specific response from the server, which could include HTML pages, graphic files, and any other information or files that are used by the browser to build a Web page that the viewer sees.

A key element of the request sent by the browser to the server is the browser's Internet Protocol Address (IP). The IP address system is critical to the operation of the Internet. It is the only way that browsers and servers know how to reach each other and know where to send files and information.

Every computer that is connected to the Internet, whether it is a browser or a server, has an IP address. Computers that are connected to the Internet all the time, like Web servers, usually have what's known as a static IP address. This IP address never changes. People with dial-up connections to the Internet usually have dynamic IP addresses—their IP addresses are randomly assigned by their Internet service provider from a large block of IP addresses every time they connect to the Internet.

Every machine that is connected to the Internet has a unique IP number. No two computers can ever have the same IP address at the same time. The IP address is different from the domain name. Several domain names can refer to the same IP address. Domain names are just a lot easier to remember than an IP address, which consists of four parts, separated by dots. For example, 143.938.3.32 is an IP address, but Amazon.com is a domain name. (We made up that IP address by the way.)

Switched any Packets Lately?

Actually, you have. If you've checked your e-mail or browsed the Web, you've been sending and receiving—switching—packets. And what exactly is a packet? A packet is a piece of information sent

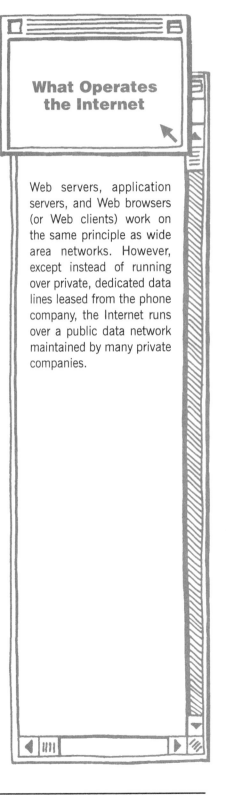

What Operates the Internet

Web servers, application servers, and Web browsers (or Web clients) work on the same principle as wide area networks. However, except instead of running over private, dedicated data lines leased from the phone company, the Internet runs over a public data network maintained by many private companies.

over the Internet. Think of it this way. Take a document like that new business plan, chop it up into little pieces, and write each on a postcard. Then mail each card. Each card has on it the same information contained in an online packet: the payload, or the information, and the to and from, otherwise known as the source and destination addresses.

Packet switching begins once the cards are delivered to the post office and begin their journey to the destination. Each one of those postcards may take a different route to get to the final address. All kinds of things can dictate how the individual postcards, or packets, get routed to the destination. When they finally arrive, they may not do so in order, but someone will sit down and reassemble them.

If you were to send that same business plan online, your computer would break it into the little pieces and send it out over the Net. Each packet may take a different route, but on arrival they are all reassembled courtesy of the TCP protocol. Rather than sitting down and putting them in order, the computer does it automatically.

The route a packet takes depends on how congested it is. Packets get sent along the least congested route at the time the packet leaves the first computer for the second. Because of this, each and every packet can go on a different route.

Web Application Servers

A Web server does the primary job of responding to Web browsers and sending Web pages across the Internet to the user. What about all of the databases, audio, video, and e-commerce that are also part of the Internet? How does all of the other cool content get down to my Web browser? More importantly, how do all of those Web sites like My Yahoo! maintain my personalized information for financial portfolios, bookmarks, and any number of the services that fit me alone? Are these handled by the Web server also? Well, sometimes they are.

Technically, the term Web server describes the Web server *software*, although the entire computer box where the Web site resides is often referred to as a whole as the Web server. The

Web server can only deliver HTML files and graphic files. Most other information that is delivered from the Web site is sent by a special server that is dedicated to a particular task—a Web application server. Some examples of these kind of servers are database servers and video and audio servers. These application servers are important because they help balance out the load from browser requests among several different computers. On high-traffic Web sites, hundreds of people making hundreds of separate requests would overload many regular servers, causing big delays and even crashes. By having application servers that handle discrete parts of a Web site, traffic is more easily balanced, creating less jams and keeping the site moving.

Cross-server Communication

So the Web server has to talk to the application server. How does it do that? The original method for cross-server communication used something called the *Common Gateway Interface* (CGI).

CGI applications are referenced within HTML pages and then run on the server to produce the desired result. They are usually run when information from the user is being delivered to a database on the server. Also, CGIs often instruct the Web or application server to deliver a customized HTML Web page back down to the user.

A CGI program can be written in any programming language, but most are written in Perl for the Web. Other popular programming languages for CGI applications are C, C++, and VB script. Perl CGIs run very fast and are easy to develop (if you know how to program in Perl!), but they are not great on heavy-traffic Web sites. They tend to bog down the site.

Microsoft Active Server Pages (ASP) work in conjunction with Microsoft Internet Information Server to deliver a plethora of interactive functionality to a Web site. ASP files are like CGI scripts in that they are little programs that run on a browser. An ASP file can contain HTML, scripts written in any language, and ASP objects or commands. When the ASP file is requested by the browser, the server reads through the code and executes any of the scripts or

DEFINITION PLEASE

Web **plug-ins** are small software programs that integrate with Web browsers to provide additional functionality and capabilities beyond those built into the Web browser. Some of the technologies commonly used in online sales presentations and interactive e-commerce Web sites are plug-ins.

Windows socket applications (or Winsock Apps) define any computer program that accesses an Internet connection. For example, your e-mail program is a Winsock App. So are RealAudio, FTP, Ping, Gopher, WAIS, and a host of other programs that do everything from synchronize the clock on your computer to update software programs.

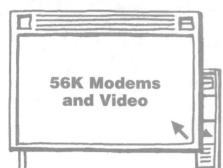

56K Modems and Video

Video files are huge; ten seconds of video averages about 4MB, and that makes for difficult downloading on most regular modems. The new streaming media creates a buffer of a few seconds of video that provides for Internet slowdowns, but if the slowdown is longer than the buffer, the video stops mid-picture.

ASP commands it contains. ASP commands (called *objects*) instruct the server to do one of the following:

Request Object—Get information from the user
Response Object—Send information to the user
Server Object—Control various aspects of the server
Session Object—Store and edit information about the user's current session
Application Object—Control other applications running on the server

The only drawback you have to remember when using ASP files is that they are proprietary to Microsoft. That means that they will only work on Web servers running Microsoft software and can cause problems with browsers other than Microsoft's Internet Explorer.

Scalability

Scalability is the key issue in distributing server load among several different computers. While you are interested in how many potential customers visit your Web site in a week or month, that is of little issue to the people who administer your server. For server administrators, the people who build and maintain Web servers, the key issue is gauging how many simultaneous users there will be at any one time—how many people will you have using your Web site at once. On big, high-traffic sites such as Amazon.com you can guarantee hundreds of thousands of simultaneous users. How many simultaneous users your Web site has is referred to as the peak load or as peak concurrent users. Scalability is important because when a Web server or an application server is overloaded, it can slow down to a crawl or even crash completely.

For this reason, many Web server administrators prefer using computers running the Unix operating system. Unix is much more robust and reliable than Windows NT, although Microsoft and many Windows NT evangelists will dispute that claim. However, Unix systems are much more difficult to set up, configure, and maintain than Windows NT. For that reason, most small to medium-size business

Web sites will have an easier time running their Web site on the Windows NT platform.

Connecting to the Internet

People connect to the Internet in a variety of ways. The most important factor for doing business online is the speed of the connection. Most consumers today access the Internet through the dial-up analog modem over ordinary phone lines. Except in a few cases, they connect to the Internet at 56 kilobits per second (or 56 Kbps), however 28.8 Kbps and 14.4 Kbps modems are still in use. Knowing this is important because 56 Kbps modems are a fast way to view regular Web pages with ordinary graphics and photographs, but they are terrible way to view any kind of video.

There are many factors affecting the speed a Web site is sent to an end-user besides the speed of the user's modem. Bandwidth is a popular term nowadays. It is used to describe an amount of data being transferred via a network connection. Bandwidth is usually measured in BPS or bits per second. Modem speeds are categorized by bits per second, but since modems are faster now, they are actually determined in Kbps, or kilobytes per second (one kilobyte is one thousand bytes). But, how much data a modem *can* transfer and how much it actually does are two different things.

In order to view Web pages, the user's Web browser must send a request to the Web server over many checkpoints on the Internet. A simple request for a Web page moves through various routers and switches, data lines, firewalls, and proxy servers, all of which take some time. Eventually it winds up at the intended destination, the Web server, which then has to deliver the Web page and all its associate files back down the same path.

To make this easier to understand, imagine you are driving from your house in New York to a friend's house in California. You will take many roads, large and small, and traffic will vary depending on where you are and the time of day. In fact, there are a million factors that will affect how long it takes to get there (even the number of times you stop for gas or food). So it is with the Internet, and download time is one of the critical factors in the success of a Web site. People do not like to wait for anything. They do not like to wait

Other Ways to Connect to the Net

Digital modems (or network adapters) such as Integrated Services Digital Network (ISDN), Digital Subscriber Line (DSL), and cable modems offer much faster connections to the Internet. But they are more expensive than regular dial-up modems, very complicated to install and configure, and have limited availability, especially outside of major cities. Their access speeds range from 128 Kbps to 1.5 megabits per second (Mbps).

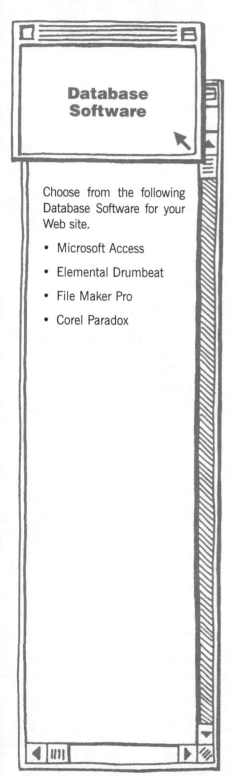

Database Software

Choose from the following Database Software for your Web site.

- Microsoft Access
- Elemental Drumbeat
- File Maker Pro
- Corel Paradox

in line at the DMV, they do not like to wait for traffic lights, and they do not like to wait while a Web site downloads. It is very easy for someone to click themselves right off your page, and if you lose them that way, they may never come back!

These and other technology issues impact the real usability of the Internet for ordinary people. It is the Webmaster's job to balance all these issues like software platforms, file sizes, and other technical questions so that the Web site is compatible with and accessible by the largest number of users. Of course, chief among these issues is download time, but many users may not be able to see flash animations, cascading style sheets (CSS), or HTML layers.

Databases

If there were only one word that the Internet has added to our business vocabulary it would be *interactivity*. The Web is one vast, interconnected network tying millions of personal computers and servers together in (usually) seamless integration. But where does all the information traveling across the Internet come from? The answer is, almost invariably, from a database.

A database is simply a place where information is stored. You probably have a database or two in your house without realizing it. A recipe box is a database. All your recipes are stored in a unique order where you can access them quickly and easily. Your telephone/address book is another database. All the people you contact from your grandmother right down to the pizza parlor are stored in a way where you can easily find the information you need.

The real power of the Internet lies in the user's ability to access huge amounts of information. If they are designed well, databases provide immediate access to the precise information you require. Whether it is a database of historical baseball statistics, the compact disc inventory of a major music retailer, or the price history of the New York Stock Exchange, databases have the ability to present and sort through huge quantities of information.

Doing business online usually requires a database of some sort, whether you are tracking products, customers, or even Web usage. There are several steps you will need to go through to integrate a database into your Web site. The first step is choosing the right technology combination of hardware and software. After you have chosen the platform the real work begins.

The second step involves the design of the database. The key to databases is that they are *designed well*. After all, your telephone/address book would not be terribly useful if you could not find the number of the person you wanted. Quality database design is crucial to maximizing the speed and extending its ability.

On the top level, databases are organized into something called *data tables*. There can be many data tables in a single database. If you think of a database as a spreadsheet with rows and columns, you are really thinking of a data table. Each data table has *records* (the subject about which you are keeping information) and *fields* (the categories of information about the record). If you use our telephone/address book example, then Pizza Galore would be a record; the address, phone number, price of a large pie, and delivery boy's name would all be fields within that record.

The first goal of good database design is to eliminate duplication of any information in any of the data tables. Another goal is to create such well-organized and logical data tables that another developer could pick up the database and understand exactly how it was developed and how it can be modified in the future.

There are two main types of databases that you can employ on your Web site: relational database or a flat database. Relational databases are much faster at handling huge amounts of information, such as a database with millions of records. SQL (structured query language) databases adhere to a standard for creating database queries and are produced by many different software companies. When moving information from one database to another, the issue of whether each database is ODBC (open database conductivity) compliant arises. Most databases in use today are ODBC compliant.

Personalization

Personalization is the term used for displaying information on a Web page that is customized for

---

Database Interface Design

How you design your database also impacts how your customer will use that database. The interface, or method your customer uses to access the database, should be a subject of good quality design. Interface design describes both the computer screens that internal employees might use to maintain the database as well as the screens that customers would use to retrieve information from a database. Good interface design involves both graphic design as well as human factors engineering.

Don't Let Cookies Crumble

You can turn your cookies off in both Microsoft's Internet Explorer and Netscape Navigator. While this gives you the utmost in privacy, it also means a wealth of Web sites will not work on your browser. There are also settings that alert you if the Web site tries to place a cookie on your computer, allowing you to refuse the cookie if you want.

a unique individual. In previous chapters we talked about the importance of personalization and how it enhances your customer's experience while at your Web site. Personalization is the technology used in all of those *MyThis* and *MyThat* Web sites that let you create your own personal home page with your stocks, your city's weather, your favorite sports teams, and other personal information that is continually updated all the time. There are actually several technologies in play to create these types of Web pages.

Obviously, the Web server and its application servers are running the show when it comes to displaying Web pages. But the server does not just magically know who you are. In order to give you the Web content you have requested, the Web server needs help from the user's own Web browser.

A Web server can store information about you on your own hard drive in something called a *cookie file*. Cookie files are built-in parts of both the Netscape and Microsoft Internet Explorer browser programs. The Web server has the ability to look inside your cookie file every time you visit that Web site. In fact, the server can store any type of information it wants to in your cookie file.

In the simplest methods of Web site personalization, however, the server simply stores a unique ID number in the cookie file. When you go to the Web site, the server reads your cookie file and retrieves this unique number. It then looks up the ID number in its database. This database is where the Web server stores all of your preferences and information. In cases like My Yahoo!, this can be the city you live in, what stocks you like to follow, what sports teams you want to see scores for, and even what news services you like to read. The Web server can then respond with a dynamically generated, personalized Web page by merging information from your database with a predesigned Web page template.

Personalization is a new trend in e-commerce. More and more smaller businesses are shying away from building huge generic sites that provides all things to all customers. Huge sites mean customers have to go through page after page of products and information that are irrelevant to them. Every page between them and the information and products they want is one more chance for them to go elsewhere to find it. Companies are now building sites that enable their customers to build their own boutiques where the content and product information is precisely what they need. Personalization like this often converts into larger order sizes and converts your occasional customer into a regular customer.

Generating your own personalization technology is a time-consuming and costly process, but it makes your Web site shine against your competitor's and makes your customer feel more at home on your site. Before undertaking any kind of development project to make your site more personalized, you really have to gather some information from your customers. We talk about information gathering methods in Chapter 12. The more information you can get from your customers the better your ability to design personalization features that will make them happy. The key to getting that information is doing it slowly and subtly. Nobody wants to fill out a long questionnaire about their habits. But if your site requires membership, you can ask a single question each time the customer logs on to your site. By the end of the month, you'll have a whole trove of information on who your customers are and what they use your site for.

If you are not an Internet-only business and have a bricks-and-mortar facility, you already have a lot of information on how your customers shop and what they buy from you. Combine that information with what you learn on the Web to help design personalization features that are right for your business and for your customer.

If you already have a preferred shopper club or other means of gathering information on your customers, build that into your Web site then offer these preferred customers a chance to take a look around their own "personal" site. They will appreciate the transition of their customer information onto the Web provided it is done in a secure way.

Prepackaged Personalization

You can have a Web site development firm build you specialized technology, or you can purchase prepackaged solutions from companies like Art Technology Group and DataSage Inc. Most prepackaged solutions require some integration from either your Webmaster or your development firm to get them to work with your existing technology. Very rarely do they integrate smoothly.

Personalize Your Customer Experience

When you combine cookies and Web databases you can create a powerful personalization package that makes your customers feel special. Think of how this information can be applied to your business. Pretend you run an auto parts shop and want to put that shop online. How can you personalize the Web experience for your customers?

You could have your customer input the types of cars they work on or own into your database. If they work on and restore classic cars, that information can be input into the database. When your customer returns to your site, the database can list what specials you are running that apply directly to that individual customer's car, and can even tell that customer you have that elusive part he or she has always wanted!

One of the newer companies offering personalization technology solutions is TriVida Corporation. The TriVida package works on suggestive selling. Based on preprogrammed settings by a business, the software suggests additional items to a customer along the lines of what they are going to purchase. (A purchase of a tube of toothpaste might bring up a suggestion of a toothbrush to go with it.) This kind of selling works well in apparel and electronics categories.

The TriVida software resides on their server, therefore the integration works smoother than packages where the software has to be worked into an existing Web site. The merchant preprograms its suggested items using HTML and JavaScript tags directly on the Web pages.

Other Hardware You Will Need

What other hardware will you need to build and maintain your Web site? As we've mentioned before, customers like to see products online. Because of the vastness of the Internet, you will be reaching potential customers from all over the world. These people cannot come down to your store and look at what they are purchasing. Some people do not even have actual bricks-and-mortar stores but do all their business online. So how do you allow these widely varied customers to see the products that you hope they will then buy?

Digital Cameras

The best way is through use of a digital camera or scanner. Digital cameras are very hot-selling items now. They allow you to take pictures without using film. Photographs are stored either in the memory of the camera or on a floppy disk. If they are stored in the camera's memory, when you are done taking pictures or the memory is full you plug a cord into the camera and into your computer, and using the software that came with the camera, you download the pictures right to your machine. If the photos are stored on a floppy, you can pull them off just like documents.

One of the huge benefits of digital cameras is that they allow you to see the picture as soon as you take it, which means if it did not come out or looks funny in some way you can retake it immediately, without waiting days for film to be developed.

Digital cameras are great ways to put your products on your Web site. Simply take a picture of your products, or several pictures from all angles, then make them a part of your site or the database architecture.

Scanners

There are other ways to get photographs up on your Web site. If you do not have a digital camera, you can take traditional photographs with a good quality camera and use a scanner to convert them to digital images.

Scanning technology has come a long way in the last several years. Good quality scanners used to be only found in printing shops and advertising agencies. They were huge machines with drums that made several passes over a picture before digitizing the images. Now you can find good quality flatbed scanners at your local office supply store for a few hundred dollars.

There are some important things to know about scanners, the biggest of which is its resolution quality or DPI.

Any kind of graphic is made up of tiny dots of color. Kind of like your television set, any solid image is not solid at all. The tiny dots of color are measured in DPI. DPI stands for dots per inch and refers to the number of dots of color you find in one inch of a photograph. The higher the DPI, or the more individual the dots, the higher the resolution and the better the graphic looks.

When you scan items that will eventually be printed out, you want to scan them at the highest resolution possible. Most commercial scanners handle 300 dpi very well, and that is a good dpi for print. Pictures on a Web site are not generated for print, they are made to be viewed on a monitor, and because of that, 72 dpi is a good scan quality for these kinds of graphics.

When it comes time to scan your pictures, there are a few things to consider. Remember, a final scan will never be as good as the original photograph, so if the original is blurry, unclear, poorly composed, or just generally bad, the scan is not going to magically correct it. In fact, it's probably going to make all the faults worse. Use good quality pictures taken with the right speed film and developed by a professional.

Scanning Techniques

You should always scan your pictures at a higher resolution than your output. For print, you should scan at 500 to 1,000 dpi. For on-screen resolution, a 300 dpi scan should be fine. You need to scan your photo at a higher resolution so you do not lose quality if you need to make modifications or edits to the photograph. There are a lot of commercially available programs that will allow you to enlarge, crop, highlight, or alter scanned or digital photographs. The most popular is Adobe's PhotoShop. However, Adobe PhotoShop is also the most expensive and one of the most difficult to use. Most Microsoft operating systems, like Windows 98 and Windows NT come with imaging software built in. These built-in programs will let you make basic adjustments to your photograph without having to lay out additional money for a program or classes in how to learn to use it.

WORKSHEET

1. How do you want to use technology on your site?

_____

_____

_____

_____

_____

_____

_____

2. How can your business benefit from a database?

_____

_____

_____

_____

_____

_____

_____

3. How can you personalize the web experience for your customers?

_____

_____

_____

_____

_____

_____

_____

Address http://chapter_eight.com

Link

E-Commerce Solutions and Online Security

DEFINITION PLEASE

E-wallets act similar to a physical wallet, allowing customers to store their electronic cash and online ordering information in a single and safe way. Many are site-specific, meaning they only work at one site.

If you have a product that requires frequent ordering, or expect your customers to order at your site often, you may want to investigate introducing an e-wallet. The customer downloads the wallet, fills out the information fields once, and the information is stored for easy transactions later.

There are some multisite e-wallets available now, like Yahoo! wallet and Microsoft's Passport. These multisite models allow you to use the one wallet at any site that accepts it. None of the existing e-wallets have taken the Net by storm, so merchants are as reluctant to sign on as users are to use them. Each group is waiting for the other to choose a clear leader in the industry.

E-Commerce Solutions

E-commerce solutions describe a suite of applications that can either be built, purchased as a single package, or purchased as individual applications. However you do it, each of the steps in the process is based on standard sets of technology.

Shopping Carts

As a customer browses around your online store, the first application you will need will be a shopping cart. This is just a cute name for a way to let customers surf around your site and click on several different products to purchase before actually filling out an order form with their address and credit card information. There are huge benefits to using shopping cart technologies. Without them, every time a person wanted to order a product he would have to select it then fill out his ordering information and complete the transaction. Want to purchase multiple items from the same Web site? Guess what, you now have to go back into the database, select the next item, and fill out that form all over again.

Shopping cart technology works much the way it sounds. Customers can select items and put them in a virtual shopping cart, then when they are ready to purchase they only need to fill out the ordering information form once. It saves time and makes the shopping experience less hassled.

The shopping cart relies on personalization technology by placing a cookie in the user's cookie file and keeping a temporary database record on the server for the user's current shopping excursion. Each time the user places another item in her shopping cart, the server is instructed to add that item to the user's current list of products to be purchased in the database. Once a user completes the transaction or leaves the site, the shopping cart is deleted.

Checkout and Accepting Payment

The next step in the process is for the user to checkout with her purchase(s). For this she must input all of her shipping and billing information and upload her credit card number. But thanks to the shopping cart technology, this only needs to be done once!

Once the customer's order and payment information have been uploaded to the server securely, it must be processed through your own order processing system. The credit card number needs to be authenticated and authorized by a credit card clearinghouse, just as it would be in your real store. Then the payment must be transferred into your bank account, called a merchant account.

To accept credit cards for online sales you first must have a "card not present" (or CNP) merchant credit card account. When a card is not present, you do not see the consumer or the card so transactions are inherently riskier.

Mostly it is a matter of assessing—and paying for—risk. The riskier your business is perceived to be by the credit card company and your business bank, the more you'll have to pay in fees to be able to accept credit card payments. This was true for the mail and telephone order business a few years ago and it's true for online businesses now. A new Internet business looks like a high-risk merchant to a lot of banks, and these new kids on the block can pay a premium to do business. As online shopping grows in popularity and Internet security gets tighter and tighter, the fees for transactions are slowly starting to come down.

In order to accept credit card transactions, you need to go to a bank that offers "card not present" accounts for online merchants. It may or may not be your own bank, but it's a good place to start. The number of banks that offer CNP accounts increase every day.

Once you get a CNP account so that you can accept credit card payments, the next thing is to get a secure Web site. You'll need to get software that allows you to set up a storefront and support real-time payments. If your site is being developed by a Web development firm, they will take care of this. There is a whole range of products and solutions from the very simple to the complex that handle building your site, and we cover those in later chapters. On the financial side, if you are going it alone, you can talk to your own bank, read trade publications, and look online for various service and product solutions.

Brick Banks and E-business

Banks view online credit card transactions in much the same way they saw mail order or telephone order transactions a few years ago. Of course, now mail and telephone orders are a big business and banks have worked out policies for handling it. As e-commerce grows, more and more banks are working out policies for their customers who wish to engage in business online.

Electronic Cash

A number of companies have been trying out new payment models so that merchants and customers can handle electronic cash. In part, this is an answer to the need for micropayments. Micropayments are small payments, from a few cents up to about ten dollars, for items like pages of information, video or sound clips, low-cost programs, greeting cards, and the like. And in part, it's simply a response to the effort to make the ability to purchase goods and services on the Web as varied and diverse as they are offline.

Two companies who are offering interesting approaches to the challenge of digital payments via electronic cash are CyberCash and Mercantile Bank. CyberCash offers CyberCoin electronic cash and PayNow electronic checks. Mercantile bank offers Ecash.

When you find something you want to buy for less than $10, suddenly credit cards are not feasible. That's because the transaction fees the credit card companies charge merchants make it prohibitively expensive to use a card for such small amounts. That's where electronic cash comes in.

To use CyberCoins, a customer initiates an electronic wallet by taking money from their checking account or advancing on their credit card and depositing it into the wallet. This process is called binding. Once the customer has money in his or her wallet, it's simply a matter of paying via CyberCoin to any merchant who accepts it. No money moves online; the only thing that moves is information. It is called a notational system because CyberCoin makes a notation of the amount of money the customer has in the wallet and how much is spent. Because the money never leaves the banking system, this kind of electronic cash transaction is very difficult to break into.

For a merchant to set up an account to accept CyberCoins, it must set up a merchant account with a bank that allows the merchant to accept credit cards. It's a good idea to have a card not present account anyway since so many people prefer to use credit cards online. Once you get a merchant ID and a terminal ID from this credit account, you can contact

ELECTRONIC CASH

CyberCoin with those numbers. In parallel, you would receive the CyberCoin software to install on your Web server.

Mercantile Bank's Ecash system works very differently from CyberCoin. With Ecash a customer in essence "mints" money right on his or her computer. Customers can even paste money into an e-mail and transfer it to friends and family as gifts.

For the customer, the first step is to fill out an application, either online or via regular mail, for a Mercantile Bank account. You must then deposit a sum of money into the account through normal means, just like starting any other kind of bank account. Once the account is opened, the customer gets an account ID and password. Then you must download the Ecash software, which authenticates the connections to the electronic bank, and the customer can download the Ecash right onto his or her computer's hard drive via the software. The Ecash system acts like a virtual ATM, and the funds are downloaded directly to the customer's hard drive. From there you can do what you wish with it. For example, you can go to an Ecash merchant, such as CDNOW, and the funds move from your hard disk to the CD-Now account. You can also transfer money directly from your hard drive wallet to someone else's electronic wallet or e-mail money right to someone.

For vendors to accept Ecash, you need to go to the Mercantile Bank Web site, fill out the application, and download the software. It is roughly the same software a customer would use with some minor modifications that allow the merchant not just to receive money but to receive money as payment.

Fulfillment

After the order has been processed, it must be picked from your inventory and shipped to the customer.

Ready-to-Open E-Commerce Stores

There is a way to get your business up and running on the Internet without knowing HTML or spending a lot of money on a development program. Many companies are now offering full-service electronic storefronts. These companies allow you to set up your Web site, design a storefront with full ordering capability, host your site, and in some cases

Payment Methods

Credit cards are still the most common means for purchasing on the Web, at least in the United States. Online transactions are about as secure or even more so than offline credit card purchases. It's not the one card that hackers are after; they want the place where a critical mass of credit card information is stored or flows. Those places are behind secure firewalls. Ordering online is more secure than giving your credit card number to someone over the phone because there is no human interaction, and even if it were somehow to be stolen, the same protections apply for online credit users as for offline users. If your card number is stolen you are not liable for more than $50 in unauthorized charges. To encourage online shopping growth, many credit card issuers even waive the liability.

Small Business and Cyber Cash

Some banks will not allow small businesses to handle online commerce at all, much less deal in electronic cash. If you are a merchant in this situation, do not fear! You can connect to CyberCash and other electronic cash providers through a third party like an Internet service provider or Web site hosting company. You should talk to both about how they help businesses set up e-commerce storefronts.

offer administrative functions that work with your existing accounting and administrative software. Companies like Bigstep.com, Yahoo! Store, freemerchant.com, and a wide range of others all make the development and running of your online store almost as easy as it can get.

There are some things to look for when deciding to use one of these online storefront services, and as with anything else related to getting your business online, doing your research now will save you money and time later. Almost all the quality storefront generators offer Web site development tools and online shopping carts, but beyond that the features vary widely and choosing one that appeals to you really lies in choosing what features you need.

Here is the rundown on a few of these online storefront generators.

Bigstep.com

Bigstep was a *PC Magazine's* Editors' Choice in November of 1999. They do not charge a fee for setting up or hosting your site, which is a great benefit if you do not have a lot of startup capital. Using their development tools, you can create a nice quality storefront, though do not expect anything fancy. Because you are not technically generating the site yourself, you need to work within the templates provided, though fonts and colors are interchangeable. They do offer a nice variety of about seventy templates, so there is no real need to worry about your site resembling someone else's.

If you are relying on the images of your products as a primary selling tool, beware when signing up with this service. Bigstep.com imposes a size limit on graphics; the entire site cannot contain more than 12MB in images. Even though you are allowed an unlimited number of pages, large-scale catalogs that utilize a lot of graphics may run into some problems showing them all.

Bigstep also does not have a feature that allows your customers to search for products that interest them, so although there is no limit to the amount of products you can offer for sale with this service, if you have a huge online store, your customers may have a difficult time finding the specific products they are looking for. Bigstep also provides no inventory control functions, so keeping a close eye on your stock is going to be up to your current tracking software.

In order to go live using Bigstep.com, you must arrange a merchant account through their service. This merchant account will cover all your transactional needs and only costs about $15 a month, plus twenty cents per transaction.

Bigstep will register your site with search engines and help you design your own e-zine as well. Bigstep has a good set of reports that track everything from site activity to purchase records, but Bigstep does not offer some of the higher-end administrative functions other sites do.

Freemerchant.com 2.0

The other *PC Magazine* Editors' Choice, freemerchant.com, is another high-quality site that allows you to quickly and easily generate an online storefront. The actual site generation tools are basic and present some of the same WYSIWYG problems that you find in page generation software. Getting the site to look precisely as you wish can require a lot of fine tuning. Like Bigstep, freemerchant.com offers a variety of customizable templates that will help you get started. But unlike Bigstep, you do not need to set up a merchant account with them. You will need to set up a merchant account somewhere though, or you'll be unable to process electronic transactions. Check the major services and decide which one is right for you.

The administrative features of freemerchant are excellent and work with a variety of external software packages like Microsoft Excel, dBase, and FoxPro. Freemerchant will also allow you to register with several of the most used search engines. The best feature of freemerchant is probably its cost. All of its site features are free with no obligation, making it an excellent way to get your business started online without high development and hosting outlay.

Like Bigstep, Freemerchant.com does not offer any product search capabilities. You can also have an unlimited amount of products for sale, but be aware that the more products you have, the more a lack of search capability is going to hurt your business. Unlike Bigstep, freemerchant will track your inventory automatically alerting customers when products are backordered.

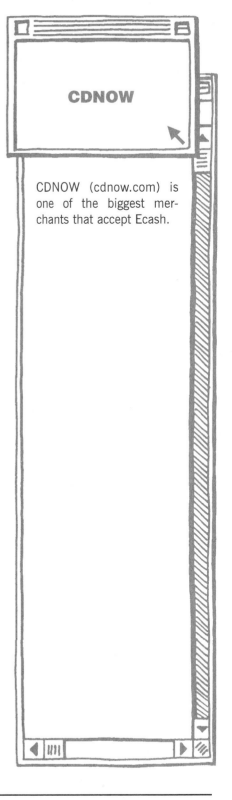

CDNOW (cdnow.com) is one of the biggest merchants that accept Ecash.

Yahoo! Store

www.store.yahoo.com

Yahoo! Store offers the same services as many other online storefronts: unlimited product capabilities and Web site generation tools. One major difference between Yahoo! Store and the other two services mentioned is that Yahoo! Store charges $100 per month for every fifty items available for sale on the site.

Most online storefront services charge a monthly fee on top of any merchant account fees, and the Yahoo! Store fee is not exorbitant by industry standards. Small stores are categorized by having up to fifty items and cost $100 per month. Large stores are categorized by having up to 1,000 items and will cost around $300 per month. Yahoo! Store does have provisions for larger stores. They will run about $300 per month for the first 1,000 items, plus $100 per month for each additional 1,000 items. This is on top of any merchant fees you will incur with your service. But, for the price, you get a lot of good features. Yahoo! Store does not have a maximum number of products, and, unlike some of the other services, they do offer a product search feature. This means storefronts with a wide array of products can let their customers search and find precisely what they need. However considering the monthly fees, large-scale stores can become very expensive.

The Yahoo! Store's site generation features are excellent, if time consuming. Because there is no size limit to the site, every product can have a graphic, a drop-down menu (great for sizes and colors), and even an extensive description. The site generation product even allows you to set different pricing for quantities and sales.

The site promotion is first-rate, if limited. Just by creating your site with Yahoo! Store you are automatically added to the Yahoo! search engine in the proper category. Yahoo! is one of the most used search engines, so that aspect of the promotion is excellent, but that is as far as it goes. You can also arrange to sell products through Yahoo! auctions.

Internet Malls

There are other ways to start and promote your store on the Web. Internet Malls are just like the old brick-and-mortar kind, offering one-stop-shopping in dozens of categories. Many I-malls also offer the same services as the electronic storefront sites just mentioned. Even if you have your own site you can still become a part of a mall. Linking procedures and membership pricing for vendors vary widely, but more and more Internet users are heading to these cybermalls rather than creating individual searches for each product they want to buy.

There are three types of Internet malls. There is a traditional full-service mall, which is self-contained, a directory-based mall, which is basically a listing of storefronts by category, and a hybrid of the two. Many search engines offer directory-type malls where all the listed shopping sites are arranged in a single directory. Sometimes they are product searchable, sometimes not.

The Internet Mall, www.internet-mall.com (part of the shopnow.com network), is one of the largest cybermalls on the World Wide Web. The Internet Mall features more than 20,000 merchants and storefronts and offers a complete range of products and services to the consumer. The Internet Mall offers one-stop business development tools, much like the storefront generators mentioned above. From domain registration to building your storefront to helping generate more customers and advertising your business, the Internet Mall's business development center is a great resource for getting started online.

Another large cybermall is the iMall. Featuring more than 1,600 storefronts, iMall offers a variety of options for site building, adding e-commerce capabilities to your current Web site, and getting a merchant listing of their mall directory. One of the most intriguing features is "bolting" e-commerce capabilities on to an existing Web site that is not enabled for commerce. If you have an online brochure but no ordering capability, iMall will help you attach shopping cart technology, start up a merchant account, and help with generating sales reports. They also offer database services for developing your catalog and product promotion within iMall, Stuffmall.com, and Excitestores.

Instant Online Stores

eCongo.com:
Free service with an unlimited number of products. A merchant account will cost $39.95 per month plus thirty cents per transaction.

IBM Homepage Creator:
$69.95 for every fifty items (maximum of 500) and fifteen pages. Merchant accounts must be set up through a service prior to enrolling.

iCat Commerce online:
$49.95 for every fifty items to a maximum of 3,000. A merchant account will cost $45 per month plus thirty-five cents per transaction. iCat also charges a merchant account setup fee of $300.

Mindspring Estore Deluxe:
$109.00 per month per 100 items with a maximum of 100. A merchant account will cost $35 per month for 100 transactions, beyond that transactions are fifty cents each.

Sitematic Catalog:
$49.95 per month for every fifty items (to a maximum of 100) and twelve pages. Merchant accounts are subject to a $50 setup fee and are $10 a month.

Guarantee Privacy

Consumers are very concerned about privacy and security on the Internet. Besides having the right security technology in place, it is critical to explain to your customers how you handle online security and why their information is safe. Besides being safe, you want your customers to feel safe as well. Explaining your security measures to your customers in a way they can easily understand will go a long way towards encouraging online shopping, as well as heading off customer service headaches. A sound policy should be in place, with a link to a copy of that policy.

The Awesome Mall of the Internet is a hybrid of a full-service mall and a directory, offering both full-service storefront hosting and advertising and directory options. The Awesome Mall of the Internet is a more entertaining mall, offering news and information and chat features in addition to a wide variety of online stores. The Awesome Mall offers hosting and site generation services through a Web site development company at a la carte pricing. Before generating your site with them, you should check their pricing against Web development costs in your area.

The Awesome Mall also offers you the ability to list your business in its directory. You can list under a few different categories for as low as $17 per month. (To get the lowest rate you have to sign on for a full year.) They also offer an advertisement option: Generate a display ad or a banner and you can choose where your ad will appear in the mall and how often. The Awesome Mall of the Internet offers great results tracking for your advertisements.

Online Security

Once you have your site up and running, you need to make sure it is secure. Merchants bear the lion's share of risk in online credit card transactions. Consumers are protected from online fraud by the same laws that protect them in the offline world. But if an online merchant ships goods and the recipient repudiates the sale, the recourse is limited. Just because the credit card authorization has been processed by the credit card company does not mean that the order was not fraudulent. If you are not careful and vigilant, you could be responsible for the cost of the merchandise you shipped. So you need security to protect your business. And, of course, customers are going to be more willing to buy from you if their credit card information is safe from interception and theft.

E-commerce has undergone a security revolution in recent years. When you are transmitting financial information like credit card numbers it is important that the information is kept safe from people who would like nothing more than to use it for their own profit. The best way to do that is through some form of encryption. Encryption is simply the process of translating data, such as credit card numbers, into a secret code.

Secure Socket Layer (SSL) and
Secure Electronic Transaction (SET)

Right now there are two protocols that help keep e-commerce information secure for both you and your customers. The first line of defense is the SSL or secure socket layer, which encrypts the information that flows between a browser and Web site. While SSL will keep your customer's credit card information safe from theft, it does not authenticate the identity of the customer, and the merchant still holds the burden of risk in any electronic transaction. A new protocol called SET (secure electronic transaction) devised jointly by Microsoft, Mastercard, Visa, and Netscape seeks to transfer the liability for electronic transactions to the customer's bank, just as it happens today in the bricks-and-mortar world.

Secure Sockets Layer, or SSL, was originally developed by Netscape to transmit private documents securely over the Internet. Originally, SSL was only compatible with the Netscape Web browser, but now it is available in the public domain. SSL is the most common method of obtaining and securing confidential user information like credit card numbers. You can recognize Web sites that utilize SSL connections because their URL begins with https:// instead of http://.

SSL is a free program, though a higher level version that costs a one-time fee of $70,000 is available. Once the SSL software is installed on the Web server, to get SSL working on your site you go to a public certificate authority like Verisign or Entrust. They check you and your business out thoroughly and issue a digital certificate. Your Webmaster (or Web development firm) gets back the digital certificate and installs it onto the server, which turns on the SSL. From there, the Webmaster or development firm decides what part of the server requires SSL and applies it through a graphical user interface. Neither the user, you, or your Webmaster needs to be an expert in security, and about 99 percent of browsers automatically recognize the legitimate digital certificates needed to run SSL.

How do you know if you need the higher level version of SSL? More and more critical business transactions are being handled online, and these will require higher level security solutions. The purchase and selling of large quantity of stock online can involve

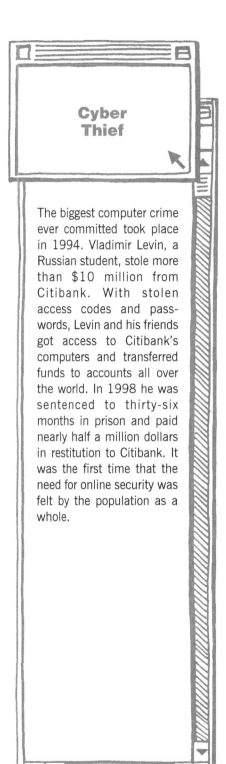

Cyber Thief

The biggest computer crime ever committed took place in 1994. Vladimir Levin, a Russian student, stole more than $10 million from Citibank. With stolen access codes and passwords, Levin and his friends got access to Citibank's computers and transferred funds to accounts all over the world. In 1998 he was sentenced to thirty-six months in prison and paid nearly half a million dollars in restitution to Citibank. It was the first time that the need for online security was felt by the population as a whole.

tens of thousands of dollars. In instances like this, both the brokerage firm and the customer may want this higher level of security. If you are merely selling books or CDs online, the amount of money involved in any one transaction probably is not enough to warrant anything deeper than the free version of SSL.

SET works by issuing digital certificates to all parties, including the customers. A merchant works with his bank to get the necessary credentials and the certificate technology while the customer works with the bank that issued his or her credit card to get a digital certificate.

Why should a customer be interested in getting a digital certificate—and why should the customer's bank be interested in assuming the liability in online transactions? Because once a consumer gets a card SET enabled, that card will be used a lot. Banks that issue credit cards like to see them being used and will be more willing to accept the risk of the transaction because it will end up generating more business for them as well as for the online retailer.

With SET, the process of getting a digital certificate will be nearly transparent for the consumer. It will probably just be another part of the application form or something simply downloaded to the cardholder's computer before he or she can perform online transactions with that card. Once the cardholder receives the digital certificate he or she never needs to think about it again; the cardholder may not even realize he has a digital certificate. He'll just know they can safely buy things with their credit cards online.

SET has not caught on in the United States very strongly yet, but Europe and Asian-Pacific markets have embraced it readily. SET is stuck in a sort of chicken-and-egg type problem. Merchants may be ready to jump on the SET bandwagon but where are the customers? On the other hand, the issuing banks are wondering if they enable their customers, where will they shop? As more and more major brand-name merchants become SET enabled, so will the customers.

Fraud Flags

There are some things you can look for that should wave potential red flags. First, you want to confirm the AVS, or address verification service response code, for the credit card transaction. AVS compares the billing address the customer inputted on their order form to the cardholder's address. While a negative response does not always mean that a credit card has been stolen, it should raise eyebrows when you look at other items. Also, know that a transaction will not be halted due to a negative AVS response. It is up to you as the businessman to look further into the transaction.

You should also pay close attention to the quantity of products ordered. Only you know if 500 widgets is a normal order or something to be suspicious of. Look at the ship to address and shipping method. Criminals want to get the merchandise they ordered before they are discovered, so be wary of large orders with ship to addresses that do not match the billing address, especially when the customer requests express shipping.

A good way to verify your customer is to check the e-mail address supplied with an order. Take a moment to check that the e-mail address does in fact exist. Is the address a derivative of a name, like John_doe@anywhere.com? Does the name match the name of the cardholder?

It never hurts to be vigilant. Precautions that may tack an extra hour onto the transaction can save you lots of time and money later. Because the fraudulent order could have been placed from virtually anywhere on earth, it is very difficult to get your merchandise back, or even bring the criminals to justice.

PKI Encryption

Internet technology is working towards solving the problem of credit card fraud online. The technology world is developing digital identification systems like PKI, or public key infrastructure, to authenticate the users at both ends of a transaction.

In the bricks-and-mortar world, proving the identity of your customers is easy. You do it every time you ask for a driver's license when someone writes a check. But in the online world, these kind of physical proofs of identity do not work. Although proving who you are dealing with is only one aspect of security in the world of electronic commerce, it's a very important aspect. What is needed is a form of electronic or digital signature that is trustworthy even

Secure HTTP and the IETF

Secure HTTP, or S-HTTP, is another protocol to transmit data securely from Web site to Web server. It works as a companion to SSL. Where SSL establishes a secure connection between two computers, S-HTTP was designed to encrypt and send individual messages securely.

Not all Web browsers and servers support S-HTTP. Both SSL and S-HTTP have been adopted by the Internet Engineering Task force as standards for e-commerce security.

The IETF is the main standards organization for the Internet. It is a large international community concerned with the growing architecture of the Internet, and it helps adopts standards for programming languages, operating systems, data formats, communications protocols, and electrical interfaces.

Using Other Secure Technologies with PKI

PKI can be used simultaneously with other encryption technologies like SSL. Think of an item to be encrypted, such as a letter in an envelope going through the mail. PKI encrypts the actual letter, making it so that nobody without the correct key can read the words on the paper. The encrypted letter then goes in the envelope and gets sent out. SSL secures the method of transport, making sure nobody can steal the letter while it is in transit.

though the signing parties may be thousands of miles apart and would not recognize each other if they sat next to each other on the bus. The public key infrastructure, or PKI, encryption coding system is such a digital signature.

To understand how PKI works, it's easier to start with the kind of code most everyone is familiar with, symmetric encryption.

A symmetric encryption system is one in which you decode a message by undoing whatever was done to it when it was coded. For example, suppose your coding system is to shift every letter in a regular message by thirteen letters forward in the alphabet. "A" becomes "M," "B" becomes "N," and so forth. To decrypt this type of message, the recipient just needs to know the algorithm (the number of letters shifted forward or backward) and shift the letters back to their original positions. The term symmetric means it works the same way in both directions. Symmetric coding was how some of the most famous codes, like the Nazi Enigma code, operated.

In symmetric encryption, the secret to the code is the scrambling arrangement. Everyone involved can use the algorithm. But for this to work, you must talk to people in advance and exchange the secret. Once the secret has been distributed among a number of people, there is no way of identifying which person actually created a specific message. A symmetric key is dependent on advance information and has no built-in way to prove authorship, which makes it useless as a way of proving identity.

PKI solves this problem by having two codes or keys instead of one. One key is public and is openly distributed to anyone with whom you may wish to exchange confidential information. This could be your stockbroker, your friend, or even an online merchant. The other key is private. Only you posses the private key, and it is unique to you. An individual's public and private keys are complementary—they work together. If you encrypt a message with your private key, your public key can decrypt it. Likewise your private key can decrypt a message encrypted with your public key. It's like a door that requires two keys to open.

If you want to send a message that is both secure and that could only have come from you, there are two steps to doing it with PKI. First, you encrypt the message with your private key. This is your digital signature. It proves that *you* sent the message since you are the only one with that unique private key. The second step encrypts the message again with the public key of the recipient. This step assures the security of the message. The message (which could be anything from ordering information to stock trading information) is now encrypted two ways and will take two keys to open.

When the recipient gets the message, he first uses his private key to decrypt it. Then he uses your public key to finish the decryption. PKI's public/private key system is asymmetric, meaning it requires different keys to encrypt and decrypt. If the recipient wants to send you a secure message, he would go about it the same way only in reverse.

The important thing to understand about public and private keys is that how they work is not what's secret. The secret is knowing the individual number that is generated that codes the message. Because the entire process is digital and handled on computers, huge numbers are selected containing, in some cases, as many as 250 digits each. One of these very large numbers is the important number in a private or public key. Figuring out such a number to break the key encoding system is nearly impossible.

But simply having someone's public key is not enough for trust. How does a merchant or customer know that the public key really belongs to who they're told it does? A merchant needs to get that public key from someplace trustworthy. That's where digital certificates come in. A digital certificate is a public key that has been verified, by a trusted third party, to come from a certain person.

Who or what constitutes a trusted third party? In the offline world the DMV is considered a trusted third party as it is the issuing body for identification like driver's licenses. In the online world, a number of companies have emerged that currently fulfill this role as certificate authorities handing out digital certificates. Three of those companies that issue and verify private and public keys are Verisign, GTE Internetworking, and CERTCO. Until a business can get digital certificates from a bank through a merchant account, companies like these are the only source.

Web Integrity and Security

There are currently four ways to guarantee customers that their credit card numbers will not be grabbed and used by a hacker. By increasing level of sophistication, they are:

1. Use "after the order" verification. You can call back, send a confirmation e-mail, etc.

2. Set up an account with a customer before a purchase. The customer provides the credit card number over the phone, and it never travels online.

3. Use digital identification. This system requires a customer to prove identity to a trusted third party, who issues a digital ID and encrypted code, which is attached to all that individual's correspondence and uniquely identifies them.

4. Secure socket layer (SSL) is a protocol that encrypts credit card data traveling via the Net to a merchant's Web site. The number is decrypted on the other end and verified either automatically or manually. SSL is built right into the browser.

WORKSHEET

1. What do I have to do to make my customers feel secure about purchasing from my site?

_____

_____

_____

_____

_____

_____

_____

2. Which technologies should I choose to guarantee secure transactions?

_____

_____

_____

_____

_____

_____

_____

3. Which banks can I deal with at my level of business?

_____

_____

_____

_____

_____

_____

_____

Address http://chapter_nine.com ▼ **Link**

Web Site Building Tools and HTML

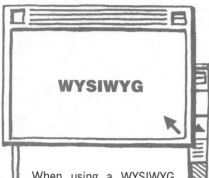

WYSIWYG

When using a WYSIWYG program, place your text, images, links, and frames on the screen as you wish them to appear on your Web site. The site creation tool will generate the HTML code for you. WYSIWYG programs are near famous for writing code with some strange-looking attributes. You will not have to worry about this odd code unless it makes your page look somehow strange.

HTML and Web Page Development

There are dozens of commercially available programs that will allow you to develop your Web site just as you would layout and advertisement on a page. These are called WYSIWYG programs. WYSIWYG stands for What You See Is What You Get, which is an apt description of what these programs do.

You do not need to know HTML to build your Web site, however, it's still good to have a basic knowledge of HTML if you are going to use one of these programs. Site generation tools can be fickle. Sometimes they generate messy code or will not allow you to do something you want. In these instances, knowing how to reprogram that part of your site yourself will give you the ability to fix your page without fighting the program for hours. Many of these site generation software packages include an HTML editor. This enables you to go into the code the program generates and make your own changes.

If you have no desire to learn HTML and are not quite ready to spend a lot of money on developing your Web site, page generation software is a good choice for you. In this chapter we will look at a variety of the most common personal and professional site creation tools. It is impossible to cover all the features of all the programs available, but we'll try to give you a good basic review of what is available, what you can expect it to do, and how much you can expect it to cost you.

Using HTML page generation software has a lot of plusses. They are quick to learn, allow great degrees of graphic manipulation and placement control, automatically check your links within your site to make sure they all connect properly, and many of them even contain FTP software to help you upload and download your site and its elements. The major drawbacks, of course, are that they often create bizarre code that would take even a professional developer time to debug, and the more features included in the software package the more it is going to cost you. But even the most expensive development package still costs less than hiring an outside development firm. If you want to get started yourself and see how things go before hiring someone to design a site, page development software is for you.

Bare-bones BBEdit v. 5.0.2

Mac systems only

$119

www.barebones.com/products/bbedit/bbedit.html

BBEdit is primarily a text editor. A text editor is the kind of program you use to write HTML code. Even though we said we were going to focus on WYSIWYG programs, we have included it in this section because it has some excellent features that can help you set up your page if you decide to code it yourself. In Web design circles, BBEdit is known as the text editor of choice for writing straight HTML code.

Like a word processor, BBEdit has an undo feature, which is invaluable for quickly undoing lines of code completely. (If you miss a tag or part of one when manually deleting it can mess up the rest of your code.) BBEdit also has menus, tool palettes, and dialog boxes that help you code most common tags. It will even allow you to assign keyboard shortcuts to your most commonly used tags so with two keystrokes you can insert them into your HTML document.

BBEdit also includes some basic site-management tools. It has an FTP client installed to help you get your site up and running. It also includes spelling, syntax, and link checkers to make sure your site is error free.

The most powerful feature in BBEdit is an easy-to-use search that allows you to search files without opening them first. This allows easy correction of things like file names or even URL locations of pictures should your Web administrator need to move things around.

There are some drawbacks to using BBEdit. Besides the fact it is not available for PC users, it does not operate on a WYSIWYG platform, so you need to know your HTML when you sit down to use it. Some beginners have complained that it is difficult to understand the interface, and the menu and tool bar structure can be confusing. Once you become accustomed to it, though, it becomes very useful.

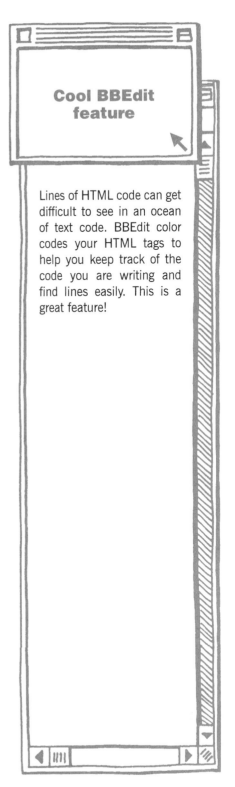

Cool BBEdit feature

Lines of HTML code can get difficult to see in an ocean of text code. BBEdit color codes your HTML tags to help you keep track of the code you are writing and find lines easily. This is a great feature!

Check Out Your Home PC

If you have recently purchased a PC, you should take a look at the software that is already installed on your hard drive. Sometimes PC manufacturers or distributors include copies of page generation software as a bonus when you purchase. Also, many times you may purchase a graphics design program or other piece of software that has a Web page generator as an added bonus or already installed with the main program. Look through what you have before you buy; it can save you a lot of money later.

FileMaker Home Page

Available for Windows and Macintosh operating systems
$99.00
www.filemakerpro.com

For basic Web page generation, Home Page is excellent. You can generate a simple online business card, with links, in just a matter of a few minutes. Add a few other pages and you can have an entire functioning site up within one afternoon.

This program has clear, easy-to-understand menus and all the important features you need are easy to find and access. Home Page offers one-click image linking and bulleted lists (which even in most word processors can be less than easy). It also includes a built-in FTP (file transfer protocol) client that will allow you to upload and preview your site without having to close out of the program. This saves a lot of time in switching between programs when you are finally ready to put your page out on the Web.

Some of the best features of FileMaker Home Page include its easy image adjustment. Altering graphics for your Web site is something many site generation programs have a problem with. HomePage offers special tools that make altering images easy. The importing tools allow you to take text from other sources and drop them into your Web page with ease. It comes with a built-in clip art library, which is useful for adding graphics to your site if you do not have a program like MasterClips. It also offers 45 site templates to help generate your site.

FileMaker Home Page offers spell and link checking capabilities and wizard-based interfaces to help beginners. But one of the most useful features in Home Page is the global find and replace. You may not think you need this until you make a simple spelling error, such as receipt, and need to change every appearance on your site. The global find and replace will check every line of text on every page.

As with any program, FileMaker Home Page has some drawbacks. Although making tables is easy, FileMaker does not show the tables on your screen exactly as they will appear in browser windows. This means that your tables may look skewed on some browsers and you might not know it. FileMaker has no support for cascading style sheets.

Nestcape Composer

Available for Windows and Mac operating systems
Free! (Bundled with Netscape Communicator)
www.netscape.com

Considering that Netscape Composer is a free program (it comes with the Netscape Communicator browser software, and can be downloaded from the Netscape Web site), it is surprisingly good. Like the other programs reviewed, Netscape composer offers WYSIWYG page composition with clear and logical menus and buttons. Netscape Composer offers a good quality table builder, which is something that many other page generation programs have difficulty with.

Netscape Composer offers FTP uploads through a simple publish command and provides a spell checker as well.

Unfortunately, Composer has some very major drawbacks that may not be offset by the fact that it is free. When creating pages in Composer, they often look very different in the browser than when you are creating it. This is especially true of images. Both their look and placement can be very different when actually published. Netscape Composer does not allow you to drag and drop images, which makes changing their position once placed very difficult.

Composer also does some strange and unexpected things. Users have reported that it adds <DIV> tags at its own whim. Some users also say that Composer makes copies of graphics and images on its own. When using Netscape Composer it is good to have a rudimentary knowledge of HTML and how it works. When strange things start happening or when the page looks different in the browser than in the program, you can make any adjustments directly to the source code rather than fiddling around in Composer until it looks the way you want. A little knowledge of HTML and an HTML tag reference card can save you a lot of headaches later.

Create Your Own Art

With the drawing and painting programs in the AppleWorks suite you can design your own images. If you are a talented graphic artist, this can be a great alternative to using stock images or clip art.

Apple Works 5.0

Mac operating systems only
Pre-installed on iMac
www.apple.com

The newest version of a program originally called ClarisWorks, AppleWorks 5.0 is a one-stop program suite. Like Microsoft Office for the PC, AppleWorks contains an excellent word processor, a drawing program, a database program, a paint program, and even a spreadsheet program similar to MS Excel. Apple Works comes pre-installed on iMacs and allows users to create and maintain Web pages with relative ease. While there is a Windows version of the software, Apple is no longer marketing it and it may be difficult to find.

All the programs in the AppleWorks suite work together, which augments every aspect of Web site generation. One of the best features in Works is the ability to design complex pages and graphics. Using the word processor, you can utilize an array of superior word processing features. Spreadsheets designed in the document can perform calculations, which is an excellent feature if you want to include payment generators or offer your customers a way to figure out tax and shipping. Surprisingly, users found that the on-screen help is actually helpful.

Unfortunately, the AppleWorks program does not display true WYSIWYG. The page as designed in AppleWorks only bears a faint resemblance to what actually appears on your browser, so you'll have to do some fiddling to get it to look the way you want. The program also does not develop true HTML code so you cannot simply go into the source code and make your fixes.

Other drawbacks include the fact that you cannot label images, align them, or eliminate borders, and probably the single biggest detractor to using this program for Web site generation is that when images are placed they become part of the document rather than being contained in a separate folder. This can make the file size of your page very large.

Adobe GoLive 4.0

Windows and Mac operating systems

$275 if purchased directly from Adobe; $299 if purchased at software retailers

www.adobe.com/products/golive/

GoLive has made a name for itself in generating code in languages other than HTML (like JavaScript) and in site management. GoLive makes link checking, HTML code proofing, and find and replace about as easy as they can possibly be.

Unlike it's predecessor, PageMill, GoLive is not a program for beginners. If you do not have a good basic knowledge of HTML and know the proper way to design and construct a Web site, this is not the program to start with. But for people who have generated their site by hand and now want to take advantage of some more advanced features, GoLive is an excellent way to do it.

GoLive lets you take two different approaches to designing Web pages. You can lay them out the traditional way, from the top down, inserting elements as you go, or you can use the Layout Grid to place images, text, and other elements directly where you want them on the page.

One of the great things about Adobe's GoLive is that it supports all or most of the newest technologies available. It is one of the newest releases (the Windows version was released in Spring of 1999) so Java, DHTML, style sheets, and even Quick Time movies are supported by the software. Unlike other page generation programs, GoLive can provide Web page previews for different browsers. Considering how so many of the programs we've listed have problems developing true WYSIWYG code, this feature on GoLive is very valuable.

Adobe Systems builds great interfaces with their programs, and that carries over into GoLive. The floating tool bars and menus are all redundant, which makes finding the commands you want to use easy for beginners.

Site management is handled easily with GoLive; broken links are not only found but repaired automatically. Searches can be conducted across all pages at once, which is invaluable, and the entire structure of your site can be presented as a flow chart. This charting feature not only allows you to change the structure at will,

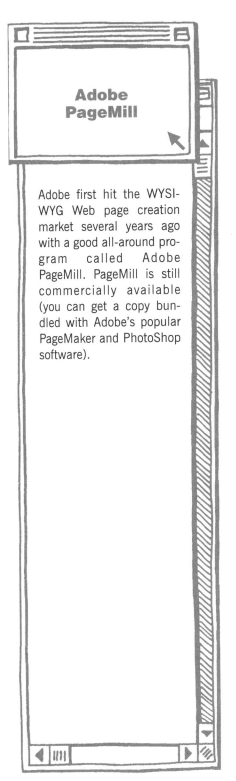

Adobe first hit the WYSIWYG Web page creation market several years ago with a good all-around program called Adobe PageMill. PageMill is still commercially available (you can get a copy bundled with Adobe's popular PageMaker and PhotoShop software).

One of the features that have made Microsoft products so easy for so many people is its **wizard**. A wizard is a small tool that enables people to follow steps at the computer's prompting. These steps are precise and help the user achieve his or her desired result. FrontPage includes both wizards and predesigned themes. These tools make site generation easy for beginning users.

but makes it easy to hand your existing site off to a development firm if you find it is time to scale it up. GoLive also has an FTP protocol for getting your site up and running quickly.

GoLive also offers an excellent editor for repairing source code, which is good, because the program can often generate bad code. The code-generating problems are not as bad as with some other WYSIWYG Web page generation programs, but when the bugs appear they can be complex, which is why knowing HTML is crucial. Also, many users have complained about the time involved in making fine changes in elements. It would be quicker in many circumstances to just rewrite the HTML code, which is just another reason why knowing HTML is vital to success with this product.

Microsoft FrontPage 2000
PC only (Windows 95/98/NT)
$105.95
www.microsoft.com/frontpage/

Early versions of Microsoft FrontPage were decidedly subpar. They would produce nearly indecipherable HTML and terrible JavaScript. The program contained no editor to change the code it generated, making many Web pages it developed unusable.

The newest version of the program, FrontPage 2000, has fixed a lot of the problems that plagued earlier versions. It is a topnotch HTML generation program that makes for easy editing. This new version includes some of the more advanced HTML features like dynamic HTML and CSS (cascading style sheets). Like the AppleWorks program is to Macintosh, FrontPage is to PCs, allowing an incredible degree of interactivity with companion Microsoft Office programs like Word, Excel, and PowerPoint. For people who want to generate online sales presentations, you can now develop them (or use existing presentations) in PowerPoint and integrate them into your Web site using FrontPage. Using FrontPage's interactivity with Microsoft Access, database functions are made easy.

One of the best things about this new version of FrontPage is that it now offers you three ways to view the page you are generating: Normal, HTML, and Preview. This allows for easy switching between WYSIWYG, code, and the final appearance of the page.

Although it is a much improved program over the original, there are still some drawbacks to FrontPage. In order to use many of the more advanced features FrontPage 2000 has to be hosted on a Windows NT server. NT Web servers are becoming more and more prevalent nowadays, but if your hosting company (or your own server) is running on Win95, 98, or Unix, you will be out of luck. Also, FrontPage requires a lot of clicking around to make changes. There are few shortcuts, and when you make a modification, the program closes the window. Every modification requires you to reopen the window, which makes delicate fine tuning more of a chore than it needs to be.

Macromedia Dreamweaver 3.0

Windows and Mac operating systems

$299

www.macromedia.com

Dreamweaver has long been considered one of the premier page development tools. It is a little pricey for the casual user, and it is considered more of a professional program than a home-based one. In this case, you get what you pay for. It is not really built for the beginner, but you hardly need to be a Web developer to use it. Dreamweaver packs a lot of punch into its package, generating some excellent sites without a lot of the problems inherent in other WYSIWYG programs.

Dreamweaver also offers a feature that allows you to create templates for your Web site with standardized background images, links, and formats. Some Web site generation programs come with templates installed but do not let you design your own. The benefit of using templates is that you do not need to recreate the basics of the site every time you generate a new page. When you alter a single part of the template on one page, you are given the option of modifying every page on the site that uses that template. This feature makes global graphics or layout changes a snap!

Dreamweaver does have a nice, basic text editor built into the software, but it also comes bundled with BBEdit (Mac platforms) or HomeSite (a comparable program for Windows) to handle any in-depth coding and editing. If you do not like either of those editors,

Getting Your Money's Worth

Some page generation software embeds a comment into its HTML code that says what program it was created with. If you decide to use a small Web development firm, have your IS department break into the source code of some of their sites you liked. If you see <!—Developed with Macromedia Dreamweaver!—> we suggest using a different developer! You are paying good money for your site; a developer should have programmers and coders of their own.

Dreamweaver Is a Dream to Work With

HTML coders and programmers LOVE Dreamweaver because, unlike some of its competitors, Dreamweaver does not alter any code you input as code unless you tell it to. With other programs, any code you input is subject to alteration by the site generation program's internal logic; they add and delete tags at will. Dreamweaver will not do this unless you direct the program to, and because of that, die-hard HTML programmers love it.

you can specify any other external editor and Dreamweaver will launch it automatically when you need to edit your HTML code.

Dreamweaver offers excellent link checking, including checking links outside your site to be sure that you do not inadvertently link to dead sites or pages. It supports CSS extensively and its site management tools allow you to manage more than one Web site, making it great for handling both your personal and your business needs. Users also report that the instruction manual is easy to understand and even easier to use.

The interface is not necessarily easy to understand. The icons are a little on the abstract side, but once you get going and get used to it, it rapidly becomes easy. The interface is also customizable, allowing you to put the buttons you use most where they are most convenient for you.

SoftQuad HoTMetaL Pro 5.0

Windows-based operating systems only
$129
www.SoftQuad.com

The newest version of SoftQuad's popular program is updated and streamlined to handle more complex functions. The entire program is more flexible than its predecessors and, above all, easier to use. It is not the best program available, but for the money it costs, HoTMetaL provides a quality product.

The manual is well written, which is a change from most software products, not just Web site generation software. It can be difficult to find what you want at times, but once you do, the instructions are bound to help you. HoTMetaL also provides video help tutorials built into the software.

HoTMetaL offers you many different options for viewing your pages as you create them. For the most part you will probably stay in WYSIWYG mode, but you can generate using pure code if you wish. HoTMetaL has the ability to let you preview your site in up to four different browsers. This is a great feature to make sure that what you see is what you actually get. Too often this is not the case.

HoTMetaL offers an excellent code checker that is easy to turn off, has a built-in library of graphics you can use, and supports both CSS and dynamic HTML. These complex functions are great for the more advanced user but can be difficult to understand for beginners. Because of this, we feel that HoTMetal is not a program for the first-time user but for someone who has had some experience with HTML and has generated a basic site.

Site organization and file transfer are also handled well with HoTMetal, and there is a reasonably complete search and replace feature. The link checker is very functional as well, checking for broken links within your site.

NetObjects Fusion 4.0

Windows-based operating systems only

$299

www.netobjects.com

Bundled with HomeSite

The newest version of NetObjects's Fusion package is a great resource for creating business-quality sites in a minimum of time. The program has a wide variety of built-in templates and themes that include a full array of buttons, text, GIFs, banners, bullets, and horizontal rules.

The code for the pages is not generated until you finish designing your site, so you cannot edit it as you go. That can be considered a drawback to advanced users and programmers, but for beginners who do not intend to change the code anyway it does not really matter. While you can add your own code to the page, you cannot change the code generated by the program. For programmers who know HTML, that presents a large problem. Unfortunately, Fusion writes code that is far from perfect. Even pre-existing code you import into the program is subjected to its at-will rewrites with some strange results.

Editing and fine tuning in the WYSIWYG views is relatively simple, allowing you to adjust everything from images to the page title without having to click through a half-dozen windows like some of the other programs we've mentioned. Some of the more labor intensive tasks (namely creation of navigation bars) are very simple with Fusion.

Fusion has full support for CSS and database connectivity, works with a wide variety of different plug-ins, and functions fairly well, though it can slow down at random times and has been known to

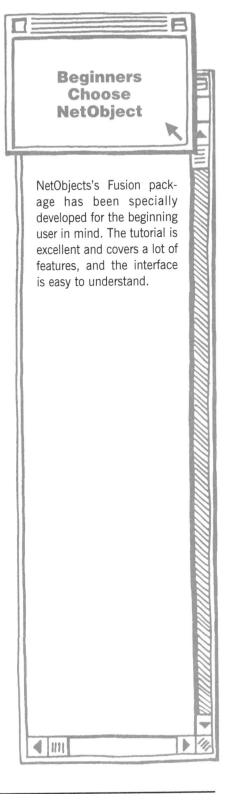

Beginners Choose NetObject

NetObjects's Fusion package has been specially developed for the beginning user in mind. The tutorial is excellent and covers a lot of features, and the interface is easy to understand.

crash unexpectedly. As with any program, it is wise to save your work often just in case.

These are just a few examples of the many Web site generation programs that are commercially available. If you decide to go this route and use a generation program, we advise that you read some additional reviews and do some comparison shopping. Prices are subject to change as newer programs come out, and versions are being upgraded almost monthly. Get a program that works well with your level of expertise. It is hardly wise to get a developing tool that requires some knowledge of HTML to produce good work if you have no interest in learning it. The most expensive is not always the best for you, so make sure you take some time to discover what program works best with your abilities, your desired outcome, and your budget. A little work now will save you a lot of money and frustration later.

Hypertext Markup Language (HTML)

So you have decided to try and build your very first Web site yourself. Maybe you only really want an online business card or you'd like to see how your site is received before you go spending a lot of money on in-depth Web development. Whatever your needs, in order to create your own Web site you need to learn a little HTML, or hypertext markup language. In this section we'll give you a few basic lessons on writing HTML code. For designing more advanced Web sites you may want to take a course in HTML programming or get a book that explains how to code your Web site in more detail. For now, we'll give you the basics to get you started.

When designing your Web page, remember that you can never guarantee with any kind of certainty that your document will look the same to your customers as it does to you. Don't waste your time rewriting and recoding your page so that it looks perfect or fits on your monitor. Other people's monitors vary, as do their settings, and one 14-inch monitor will render all that time completely useless.

Of course, you still want to write your documents so they look pleasing to most people. To do that, you need to think like most people. Most browsers are set by default to display text in a very common font, like Times or Times

New Roman, at a point size somewhere between 10 and 15 (usually 12). You are going to spend a considerable amount of time arranging and engineering your page, but you shouldn't waste your time worrying how your Web site will look to someone who has his display set in an untraditional font or at a strange size.

To compose your HTML document you can use any word processing program, but many of them have autoformatting options that if you don't know how to turn off can affect the document. Because of that we recommend using Notepad, Wordpad, or another text-based editor. Both Notepad and Wordpad can be found on all Microsoft operating systems later than 3.1. Look in your start menu under accessories.

Tags

HTML language is composed of tags. Tags are formatting codes used in HTML documents. They indicate how parts of a document will appear when displayed by browsing software like Netscape or Internet Explorer. HTML tags are always enclosed by angle brackets that look like this: < or >. Tags are not case sensitive. That means it doesn't matter whether you type the tags in uppercase or lowercase letters. Most programmers type their tags in all uppercase letters because that makes it easier to pick them out of the document. After all, something that looks like this: <TAG1> is easier to see in a long text document than something like this <tag1>.

HTML tags are usually found in begin-end pairs. The first tag indicates the start of a function. For most HTML tags, a second concluding tag echoes the first but begins with a slash (/). For example, all HTML documents must begin with a piece of code that marks the document as written in HTML. That code is a tag, and that tag looks like this <HTML>. The concluding tag, that is, the tag that indicates the end of the document, looks like this </HTML>. Using these tags in this way enables the Web browsers to know where the HTML in a document begins and ends. In another example of paired HTML tags, the tag <B> begins marking text in bold and </B> ends the bold text.

A nice way to think about HTML tags is as little containers. Any text or code that appears within tags has the rules of that tag

What Software Can't Do

Keep in mind that these software development programs are good all-around tools. Do not expect them to generate full out interactive e-commerce Web sites. For a good quality interactive site you will need to hire a developer.

Web Browsers Affect Your Site

There is one thing you should remember when coding your own Web site: Web browsers like Netscape and Microsoft's Internet Explorer were written by different people, and because of the differences in programming any given Web page will look different on different browsers. Sometimes, depending on how your customer has their preferences set, the Web page will look differently on two different versions of the same browser!

applied to it. For example, anything that appears between the <HTML> and </HTML> tags is written in HTML

Not every HTML tag appears in pairs. Some tags, such as those denoting line breaks, appear on their own. Tags like this are called empty tags. For the most part you'll be dealing in these begin-end tag pairs.

With all that said, it's time to learn what some of the tags are and what they mean.

As we said before, the first and last tags must always be <HTML> and </HTML>. HTML documents have two parts to them: the head and the body. Document tags are used to divide your Web page into these basic sections.

The body of the HTML document is the real meat of your Web page. All your text and graphics go in the body of an HTML document. The head of the document contains the document title, which appears both at the top of the browser's document bar and in the history file. It will also be the default name for the bookmark if your customer decides to mark the page.

<HEAD> and </HEAD> denote anything that goes in the header of your document. In this instance, all we are interested in is the title. <TITLE> and </TITLE> are the tags that indicate the document title. So if you are creating a document called The Bass Fisherman's Catalog, your HTML document header would look like this.

```
<HTML>
<HEAD><TITLE> The Bass Fisherman's Catalog
</TITLE><HEAD>
```

If you added the </HTML> tag:
```
<HTML>
<HEAD><TITLE> The Bass Fisherman's Catalog
</TITLE><HEAD>
</HTML>
```

When viewed on a browser, the Web page would have The Bass Fisherman's Catalog in the title bar and a completely blank page. It would be a complete document and programmed correctly, but it would be very boring. You are going to want to have something on your Web page and that information will be contained in the body, between tags <BODY> and </BODY>.

Headings

Headings (not to be confused with the HEAD of the document) are used to set apart sections of your document. Something like:

Bass Fishing Bait

is an example of a heading. The opening tag for a heading is <H?> and the closing tag is </H?> where the ? is the size of the heading. Headings can be in one of six sizes with 1 being the most important header (and therefore the largest) and 6 being the smallest header. The default settings for most browsers has the 6 heading as almost fine print, but remember people can change these settings to be whatever they want.

Headings are always assumed by HTML to exist on a line by themselves, and a line break is automatically inserted when you close the tag. So the line of code, <H1> An introduction to Bass Fishing </H1>, will look like this:

An introduction to Bass Fishing

The same code with a different size, <H2> An introduction to Bass Fishing </H2>, would look like this:

An introduction to Bass Fishing

Remember, because the heading tags automatically insert a line break, you cannot use them to highlight text in the middle of a sentence of paragraph. If you did, it would look like this:

Bass fishing is a very
Exciting
sport if you have the right equipment.

There are certain tags, called text effect tags, that will allow you to highlight text. We will explain text effect tags later in this chapter.

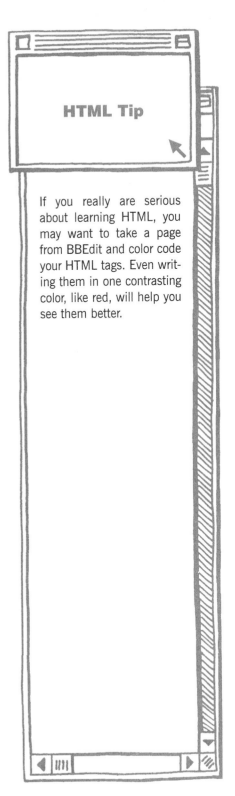

HTML Tip

If you really are serious about learning HTML, you may want to take a page from BBEdit and color code your HTML tags. Even writing them in one contrasting color, like red, will help you see them better.

Paragraphs and Line Breaks

As with any text document, paragraphs are important for maintaining clarity and ease of reading. Paragraphs are just as common in Web pages as they are in this book. The beginning of a paragraph is marked by <P> and the end by </P>. One neat thing about working in HTML is that how you type your text doesn't matter. If you type code like this:

```
<P> The most interesting thing about Bass
Fishing is the many places you can do it. You
can fish for bass in lakes, streams, and some-
times even in shallow creeks. </P>
```

Or like this:

```
<P> The most interesting thing about Bass
Fishing is the many places you can do it.
    You can fish for bass in lakes, streams, and
sometimes even in shallow creeks.</P>
```

You will still get a paragraph that looks like this:

The most interesting thing about Bass Fishing is the many places you can do it. You can fish for bass in lakes, streams, and sometimes even in shallow creeks.

No matter how much white space you put between words, how many spaces or carriage returns, HTML will always format the paragraph with one space between words. But what if you really want to end a line after a specific word but don't want to start a new paragraph? For this you would use a tag called a line break. Line breaks are one of those tags that don't come in pairs. There is no need to begin and end a line break because they are really one-time occurrences. To break a line you use the <BR> tag. So if you type code that looks like this:

```
<P>The most interesting thing about Bass
Fishing is the many places you can do it. <BR>
You can fish for bass in lakes, streams, and
sometimes even in shallow creeks.</P>
```

Your output would look like this:

The most interesting thing about Bass Fishing is the many places you can do it.
You can fish for bass in lakes, streams, and sometimes even in shallow creeks.

Preformatted Text

While most standard text doesn't depend on line breaks or special spacing, some things do. For example, poetry and song lyrics depend heavily on where you break the line and the placement of words. There is a way to include text like this on your Web site without using the <BR> tags. This is called using preformatted text. When using preformatted text it is important to keep two things in mind: preformatted text will appear on the screen in a typewriter-like font (this is really a monospaced, fixed-width font), and it will appear *exactly* as you typed it including carriage returns and spaces. You have to be careful to remember to hit your carriage returns, even if the text automatically wraps in your word processing program. If you don't, the words will continue on the same line indefinitely, forcing visitors to your site to scroll to the right until you ended the preformatted text or until they get tired and move on.

To insert preformatted text into your document you use the paired tags <PRE> and </PRE>. For example, if you typed this text using the standard HTML paragraph tags:

```
Mary had a
little lamb          whose fleece
was white as snow.
```

The code would look like this:

```
<P> Mary had a
little lamb                whose fleece
was white as snow. <P>
```

But the text would appear like this:

Mary had a little lamb whose fleece was white as snow.

In order to get the text to appear with the line spaces and breaks you want, you need to use the preformatted text tags. The new code would look like this:

```
<PRE> Mary had a
little lamb                whose fleece
was white as snow.</PRE>
```

And the text would appear like this:

```
Mary had a
little lamb        whose fleece
was white as snow.
```

HTML is not a difficult language to learn once you know all the tags. Sometimes it is helpful to keep a handy reference card or notebook nearby when coding your Web page so that you can refer back to it on some of the tags you don't use as often.

Now that you have a header and some body text, we'll put the whole page together. The Bass Fishing page we've constructed so far looks like this in HTML.

```
<HTML>
<HEAD><TITLE> The Bass Fisherman's Catalog
</TITLE></HEAD>
<BODY>
<H1>An Introduction to Bass Fishing</H1>
<P> The most interesting thing about Bass
Fishing is the many places you can do it. You
can fish for bass in lakes, streams, and some-
times even in shallow creeks.</P>
</BODY>
</HTML>
```

Don't forget to end the body with the body end tag </BODY> and to end the HTML document with </HTML>.

Horizontal Rules

Of course, a page like this would look rather dull and boring. The text is plain, and there is no graphic or background. Now it's time to add some design elements and text effects to your HTML document. The horizontal rule is a nice effect. It allows you to mark off sections of a document. A horizontal rule is a line drawn across the page like this:

You can make horizontal rules in HTML without having to draw the line manually using the <HR> tag. Like the <BR> tag for line breaks, the horizontal rule tag is empty. That means it does not have a closing pair. There are some interesting attributes to the <HR> tag. When making a horizontal rule, you can choose how long the line is (how much of the screen does it take up), how thick the line is, and whether you want the line shaded or just a box. You do this by changing the *width, size,* and using *noshade.*

Width for horizontal rules can be described by fixed pixel width—how many pixels you want the line to be—or by a simple percentage of the screen. Either way, the tag is formatted the same: <HR width=?> where ? is either a pixel number or a percent followed by the percent sign (%). This will determine how far across the screen the horizontal rule will travel. Unless you align the rule to the left or right, the width will be determined with the rule resting perfectly on center. We will get to aligning in a minute.

For the thickness, or size, of a rule, you use the term size in the tag. So if you wanted a rule that traveled the length of the screen and was a certain amount of pixels thick, your tag would read: <HR size=?> where ? is the number of pixels wide or the percentage of the screen. You can combine attributes within a rule to get it to look many different ways. For example:

```
<HR width=75% size=10>
```

will produce a horizontal rule that travels three-quarters of the way across the screen and is 10 pixels thick. If you wanted to make the line an unshaded box, you would add the term NOSHADE, making the code look like this:

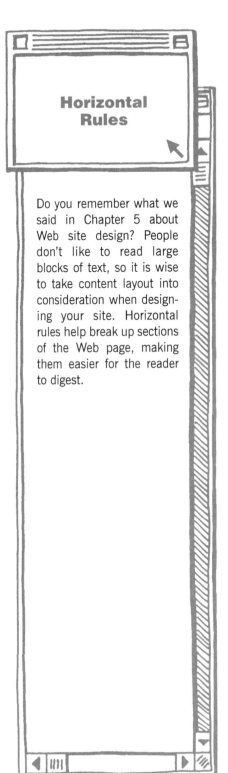

Horizontal Rules

Do you remember what we said in Chapter 5 about Web site design? People don't like to read large blocks of text, so it is wise to take content layout into consideration when designing your site. Horizontal rules help break up sections of the Web page, making them easier for the reader to digest.

```
<HR width=75% size=10 NOSHADE>
```

Horizontal rules help keep different sections of text apart and can block the top and bottom of your page. Try some out in varying thicknesses and lengths until you find one you like.

Lets add a horizontal rule into our HTML document about Bass Fishing to set off the section after we finish talking about where you can find bass.

```
<HTML>
<HEAD><TITLE> The Bass Fisherman's Catalog
</TITLE></HEAD>
<BODY>
<H1>An Introduction to Bass Fishing</H1>
<P> The most interesting thing about Bass
Fishing is the many places you can do it. You
can fish for bass in lakes, streams, and some-
times even in shallow creeks.</P>
<HR width=75% size=40>
</BODY>
</HTML>
```

The horizontal rule we added will be a solid line that takes up 75 percent of the screen. The rule will be 40 pixels thick and appear just underneath the paragraph about places to find Bass.

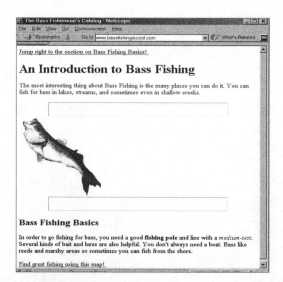

Text-Effect Tags

Earlier I mentioned text-effect tags that will allow you to emphasize text within a paragraph. Let's add a new header and new paragraph to our HTML document about Bass Fishing, and then we can highlight some of the text we want to emphasize.

```
<HTML>
<HEAD><TITLE> The Bass Fisherman's Catalog
</TITLE></HEAD>
<BODY>
<H1>An Introduction to Bass Fishing</H1>
<P> The most interesting thing about Bass
Fishing is the many places you can do it. You
can fish for bass in lakes, streams, and some-
times even in shallow creeks.</P>
<HR width=75% size=40>
<H2>Bass Fishing Basics</H2>
<P> In order to go fishing for bass, you
need a good fishing pole and line with a
medium-test. Several kinds of bait and lures
are also helpful. You don't always need a boat.
Bass like reeds and marshy areas so sometimes
you can fish from the shore.</P>
</BODY>
</HTML>
```

As you can see, we've now added a secondary heading, which because it is an <H2>, will be smaller than that of the main heading. We've also added a new paragraph about bass fishing equipment. Now you want to emphasize some of the equipment that your customers will need. You want your text to look like this on the screen.

In order to go fishing for bass, you need a good fishing pole and line with a *medium-test*. Several kinds of bait and lures are also helpful. <u>You don't always need a boat</u>. Bass like reeds and marshy areas so sometimes you can fish from the shore.

Text-Effect Tags

You should take care when using text-effect tags. Bold, underline, and italicized text should be used to emphasize text or to indicate links. Overuse of these effects can make your text difficult to read (this is especially true when people have reset their browser preferences).

Of course, this would look really strange on a page, but we're just using it as an example. You can bold, underline, and even italicize lines within a paragraph using these text-effect tags. Text-effect tags are paired, so be sure to use the closing half of the pair or the browser will make everything after the opening tag respond to the effect.

To make text bold use <B> and </B>. To italicize text use <I> and </I>. To underline text use <U> and </U>. So the HTML code for the paragraph about bass fishing equipment would look like this:

<P> In order to go fishing for bass, you need a good <B>fishing pole</B> and line with a <I>medium-test.</I> Several kinds of bait and lures are also helpful. <U>You don't always need a boat.</U> Bass like reeds and marshy areas so sometimes you can fish from the shore. </P>

Changing Font Attributes

Body text in HTML is automatically set to a certain height, but, like headings, individual users can change those settings to whatever they want. Most users don't, though, so you can expect your body text to appear uniform at somewhere between 10 and 15 points. You can increase or decrease the font size of your body copy by using the size attribute to a FONT tag. If you are typing default text, that is, text that will appear in black with the default font style and in a default size, you do not need to use a FONT tag. If any of these attributes change, you must put <FONT?> in front of your text, where ? is a font attribute such as size, color, or style.

The HTML tag for changing size is <FONT SIZE=?> where ? is either a + or - followed by the number you wish it to increase or decrease. For example <FONT SIZE=+4> will increase your font by 4 sizes. <FONT SIZE=-2>, will decrease your font by 2 sizes. Font size is a pair-dependent tag so you must make sure to end the tag with </FONT> when you are finished

You can continue to increase or decrease font size with every word, but it can only do so relative to the default size. This means that if you increase the font size in one word and then wish to increase the font size again in the next word, you cannot do this:

```
<FONT SIZE=+2>Bass is a good fish to
eat.<FONT SIZE=+2> You can fry it or broil
it.</FONT>
```

and expect the second sentence to be two points larger than the first sentence. If you wish to make the second sentence two sizes larger then the first, you must end the first increased font size, then increase it again by 4. It would need to look like this:

```
<FONT SIZE=+2> Bass is a good fish to eat.
</FONT><FONT SIZE=+4> You can fry it or broil
it. </FONT>
```

In addition to changing the font size, you can also change the font itself. The FACE attribute (short for typeface) tells the browser what font to use for a particular block of text. You can choose any font you like, but doing this is a common pitfall. Not all browsers have all fonts installed. There are some fonts that you can feel relatively safe in using. Arial, Verdana, Helvetica, and Impact are considered common fonts now. You can download fonts off the Internet or install them from graphics design programs and some print design packages. It isn't advisable to use any font that didn't come pre-installed with your computer to design your Web site. Even some pre-installed fonts are not universal, so when choosing the design scheme for your site, try to do so with as few fonts and as common fonts as possible.

Because not all browsers recognize all fonts, the FACE attribute allows you to list more than one possible font in descending order of preference. This gives you a better chance of finding a font that your customer or visitor's browser will recognize.

The FACE attribute works with the <FONT> tag. The tag would look like <FONT FACE="?"> where ? is the name of the font you wish to use. Remember, all <FONT> tags, regardless of attribute, must be paired with an end tag. When you want to change your font again or return to the default you must use </FONT>.

Logical Text-Effect Tags

There is another way to highlight text in an HTML document. This is called using logical tags. The tags <B>, <I>, and <U> are called formatting tags; they indicate the way text should be formatted. Logical tags do the same thing but in a format more appropriate to each browser. For tags like strong (<STRONG>) and emphasis (<EM>), the use of logical tags is often no different than formatting tags. There are formatting tags like <ADDRESS> that allow you to type in a mailing address and have it appear in the correct format without having to worry about line breaks. Like formatting tags, logical tags appear in begin-end pairs and must be ended with the slash version of the tag.

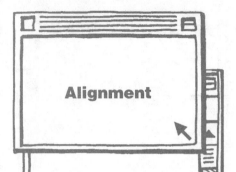

Alignment

Many tags, such as headings, paragraphs, and images (explained below), support align attributes. Align attributes allow you to line up text or images at the left margin of a page, in the center of a page, or at the right edge. To align text you would use either ALIGN=LEFT, ALIGN=RIGHT, or ALIGN=CENTER in your tag. For example, if you wanted to change the heading, "An Introduction to Bass Fishing," in the above example to align in the center of the page, the code would read like this: <H1 ALIGN=CENTER>An Introduction to Bass Fishing</H1>. The align attribute only needs to be in the first half of the tag pair.

In looking at our sample Web site, if you wanted to change the font style of our first sample paragraph to Arial, your code would look as follows:

```
<P><FONT FACE="ARIAL"> The most interesting
thing about Bass Fishing is the many places you
can do it. You can fish for bass in lakes,
streams, and sometimes even in shallow
creeks.</FONT></P>
```

If you wanted to specify alternate fonts for browsers that may not recognize Arial, you would add them to the code in descending order of preference separated by commas. The new code would look like this:

```
<P><FONT FACE="ARIAL, HELVETICA, VERDANA">
The most interesting thing about Bass Fishing
is the many places you can do it. You can fish
for bass in lakes, streams, and sometimes even
in shallow creeks.</FONT></P>
```

Images

Now you know how to construct a basic Web site and format your text. But you are missing one of the things that really defines the Web as a medium. You are missing graphics. Now it is time to add images to your page. It is important to mention here that although images are part of a Web document visually, in reality images and graphics are all separate files. If you have a Web page with text and four graphics, in order to have the page look right you need a total of five files: one for the page formatting and the text (that is, the HTML document) and four separate image files. All the necessary files are stored on a Web server, and each server administrator has a separate way of storing those images.

In order to add your .gif or .jpeg graphic to your page, you use the <IMG> tag. This tag is also an empty tag and requires no closing pair. However, just putting <IMG> into your document won't do anything. You need to let the browser know where to find the image.

For now, we'll assume that the images are being stored in a directory called pics on the server www.bassfishingiscool.com.

In order to make your <IMG> tag work, you need something called an SRC attribute. SRC stands for source, which tells your browser what the source of the image is or, in other words, where on the Web server to find the image. The whole tag looks something like this <IMG SRC="?"> where ? is the URL of the graphic. For our example, let's say you had a picture of a bass you wanted to put on your page. This picture is called basspic.gif. The image tag you would use would be <IMG SRC="www.bass-fishingiscool.com/pics/basspic.gif>.

When you place image tags in your HTML document, the browser puts the graphic precisely where the tag is located. If you put your tag in the middle of a sentence, then the graphic will go right in the middle of the sentence. In the example page we've been building, let's say you wanted your picture of the bass to go between the two sections of text, set off by horizontal rules. The new document would look like this:

```
<HTML>
<HEAD><TITLE> The Bass Fisherman's Catalog
</TITLE></HEAD>
<BODY>
<H1>An Introduction to Bass Fishing</H1>
<P> The most interesting thing about Bass Fishing
is the many places you can do it. You can fish for
bass in lakes, streams, and sometimes even in
shallow creeks.</P>
<HR width=75% size=40>
<IMG SRC="www.bassfishingiscool.com/pics/basspic.gif">
<HR width=75% size=40>
<H2>Bass Fishing Basics</H2>
<P> In order to go fishing for bass, you need a
good fishing pole and line with a medium-test.
Several kinds of bait and lures are also helpful.
You don't always need a boat. Bass like reeds and
marshy areas so sometimes you can fish from the
shore.</P>
</BODY>
</HTML>
```

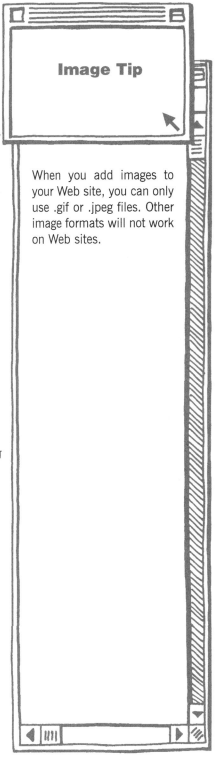

Image Tip

When you add images to your Web site, you can only use .gif or .jpeg files. Other image formats will not work on Web sites.

Placing Images

Remember, placing an image is just like placing text. If you don't otherwise specify where on the page an image goes, it will automatically go right where you typed its tag. You can place images with more specificity by using align attributes when placing your pictures. Using our Bass Fisherman's Catalog example, if you wanted to put the image in the center of the screen between two horizontal rules, you would change the tag to include ALIGN=CENTER. The new tag would read: <IMG SRC="www.bassfishingis-cool.com/pics/basspic.gif ALIGN=CENTER>.

Because line breaks are automatic when using a horizontal rule, you don't need to put a line break before or after the bass picture. If you were placing the picture within the text, though, unless you wanted to have it appear mid-sentence you would have to set the picture off with <BR> tags.

HTML is a very logical language, and if you take the time to think about how you are constructing both your tags and your page, you will have a simple site up and running in no time!

Do you remember when we said it is helpful to think of tags as little containers? Now that you know some of the basics of HTML and what tags do, you need to be careful of overlapping tags. The overlapping of tags occurs when tag A begins followed by the beginning of tag B, then tag A closes and tag B closes. The proper way to open and close tags are to begin tag A, begin tag B, close tag B, then close tag A so that that B is completely contained by the attributes of tag A. In other words, container B is entirely enclosed within the larger container A.

Let's say you wanted to have a sentence that is bold and one font size bigger. This is an example of the wrong way to order your tags.

```
<FONT SIZE=+1><B>Bass tastes
good.</FONT></B>
```

You need to close the bold container before you close the font size container. The right way to order your tags so they don't overlap is:

```
<FONT SIZE=+1><B>Bass tastes
good.</B></FONT>
```

As you can see from this example, the bold tag container is closed and neatly contained by the font size tag.

Adding Color

Now that you know how to add your images and set up your text, it's time to add color to the page. Background and text colors are important to make your site exciting and engaging. As with any other design issue, you have to give serious thought to what kind of computer other users have when deciding on your color scheme. While you may have a video card that allows for millions of colors, there are a lot of folks out there still using the VGA palette of 16 colors or the SVGA palette of 256 colors. While you may pick the perfect aqua blue for your background, older computers may not be able to register that color and the results would be very unpredictable. So give some thought to your color scheme.

When the time comes to add color to your background or text, you need to use something called the hexidecimal color code. The hexidecimal color code is a six-digit number that specifies the amount of red, green, and blue needed to create a certain color. This is called RGB coloring. If you've ever gotten really close to your TV and looked at the dots that make up the image, you can see that they are either red, green, or blue. The amount of each color in a particular area determines the overall look of that area. Color works the same way on a computer monitor. Different values of red, green, and blue make up different colors. The hexidecimal code assigns two digits for red, two for green, and two for blue, in that order. Each digit is a value from 0 to F in the hexadecimal system. The hexadecimal color system uses 0 1 2 3 4 5 6 7 8 9 A B C D E F, with 0 being a null value and F being the highest value. So if the first two digits representing the red values are full (FF) and all the others are null, the hexidecimal code tells the computer to paint the area (the background or text) with full red and nothing else. The hexidecimal code would look like this:

```
#FF0000
```

In order to change the color of text you need to use the FONT tag with a COLOR attribute. Therefore, the tag for changing the color of text is <FONT COLOR="?"> where ? is the hexidecimal code for the color you want. Font color tags are paired, so in order to return to plain black text or to change to another color you must close the first tag.

Let's look at our sample Web page one more time:

```
<HTML>
<HEAD><TITLE> The Bass Fisherman's Catalog
</TITLE></HEAD>
<BODY>
<H1>An Introduction to Bass Fishing</H1>
<P> The most interesting thing about Bass
Fishing is the many places you can do it. You can
fish for bass in lakes, streams, and sometimes
even in shallow creeks.</P>
<HR width=75% size=40>
<IMG SRC="www.bassfishingiscool.com/pics/basspic.gif">
<HR width=75% size=40>
<H2>Bass Fishing Basics</H2>
<P> In order to go fishing for bass, you need
a good fishing pole and line with a medium-test.
Several kinds of bait and lures are also helpful.
You don't always need a boat. Bass like reeds and
marshy areas so sometimes you can fish from the
shore.</P>
</BODY>
</HTML>
```

Let's change the color of the text in the first paragraph to blue. To do that you would add <FONT COLOR="0000FF"> after the first paragraph tag (<P>) and </FONT COLOR="0000FF"> before the tag that completes the pair (</P>). The new page would look like this:

```
<HTML>
<HEAD><TITLE> The Bass Fisherman's Catalog
</TITLE></HEAD>
<BODY>
<H1>An Introduction to Bass Fishing</H1>
<P> <FONT COLOR="0000FF">The most interesting
thing about Bass Fishing is the many places you
can do it. You can fish for bass in lakes, streams,
and sometimes even in shallow creeks.</FONT
COLOR="0000FF"></P>
<HR width=75% size=40>
<IMG SRC="www.bassfishingiscool.com/pics/basspic.gif">
<HR width=75% size=40>
<H2>Bass Fishing Basics</H2>
<P> In order to go fishing for bass, you need a
good fishing pole and line with a medium-test.
Several kinds of bait and lures are also helpful.
You don't always need a boat. Bass like reeds and
marshy areas so sometimes you can fish from the
shore.</P>
</BODY>
</HTML>
```

The hexidecimal color system allows you to apply plain color backgrounds to your Web page using the background color tag. The background color tag is an empty tag, having no pair to complete it, and it works in conjunction with the <BODY> tag we talked about earlier. The <BODY> tag tells the browser what part of the HTML document to display as the page. In order to format that with a background color, you need to ad BGCOLOR="?" to the <BODY> tag, where ? is the hexidecimal color code you want to use. Say you'd like your bass fishing page to have a pale blue background. You would change the <BODY> tag to read:

```
<BODY BGCOLOR="00FFF">
```

Hexidecimal Color Code

It is often helpful to think of the hexidecimal code as a painter's palette where you mix different amounts of red, green, and blue to get the color you want. What happens when you mix red and blue? You get purple. So the hexidecimal code for a rich purple would be #FF00FF. This mixes equal parts of red and blue. There are 16.7 million different colors in the hexidecimal color system: #000000 is white (the absence of color) and #FFFFFF is black (the total saturation of color). Black is the default color for HTML text. You don't need to specify it. You only need to specify color when you are changing from black.

Sometimes you don't want to use plain color as your background. There are a wealth of nice background images you can get right off the Web. Even some clip art packages like the MasterClips series contain images suitable to use as backgrounds in your Web site. To set an image as your background you need to combine what you learned about placing an image with what you learned about setting background color. Remember, you can only have one <BODY> tag, so of course your selection will have to go there. As with an image, you need the URL where the picture is stored on the Web server, but you place it like you would background color by using the BODY BACKGROUND tag. The BODY BACKGROUND tag works the same as the BG COLOR. For example, if you wanted that bass picture (basspic.gif) we talked about earlier to be your background for this page, your body tag would read:

```
<BODY BACKGROUND="www.bassfishingiscool.com/
pics/basspic.gif">
```

This tag sets your background image as the bass picture titled basspic.gif.

Linking Everything Together

Now that you've built the first few pages of your Web site, it's time to link them all together. The linking system is what makes the World Wide Web a web. The system of links that connect one page to another and one Web site to another is the true hallmark of the Internet. One of the special things about links is the ability to enhance documents by providing more information, starting a movie, or playing a sound. Let's say you had a great article on types of bait that you wanted to make available to your customers. By placing a link on the word *bait* within your block of text, your customers could click right on that link and take them to the article about bait. Customers who weren't interested in learning about bait would just read on.

When constructing a link (links are sometimes called hyperlinks) the first thing you need is the URL of the page you are linking to. This can be another page on your Web site or the URL

Finding
Backgrounds

There are hundreds of sites on the Internet where you can find backgrounds for your Web site. A search on any search engine will produce at least a half dozen places to start, and many of those sites have links to other sites with background images you can save and use. When you see a background image you like, just right click on it with your mouse and use the "save picture as" command. Make sure you remember where you saved the picture and what name you used. It can be hard searching your entire hard drive for that elusive background.

Make sure the background you are saving comes from a site that offers it for free. While you can still use the "save picture as" command for other backgrounds, that is considered a violation of copyrights. Saving backgrounds that are being offered for sale or saving a picture from another Web site and using it as your background is unethical and, in some areas, illegal. You don't want someone stealing your logo or corporate image and using it as a background or other graphic on their Web site. Don't do it to them either.

To protect yourself from people who snatch graphics off Web sites, you may want to include a copyright notice at the bottom of every Web page on your site. It can be as simple as the copyright symbol and the year you put your site up or as complex as your industry warrants. This won't protect you from people who snatch graphics, but if you see your logo or images on someone else's Web site, in some jurisdictions it will give you some recourse.

Remember, the World Wide Web is so vast that the graphics snatcher may be doing business in another state and another country. If you are really worried about proprietary information or images being pulled off your Web site, consult an attorney who specializes in copyrights and intellectual property.

of a different site. It can even be the URL of a specific page within another site. (If the article you found was in an online magazine you would want to link to the page with the article, not the home page of the site.)

Once you know the URL, you need to decide which word or words on your page will act as the link. These words act as a kind of "hot spot" where people can click to travel to the specific article or to another Web site.

By using this code, the words "Go visit USA Today for the latest area weather" would be underlined and colored the default link color, indicating them as a hot spot. By clicking on them the user would be taken to the *USA Today* Web site at www.usatoday.com

Let's try it within our document. We wanted to link to that interesting article about bait we found at www.baitfishermans.org. So the new code for the second paragraph in our document would be:

<P> In order to go fishing for bass, you need a good fishing pole and line with a medium test. Several kinds of <A HREF/=/"www.baitfishermans.org">bait </A> and lures are also helpful. You don't always need a boat. Bass like reeds and marshy areas so sometimes you can fish from the shore.</P>

Now the word *bait* would appear in a different color and be underlined. Anyone clicking on the hot spot word would be taken to the www.baitfishermans.org Web site where they could read all about different kinds of bait. To go back to your site, they just have to click the BACK button on the browser.

A link doesn't only have to take you to a document or a new Web site. By using the anchor tags you could link to graphics, sounds, movies, or any other kind of file stored on a Web server. Linking like this becomes particularly useful when you have large graphics you don't want to display on a page (because they would slow the download time) but you still want your customers to have access to the information. A good example of this would be a map to your store. A map graphic would make a pretty large file, but having a map so your customers can find your business is a good idea. By linking to that map, only customers who needed it would follow the link and you wouldn't slow down the download and operation of your site for everyone.

Linking to a graphic is done the same way as linking to a site. Remember earlier when we included an image in our Web page? That image was stored on the Web server in the same way your map will be. For our example we'll say that a map to some great fishing holes is called map.gif and is stored in the same pics folder the bass picture was.

To create a link to the map, you would use the anchor tags like this:

```
<A HREF="http://www.bassfishingiscool.com/pics/map.gif">
Find great fishing using this map! </A>
```

When your customers clicked on the hot text, "Find great using this map!" the map titled map.gif would open in the browser window so your visitors could see it. Clicking BACK on the browser would take them right back to the page with the link.

Let's add this link to our document!

```
<HTML>
<HEAD><TITLE> The Bass Fisherman's Catalog
</TITLE></HEAD>
<BODY>
<H1>An Introduction to Bass Fishing</H1>
<P> <FONT COLOR="0000FF">The most interesting
thing about Bass Fishing is the many places you can
do it. You can fish for bass in lakes, streams, and
sometimes even in shallow creeks.</FONT
COLOR="0000FF"></P>
<HR width=75% size=40>
<IMG SRC="www.bassfishingiscool.com/pics/basspic.gif">
<HR width=75% size=40>
<H2>Bass Fishing Basics</H2>
```

How to Find a Link

Links are generally underlined and appear on the browser as a different color than the rest of the text. The default color for links on most Web browsers is blue, but as with many other aspects of site viewing, this, too, can be changed.

To create a link you use anchor tags. The anchor tags are another example of a begin-end pair. The anchor tags are <A HREF="?"> and </A> where ? is the URL you wish to link to. HREF stands for Hypertext Reference, which tells the browser what file it is referencing and where it can be found (the URL).

Anything you type between the anchors becomes the "hot spot" text. For example, if you were going to link your page to the home page of the *USA Today* newspaper, the link would look like this:

<A HREF="www.usatoday.com">

```
<P> In order to go fishing for bass, you need a
good <B>fishing pole</B> and line with a <I>medium-
test.</I> Several kinds of bait and lures are also
helpful. You don't always need a boat. Bass like
reeds and marshy areas so sometimes you can fish
from the shore.</P>
    <A HREF="http://www.bassfishingiscool.com/pics/map.gif">
Find great fishing using this map! </A>
    </BODY>
    </HTML>
```

As we add each line of code, you can see how the document starts to take shape. Go back and look at the HTML document now. Can you understand what each line of code does?

Images and graphics are often used on Web pages as links. An example of this is the banner advertisement. Banner ads are images, sometimes animated, that when clicked on take you to a new Web site. Image links are more visually pleasing than just a plain text link. For example, if you take the link to the map we used a moment ago, rather than use text to point out the link you could use a picture of a compass. Or for your bait article, rather than insert the link into the text, you could have a link at the end with a graphic of some bait that would take the visitor directly to the bait article.

To use images as links you need to combine what you've learned about the construction of a link and the placement of an image. You still need to start by determining the URL you are linking to and the image you want to use. For our example, let's say you wanted to link to the *USA Today* Web site with a picture of a newspaper. We'll call the newspaper graphic news.gif and store it in the same place we've been storing all our images (this keeps Web server administrators happy). So the image source is www.bassfishingiscool.com/pics/news.gif, and the URL we are linking to is www.usatoday.com. Now let's construct the code. <A HREF="?"> </A> where ? is the URL for the link. You remember from constructing links that the text you want as a hot spot goes between the begin-end pair. In this case, there is no text, just an image, so you would place your image tag here. < IMG SRC="X">

Where X is the URL of the image that will be placed. The entire code looks like this:

```
<A HREF="?"><IMG SRC="X"></A>
```

In our example, the completed code would look like this:

```
<A HREF="http://www.usatoday.com"><IMG
SRC="http://www.bassfishingiscool.com/pics/news.gi
f"> </A>
```

Since there is no text associated with this link, just the image, you close the pair right after telling the browser where to find the linked image.

Mailto

There is another kind of link called a mailto. Mailto links don't take you to a new Web site, but they open a message in your default e-mail browser so you can send mail to the Webmaster or anyone specified by the mailto link. Often this kind of link is used to solicit feedback for a site or allow the visitor to ask questions or get help.

When constructing a mailto link you also use the anchor tags. You also use the HREF="?" part of the tag, only with one minor change. You need to specify that you are not linking to a URL but to an e-mail address. You do this by including the mailto: qualifier before the address. For our example, let's say that the Webmaster for this Bass Fishing Web site is fisherman@bassfishingiscool.com. In order for you to create a mailto link for that address, you place that e-mail address between the double quotes in the anchor. It should look like this:

```
<A HREF="mailto:fisherman@bassfishingiscool.com">
Send questions, comments, or feedback to the
Webmaster! </A>
```

Now when a visitor clicks on the hot text, "Send questions, comments, or feedback to the Webmaster!", it opens up a new message in

his or her default e-mail program. This automatically puts fisherman@bassfishingiscool.com in the To: line. All the visitor has to do is type a message and hit send. As with links, the words appearing between the anchors can be anything from "Send me mail!" to "I love to get mail, send me more!" The actual text doesn't matter, all it does is act as a hot spot for people to click.

Navigating Within a Document: The Name Attribute

There is one other type of anchor that is of particular interest. Adding the NAME attribute to an anchor tag allows you to jump directly to a spot on a page. This is a great feature for finding specific things of interest in a long document. Rather than waiting for the entire page to load and then scrolling around to find what interests a particular visitor, a surfer can hit a single link that will take him to the chapter, subheading, or area he is interested in. NAME attributes add speed and convenience to your Web site, which helps make yours stand out to your customers among a crowd of competitors.

Named anchors are very similar to regular links in their construction. There are two parts to a named anchor, not just a begin-end pair. You must create the link and then tell the browser where the other end of the link is.

This is how the first part of a named anchor looks: <A HREF="#?"> where ? is any text you care to use that appears later in the document. The pound sign (#) in the anchor lets the browser know that it isn't looking for a completely different URL (since the tags look very similar) but that it is looking for a name within the document. When using named anchors, a logical choice for the text would be a chapter number or section name.

In our Bass Fishing example, the header Bass Fishing Basics would be good to link to. This way customers can automatically jump down from the top of the document to the Bass Fishing Basics section instead of scrolling to it. (Of course, our sample document is too small for this to really be effective, but if you were writing an entire book on bass fishing, name anchoring each chapter heading would make finding specific information much easier.)

So the code for a named anchor to the Bass Fishing Basics section would look like this:

```
<A HREF="#Bass Fishing Basics"> Jump right
to the section on Bass Fishing Basics! </A>
```

But how does the browser know where to jump to? You could have used the words "Bass Fishing Basics" dozens of times in a particular document. In order to make sure that visitors clicking on your hot text will actually reach the section they want, you have to mark that section with another anchor tag. This tag looks like this: <A NAME="?"> where the ? is the same text you used in the first anchor tag. It is important that the text in the first tag and the second tag are identical. For our example, the first half of the named anchor would be:

```
<A HREF="#Bass Fishing Basics"> Jump right
to the section on Bass Fishing Basics! </A>
```

And the second half would be:

```
<A NAME="Bass Fishing Basics"></A>
```

Here is how these two lines of code fit into our document. (Because our example page is getting a bit long, we have made the inserted code bold so you can find it.)

```
<HTML>
<HEAD><TITLE> The Bass Fisherman's Catalog
</TITLE></HEAD>
<BODY>
<A HREF="#Bass Fishing Basics"> Jump right
to the section on Bass Fishing Basics! </A>
<H1>An Introduction to Bass Fishing</H1>
```

More Aligning

As with any other tag containing images, you can also use the ALIGN tags to move the linked image to the right or left margin or have it centered on the page. To align the image in the *USA Today* example on the right, you would add ALIGN= RIGHT to the image source part of the tag. The new code would look like this: <A HREF="http://www. usatoday.com"><IMG SRC= "http://www.bassfishingiscool .com/pics/news.gif" ALIGN=RIGHT></A>

```
<P> <FONT COLOR="0000FF">The most interesting
thing about Bass Fishing is the many places you
can do it. You can fish for bass in lakes,
streams, and sometimes even in shallow
creeks.</FONT COLOR="0000FF"></P>
   <HR width=75% size=40>
   <IMG SRC="www.bassfishingiscool.com/pics/basspic.gif">
   <HR width=75% size=40>
   <A NAME="Bass Fishing Basics"></A><H2>Bass
Fishing Basics</H2>
   <P> In order to go fishing for bass, you need a
good <B>fishing pole </B>and line with a
<I>medium-test.</I> Several kinds of bait and
lures are also helpful. You don't always need a
boat. Bass like reeds and marshy areas so some-
times you can fish from the shore.</P>
   <A HREF="http://www.bassfishingiscool.com/pics/map.gif">
Find great fishing using this map! </A>
   </BODY>
   </HTML>
```

Now a visitor to the site could click on the hot text "Jump right to the section on Bass Fishing Basics!" and skip your introduction to bass fishing. The browser would automatically jump down to section two where we marked the other half of the named anchor.

Advanced HTML

The information covered thus far will help you create a basic Web site, such as an online business card. If you want to create an online brochure or a more in-depth method of selling your products online, you will need to know a few other intricacies of HTML

Lists

There are three types of lists you can create in HTML. They are unordered, ordered, and definition lists. The most basic type of list is the unordered.

Unordered lists are characterized by items in a plain list format. Bulleted lists are a common way of referring to unordered lists, and a bulleted list is precisely what the unordered list tags create. The most common bullet is a small black circle, but all browsers view the bullets differently and the settings can be changed by the user.

To begin an unordered list you use the <UL> tag. This tag requires an end tag that looks like this </UL>. The items that go in your list must be marked as list items, and to do that you use the <LI> tag. So, a basic unordered list of bass fishing equipment would look like this:

```
<UL>
<LI> Fishing Pole
<LI> Good Quality Line
<LI> Bait
<LI> Lures
<LI> Hooks
</UL>
```

And on your Web page, the list would appear like this:

- Fishing Pole
- Good Quality Line
- Bait
- Lures
- Hooks

Only list items can go inside an unordered list. If you wanted to make a heading to this list, it would have to appear before the <UL> tag. Almost anything can go inside a list item, from images to links to another sub list. As long as you precede the entire line with a <LI> tag, you can format the information as you would anything else.

Sub lists (sometimes called nested lists) are useful to give information about a list item. For example, to give some information on types of bait, you would use a sub list. That sub list would be constructed using the same list format:

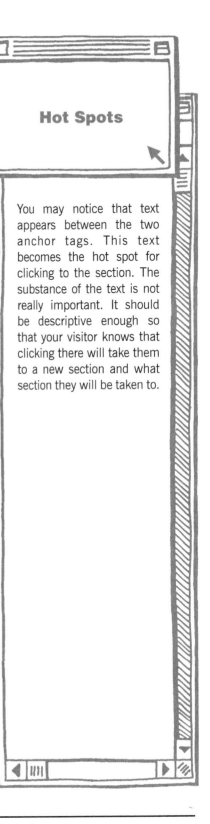

Hot Spots

You may notice that text appears between the two anchor tags. This text becomes the hot spot for clicking to the section. The substance of the text is not really important. It should be descriptive enough so that your visitor knows that clicking there will take them to a new section and what section they will be taken to.

```
<UL>
<LI> Fishing Pole
<LI> Good Quality Line
<LI> Bait
<UL>
<LI> Worms
<LI> Sardines
<LI> Hand-Tied Flies
<LI> Lures
<LI> Hooks
</UL>
```

Remember what we said about logical construction of your tags? When dealing with nested lists, it is especially important to make sure that your begin-end pairs are all contained within each other. The above nested list would appear in a browser like this:

- *Fishing Pole*
- *Good Quality Line*
- *Bait*
    - *Worms*
    - *Sardines*
    - *Hand-Tied Flies*
    - *Lures*
    - *Hooks*

Some browsers will put a different bullet in front of a nested list. In theory, you can use as many nested lists as you want on your Web site. However, nested lists can be difficult to look at, so be careful how often you use them. They should be saved for when they are absolutely necessary.

Ordered lists are different from unordered lists in only one respect. Instead of putting a bullet in front of the list, the browser will automatically generate a number sequence in front of the list items. As with unordered lists, only list items may appear within the <OL> and </OL> tags, but once items are formatted as such they can contain any HTML element. List items are marked the same way in ordered lists as in unordered lists. So the same list created as an ordered list instead of an unordered one would look like this:

```
<OL>
<LI> Fishing Pole
<LI> Good Quality Line
<LI> Bait
<LI> Lures
<LI> Hooks
</OL>
```

The third kind of list, a definition list, is rarely used in creating personal Web pages but may be of some use in creating commercial pages. A definition list creates an unordered list with items and their definitions. As with all lists, it is contained within a begin-end pair, in this case <DL> and </DL>. But unlike the other two kinds of lists, definition list items come in two kinds: the definition list term and its definition. <DT> stands for the definition list term, and <DD> for the definition list definition. When used correctly in a definition list, the browser arranges the elements so that each item is associated with its corresponding definition. While the exact way the different elements are displayed will vary from browser to browser, the most common way is to put the definition on a separate line indented slightly.

Here is the markup for our list, with definitions:

```
<DL>
<DT> Fishing Pole
<DD> The basic method of catching fish. A
fishing pole consists of a rod and a reel.</DD>
    <DT> Good Quality Line</DT>
    <DD> Line comes in many kinds of weights, or
tests. The heavier a test, the larger the fish
you can catch. Bass are not heavy, so a good
medium-test will be fine.</DD>
    <DT> Bait</DT>
```

```
<DD> Bait can be anything that will entice a
bass to strike your hook. Sardines and worms
are popular, as are hand-tied flies.</DD>
    <DT> Hooks</DT>
    <DD> Hooks come in many shapes and sizes,
with many barbs. A standard hook with two barbs
is sufficient for bass fishing. </DD>
    </DL>
```

In a browser window, the list will often look like this:

Fishing Pole

The basic method of catching fish. A fishing pole consists of a rod and a reel.

Good Quality Line

Line comes in many kinds of weights, or tests. The heavier a test, the larger the fish you can catch. Bass are not heavy, so a good medium-test will be fine.

Bait

Bait can be anything that will entice a bass to strike your hook. Sardines and worms are popular, as are hand-tied flies.

Hooks

Hooks come in many shapes and sizes, with many barbs. A standard hook with two barbs is sufficient for bass fishing.

For commercial purposes you may want to use definition lists to describe some of your product lines or even some of the benefits of individual products.

An HTML Glossary

anchor \<A>. The anchor tag defines a section of text as either a hyperlink (using HREF) or as the target of another hyperlink (using NAME). The anchor tag is used to link to other pages or to other sections within the same page.

body \<BODY>. The body tag is used to define the main portion of an HTML document. All material between the BODY tags is shown in the browser display window.

boldface \<B>. Text between the boldface begin-end pair will appear in bold.

comment \<!— *comment* —>. Any text written between the comment begin-end pair will not be displayed in the browser display window. This is useful for marking sections and areas for future improvement or increased scalability.

definition list \<DL>. Defines a list of term-definition pairs; typically used to create glossaries. There are two components of a definition list: definition list definition and definition list term.

definition list definition \<DD>. Defines the definition in a term-definition pair of a definition list.

definition list term \<DT>. Defines the term in a term-definition pair of a definition list.

header \<HEAD>. Header tags define the header information for a document, such as the TITLE (required) and any other header elements.

headings \<H1>—\<H6>. All text appearing between heading begin-end pairs will be separated from other text and will appear in a different style and at a larger size so as to make its special status obvious. Section titles and even document names are the usual uses for headings.

horizontal rule \<HR>. Creates a line that runs the width of the browser window. There are ways to modify the length, height, and appearance of a horizontal rule.

HTML \<HTML>. Defines an HTML document. The HTML begin-end pair marks for the browser what part of the document is written in HTML.

image \<IMG>. Causes an image to be placed in the HTML document at the point where the tag occurs. The graphic file's location is specified using the SRC attribute. Other commonly used attributes are ALIGN and ALT.

italics \<I>. Causes text to be italicized.

**line break \
.** Forces the current line of text to end at the point where the tag occurs and any subsequent text or HTML elements to be displayed beginning at the beginning of the next line on screen.

list item \<LI>. An element of either an ordered or unordered list. Use of the closing tag (\</LI>) is optional.

ordered list \<OL>. Defines a list of items that are automatically ordered; typically, this is a sequential numbering from one to the number of list items.

paragraph \<P>. Defines a section of text as being a paragraph. The closing tag (\</P>) is technically optional, but its use is strongly recommended.

title \<TITLE>. Defines the title of the document, which will appear in the history list and any bookmarks that are set.

typewriter text \<TT>. Causes text to be displayed in the browser's defined monospace font.

underline \<U>. Causes text to be underlined; not supported by all browsers.

unordered list \<UL>. Defines a list of items that are automatically marked with a bullet, typically a solid disc or asterisk.

PART THREE

MAKING MONEY FROM YOUR SITE

Add items to Cart

★★★ Ratings & Reviews

Compare Prices

Find Products

Buy Now!

Address http://chapter_ten.com

Link

Marketing Your Site

Marketing Overview

What exactly is marketing and why do you need it? You may say to yourself, "Are not people surfing the Web all the time? Will not they come across my site?" Once the Web site is built and the devices for ordering, purchasing or contacting are constructed, you need customers. Marketing is the mechanism for encouraging people to visit your site. Expecting that brave and hardy souls will find their way to your site by meticulously searching the Web and discovering your address is expecting too much. It's like offering a new item in a grocery store without advertising—you may see it, you may not—but if it is advertised and promoted, you may even come into the grocery store looking for it!

Marketing in the physical marketplace is directly related to marketing on the Internet—the same strategies and tactics work. This includes identifying the target audience and their needs, creating a meaningful and unique message, and notifying customers via advertising. If you are disciplined about developing your marketing strategy, you are well on your way to developing effective advertising that will drive qualified users to seek your business. However, before you can develop an effective marketing strategy, you must look at your marketing objectives first.

Marketing Objectives

There are many kinds of marketing objectives—building awareness of your company or product, gaining first-time buyers, increasing buyers' use-up rate or frequency of purchase, and capturing a share of the competitors' business. Some companies look at expanding a category of goods or services. One example is the category of starchy side dishes (such as rice, pasta, potatoes). By adding a completely new entry to the market, such as polenta or tabuleh, a company can expand its sales. Your company could approach your category of goods or services this way, too. Sometimes service organizations achieve this by *bundling services*. Bundling services is a way of achieving a point of difference by offering a new type of service along with an old one, for example, a travel agency booking combined with educational materials about the destination.

Advertise Your Site Everywhere

Spending money to advertise on the Web has become big business. Net advertising was over $4 billion in 1999. However, you should also advertise your Web site on traditional media venues. This can help build awareness, brand or company recognition, and credibility. Repeated exposures to a message—using a variety of media—helps persuade users and potential users to hire you. Some advertising agencies claim that unless an advertising message is seen three or more times the audience does not remember it at all.

Whatever your product or service, you will probably want to entice new users to try your product (first time purchase), and you will want to retain your current users (not let them go to the competition).

Trial Marketing

Traditional methods of attracting first-time customers work the same way on the Web as they do in the physical marketplace. These methods include incentives such as an offer of free services, a membership program that provides valuable information or discounts, or using a loss leader product. A loss leader product is an item that is valuable (or frequently used) by consumers, which is offered at an extreme discount in order to build traffic and incentivize the purchase of other, more profitable items. The loss leader product *is* the promotion. Examples of loss leaders in the grocery store include toilet paper and paper towels. While the shopper is in the store (or at your site), the customer buys other products, too. Have you ever had the experience of going to the store for one thing and buying another? This can be your strategy too.

Repeat Marketing

Establishing repeat business, ongoing business from old customers, is often the key to a successful, long-term business. Keeping current users happy is the primary goal of many profitable businesses, and they will go to great lengths to keep a customer happy. The reason for this is simple. That customer represents not only the current sale but years of future sales and potentially new customers.

How do you keep customers happy? Service is key for repeat. Put yourself in your customers' shoes. What are the real reasons a customer would come back? Sometimes a product is cheaper or delivered faster than another company. Sometimes a firm offers a unique product, which is unobtainable elsewhere. But these reasons are why customers are at your doorstep. They are not the keys to a *truly loyal* user. Service is the real reason for loyal customers. Truly loyal customers are valuable, certainly because of their business, but also because they are willing to endure the growing pains

Red Herrings

Sometimes companies will play a game with their potential customers where they scare or intimidate them into investigating the product. An example of this approach is when you get a piece of junk mail and it looks like a bill. You open it up only to discover that it's really an advertisement. Likewise, Internet companies send red herring e-mails to potential customers. On the Web, some ads are designed to look like a Windows warning message in order to provoke the potential customer into opening the message. Others take a humorous play on Windows warning message. In any event, this strategy to get new users is ill-advised. Many people will be so annoyed that they will be certain to never use your product!

Share Your Greatness

Never, ever be afraid to tell your customers why you are better, but try to avoid shameless self-promotion. There is a fine line between touting the success of your business and what is viewed by customers as a cyber-ego trip! Give examples of the added value customers get by doing business with you. Use testimonials. Do anything you can in a substantive way to let your potential customers know why you are the best in your industry.

of your company. They also can act as brand advocates in their communities.

Finally, tell your customers over and over why their choice—your company—is better than any other.

Developing Your Marketing Strategy: A Step By Step Plan for Effective Advertising

There are definite steps that all advertising people take to ensure a successful marketing and advertising campaign. Whether they be an in-house marketing department, a full-service ad agency, or even the neighborhood small business owner who builds his own campaign, they follow the same four steps:

1. Defining the Audience
2. Developing Creative
3. Media Planning
4. Measuring Success

Defining the Audience

Defining the target audience for your product is probably the single most useful marketing exercise you will do. It is absolutely critical that you decide who will be the market for your goods or services. Even if the audience is broad, even if there are diverse groups potentially interested in your product, it is crucial to sketch them out.

You already defined your target audience when you were planning your Web site. You decided who your product would best suit, and you looked carefully at how you do business with them in Chapter 3. Now it is time to look at those customers and determine what message will reach them and imprint on their memory your business and your business Web site.

Defining your audience is important because if you know whom you wish to reach with your advertising messages, you will be in a position to evaluate both your message and your media options against a *criteria*. Having a criteria is an important tool to cut through a maze of creative and media options. Really, all of the strategies (marketing, creative, and media strategies) function as criteria. These outlines become working documents. These should not be put away in a drawer after the exercise is over. Rather, they can become the bible for achieving viable advertising, and a viable business. These strategic criteria can also act as consensus builders within an organization, even if it is a small one. The agreed-to target audience can be signed off by the principals in the company so that when opportunities arise to advertise or promote the company, the guide acts as arbiter.

There are at least four dimensions along which to define your audience. These dimensions will provide the parameters for your target audience. They are demographics, psychographics, category usage behavior, and shopping behavior.

Demographics

Demographics are the external attributes of your target audience. They include tangible facts about people such as level of education, level of income, geographical location, age, marital status, presence of children in household, homeowner/apartment-dweller, ethnicity and gender. Some marketers look at the total picture of a demographic target and describe the group by lifestage or lifestyle.

Targeting teens is an example of lifestage marketing. Teens are at a particular lifestage—adolescence—which is characterized by behaviors, attitudes, and circumstances that other groups do not share. Targeting seniors is another example of lifestage marketing. This is not a question of who is at home in the afternoon or who has free time. Lifestage marketing is addressing a totality of circumstances that creates a unique group.

Lifestage is different from lifestyle. Lifestage addresses what stage of life the consumer is passing through, whereas lifestyle addresses *how* the consumer chooses to live. An example of a brand marketed to lifestyle is Ann Taylor. This retailer primarily addresses the fashion needs of young, professional, working women. On the other hand, maternity shops address the fashion needs of a particular lifestage.

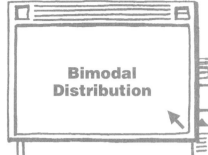

Bimodal Distribution

Occasionally when you are defining your audience you will discover that you have two groups who are about as distinct as you can get (elderly suburban women and young urban men!). When developing your creative strategy you have to look at each subgroup differently because the message you use to reach one group will not have the same impact as the strategy you use on the other.

Successful Lifestage and Lifestyle Marketing Campaigns

One example of a successful lifestage marketing campaign is that by Playtex nursing products. Playtex targets women in the stage of early motherhood. They focus their advertising on magazines like *Parents*, whose content is specifically generated for women in this stage of life. They promote their products in conjunction with other products and services associated with early motherhood.

Automobile manufacturers have targeted a lifestyle with the advent of the minivan. These vehicles were marketed to a type of women, the "soccer moms," who, while they may fit into any one of a number of lifestages, are primarily distinguished by their lifestyle. They are constantly on the go and often transport multiple children, needing a vehicle of larger size and capability than the traditional car.

Psychographics

Psychographics are the attitudes of your users and your competitors' users. The psychographic landscape can also include the attitudes of nonusers of the category. The word psychographics is really another word for mindset. It should also include insights into the reasons people use the category and a particular brand.

Understanding the mindset of your user is sometimes difficult, but it always pays off. The best way to grasp your customers' perspective is through the use of focus groups. This is *qualitative* market research. Focus groups are essentially a discussion group of your users, gathered together to talk about their feelings and attitudes about your product, your competitors' products, and the category as a whole. It is often eye-opening to simply gather a group of your customers to talk about what they like best and least about the products or services available in the category. You will learn things that they would not otherwise mention, often simply because they were not asked!

If you decide to try a focus group, consider talking to your competitors' users, too. They will be able to explain why they choose that competitor and what you need to do to become their favorite product or service. Another interesting group is nonusers. These are people who do not buy goods or services in the category. Why are these people worthwhile to talk to? The answer is that some of these people might be interested in your product or service but some obstacle is preventing them from purchase. Your job is to discover that obstacle and decide if you can overcome it. If you do, you will be expanding your base of users, always an outstanding achievement because these new users tend to be more loyal than someone who has switched from another company.

Category Usage Behavior

Usage behavior is a descriptor of how people use the goods or services in the category. So in addition to saying that your target audience is adult working mothers, you can also qualify them by their behavior in the marketplace. Examples include competitive users, nonusers, your users, heavy category users, light users, periodic users, and more. There are those who use only a certain flavor, color, or size. Take me, for example—I only chew cinnamon gum, I am a light gum user but only cinnamon. There are those who use a product only at a certain time of year or day. For example, some people only buy apples in the fall. Others buy them year round. Dividing your potential customers by their usage behavior can give you insights as to how and when to deliver messages to them and provide keys to their needs and wants.

There is a really useful notion about a customer's attitude toward products. It is called the "share of requirements" concept. Even though this has a fancy name, the concept is straightforward. Each user of a product has a certain number of occasions to use that product. This is the customer's "requirements." For example, I "require" lunch away from home five days a week—Monday through Friday. Most of the time, let's say 60 percent of the time, I buy my lunch at the fast food place around the corner. The rest of the time, 40 percent of the time, I buy from the deli. The deli is more expensive, but I like the food better.

Using the share of requirements notion, the fast food place has a 60 percent share of my requirements, and the deli has 40 percent. This concept can work for your business if you know whom you are competing with and how your company and your competitor fills a customer's share of requirements. The deli, if they want more of my business (a greater share of requirements), needs to make me into a more loyal customer. Retaining loyal customers, as we have said earlier, is one of the *most* important and profitable tasks of any business owner. In the case of the deli, they began handing out cards that were punched every time a customer bought a sandwich. When your card is punched ten times you get a free sandwich. This was a device that worked well with me because I

The Importance of Psychographics

The mindset or psychographics of customers is important because it is the key to understanding their wants and needs—both functionally and emotionally. It is impossible to uniquely and meaningfully fill their wants and needs with your service if you do not understand what they are. This level of understanding is often the difference between a successful product or successful advertising and a "me-too" message. Do not be an also-ran; take the time to grasp what your customers and potential customers really want. Communicate that in your message.

Seek Out Loyalty

A loyal customer will actually overcome hurdles of price and inconvenience to purchase goods or services at your business. Have you ever driven out of your way to see your favorite lady behind the counter or because you know a certain business will stand behind its products? These are the aspects of service that can create loyalty and a willingness to seek out your special offering.

kept using the card (kept coming back). And their lunches were competitively priced versus the fast food place.

Let's use another example in a local community and business setting. Let's say a customer buys gifts at two local gift shops. The customer divides her purchases roughly evenly between the two shops. One is closer to her house and the other is farther away and offers slightly more expensive wares. If the gift shop that is more expensive and farther away wants more of the customer's business, it needs to develop the quality of loyalty in that buyer. Loyalty is gained, as it is in all areas of life, from trust, relationships, and service. The Internet, which reaches people on an intimate, immediate level can help cement loyalty in customers by making their purchases easier and offering the services and value-added items that make a customer a repeat customer.

How Consumers Decide What Product or Service to Buy

The way a customer decides to make a purchase is called a decision hierarchy. This term describes the decision tree, or decision-making process of the buyer. Decision trees are different for each category of goods or services.

The factors that come into play when making a purchase decision include brand name, price, product features (flavor, color, fragrance), size, shopping outlet, convenience, and speed of delivery. The decision tree is the order in which these factors are decided upon. For example, when it comes to choosing a car, a customer may decide what type of car she wants first (say, a sports utility vehicle). Next she may decide on certain features of the vehicle, including moon roof, child safety features, and color. Her brand choice may be narrowed by which makers offer her choices of features. The brand may be the next decision, or possibly the price. Finally, after lots of looking around she may decide on a certain dealership that offers her an excellent price or the one that can get the vehicle the fastest.

Everyone's decision tree is slightly different. If you conduct a focus group or two, you will probably find that there are groups of people who put price first. Another group puts brand first. Yet another holds all options to a standard of desired features. These groups of users can be a way to divide your market *psychographically*. Each group can be addressed and lured according to what is important to them. Armed with this information you can prioritize your target audience.

You can even label the groups by mindset. Continuing with this example, there are price-conscious status shoppers, price-is-no-object shoppers, technology-first shoppers. These groups are based on this example, but you can get specific about your customers' mindsets by talking to them.

How can I use this information? Let's pretend I have a car dealership and I know that most of my shoppers are price-is-no-object-status shoppers. If I want to capture business from the more price-conscious shoppers (without sacrificing image), I could do a direct-mail campaign featuring price or value advantages of my dealership. The direct-mail campaign has the beauty of not notifying the other spenders.

The key to the decision tree is using it appropriately for each group of your customers. The decision tree for Web shoppers is slightly different, relying more on page design and good content. In the online world, customers can click over to your customer with more ease than visiting them in the bricks-and-mortar world. The lures you must use focus more on keeping your customer on your Web site because if they come to look and if the site offers them what they need, they will often stay to buy.

Shopping Behavior Translates into Web Behavior

The activity of shopping itself influences purchase decisions. Conventional shopping behaviors roughly translate into Web shopping behaviors. However, the Web offers unique challenges and opportunities, too.

Like traditional shopping, there are both impulse purchases and planned purchases. If you remember, we used these terms to help categorize your products way back in Chapter 2. Now we will use them to help you determine a sales and marketing strategy for both types. The other types of products will fall somewhere on a spectrum between impulse purchases and planned purchases, so your strategies must adjust accordingly. Think of your final marketing strategy like a Chinese menu. You will take some items from

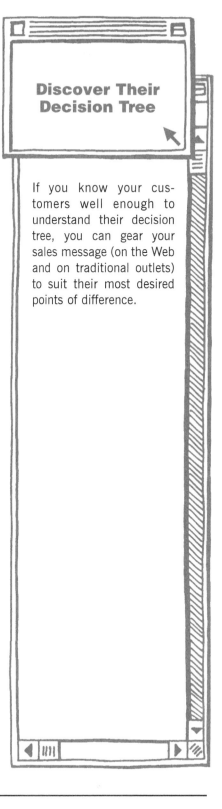

Discover Their Decision Tree

If you know your customers well enough to understand their decision tree, you can gear your sales message (on the Web and on traditional outlets) to suit their most desired points of difference.

column A, some from column B, and use them together to make a good, solid plan that will help your business.

1. *Impulse buys* are usually small items that are perceived as low-risk purchases. These are often low in price, disposable (or have limited life of use), commodities, gift purchases (no consequences for the purchaser), and high use-up, frequently bought items. Examples include paperback books, CDs, specialty foods like imported coffee or chocolates, and a casual sweater or scarf. These type of products can compete solely on price and delivery—perfect opportunities for a Web-based business. Consequently, you will probably want to develop ads and pitches that discuss those things.

2. *Planned purchases* are more expensive and are given more time and consideration. These are closer to investments for the customers. These items have many different features and options, higher prices, and higher values. They include purchases such as cars, boats, and vacation homes, all the way down to an expensive watch. In terms of services, many purchases are planned.

   Customers research a lawyer, doctor, cleaning service, a new school, a day care center, or a personal trainer. The role of the Web here is often to help the customer in her decision-making process. You can help her figure out what she wants and needs and help her make her purchase decision. This is a decision that she wants to be happy with a year down the road.

Beyond impulse and planned purchases, people have certain behaviors when searching for goods and services on the Web. They use Yahoo!, Lycos, and other search engines and they also see ads on related Web sites that they are visiting. There are four ways that consumers receive notice about a site on the Web:

- Selecting a site from an industry direction
- Typing in a keyword search

- Seeing an ad in front of them
- Taking the advice of a friend or colleague

When it comes to a specific ad, it is important to understand the technical expertise of your users and how much you are asking them to do. A specific offer should outline the terms of the offer and what a customer will need to divulge about herself, as well as price and delivery schedule. Web users like offers that clearly detail the level of information required to complete the transaction because they are concerned about privacy issues.

Fears about doing business on the Web are wide-ranging and not always rational. They include fears of being inundated with e-mails, fears of being personally contacted (on the phone or mail), fears of exposure of self, fears of credit card abuse, and fears of identity fraud. These fears are often fostered by the media looking to make an interesting story about the Internet.

To have a successful business site, it is paramount to reassure customers about credit card security and the confidentiality of their identity. It is important to reassure customers about this—and to back it up with integrity. Some businesses have burned their customers. Web site businesses have abused customers by using their e-mail address in inappropriate ways. Some sites have sold their address list to other sites that will spam them.

Customers will be more likely to buy a well-known item when shopping on the Web. You should make every effort to be the brand name they will think of first. This means that advertising on traditional channels will pay off when it comes time for your customer to go online. Ways to get your name in front of consumers (without advertising on the Super Bowl) include placing ads in local newspapers and magazines, trade journals, or specialty associations if appropriate. Use outdoor advertising and direct-mail advertising. Sometimes other local non-competing businesses will let you post an advertisement in their foyer. There are many ways to get your name out locally. Sponsor a little league team. Sponsor runners in the marathon or a local charity function (be sure to get your banner up!). Remember to always include the name of your business, a slogan about the nature of your product and its point of difference,

Get Customers to Know You

Because of the general wariness of users, most buyers on the Web search out brand name items or names with which they are personally familiar (i.e. a local business). They will buy from a known quantity rather than an unknown because the issue of trust is so important. This affects the decision tree in purchasing. Amazon.com sells lots of books because of its price and speed of delivery—but also because people know it. Customers figure that a well-known brand name will not risk its reputation to rip someone off. Further, many people have already used the service successfully, which helps reduce the risk in the mind of the new user.

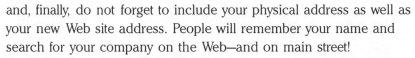

The objectives of creative development are to generate a **guide**. This guide is used to produce the marketing materials—"sell" copy, logos, slogans, personality, look and feel, and descriptions and depictions of products and services.

and, finally, do not forget to include your physical address as well as your new Web site address. People will remember your name and search for your company on the Web—and on main street!

One final word about the benefits of shopping online and being a business that is known for online sales. The feeling of safety is critical to clinching a sale. When customers feel safe and comfortable doing business online, they can also feel hip and in-the-know. This is a little bit of the bandwagon mentality. Like at high school— if he is cool and I am his friend, I am cool. This accounts for customers bragging that they bought a book from Amazon.com. Do people brag that they checked a book out of the library? Checking a book out of the library is low tech, and it's been done. It is not a daring new feat. Reading and supporting the community is still worthwhile, even moral, but it's not hip like ordering online. Your customers can brag that they bought something from your company online if they feel confident and safe about their purchase and their confidentiality. Let your customers feel like they are part of an insiders' club. Reinforce this feeling with an e-mail thank-you note or even a badge such as a baseball cap with your company's e-mail address on it.

Developing Creative

After you have defined your audience, the next part of our step-by-step marketing plan is developing the *creative*. The word *creative* in marketing circles is used as a noun to describe the advertising message, or any aspect of the product or service that communicates messages and feelings. Any description or depiction conveys a personality or an attitude, in addition to strictly conveying information. The personality and attitude of the brand is as important as how the product described.

This is the arena where advertising copy, which includes slogans and product descriptions, comes into play. Graphic style—colors, shapes, and feeling—also matters. The editorial environment also plays a part in the communication about the product or brand. For example, a message delivered in the *New York Times* may be perceived differently than if it is delivered in the *Utne Reader*. This is not only a question of the audience, but also a question *of context*.

Everything you say or show about your product communicates *something* to your audience. The trick is to use all aspects of communication deliberately and effectively.

It is sometimes important to communicate how to access these goods, if that is not obviously apparent to the buyer. (Absolut Vodka does not advertise where to buy it, for example.) This communication is done in the form of messages to your users. These messages are found in advertisements, on packages, on the Web, and in any other way that you communicate with users and potential users. Bear in mind that though your messages are geared to the shopper, they also communicate with your competitors and suppliers.

Before writing copy and developing graphics, you need to decide who you want to be in the mind of your customer. Words and pictures deliver more than just facts. Their tone and manner communicate personality. Consider the difference between these two ways of encouraging a customer to purchase again: "Thanks for your business, please call again" and, "Y'all come back now!"

The personalities of health care and financial sites, such as the American Cancer Society and DLH direct.com are geared to encourage the confidence and credibility of the buyer. Entertainment sites, such as mtv.com and the sci-fi channel, have personalities that sell fun and playfulness.

Remember that the person seeing your ad will have developed a preconceived idea about what he will experience at your Web site. As a general rule of thumb, you want to make good on those expectations. The personality and performance of the ad itself should act like a teaser of what's to come. Ads are like accessories to your site, they are like matching shoes to your outfit. If they do not match, the user is disappointed. Have you ever seen an ad for a movie that did not turn out to be what you expected?

Point of Difference

The objective of creative development is to communicate the type of product you are offering. You need to develop messages that make sense to potential customers and that convince them that you can fulfill their needs *in a way that no other company can.* That unique quality is your *point of difference.*

Brand Equity

Brand equity is the meaning your customer equates with your product in their mind. This may or may not be accurate, yet it is what the customer believes. For example, Bausch & Lomb's brand equity is in high-quality vision care. People believe their products are of a higher quality. Brand names and their clout with consumers—both meaning and trust—go a long way on the Web. The Web is a newfangled thing to many surfers, who are put at ease when they see a brand name or even locality they trust.

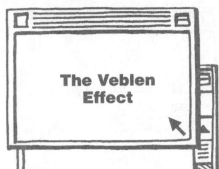

The Veblen Effect

The *Veblen Effect* is the way a customer's perception of a product changes based on that product's price point. Customers may view high-priced items as being of a high quality, while identical items priced and marketed in a lower bracket are viewed as being of a lesser quality.

A company or brand's point of difference can be emotional, for example, Johnson & Johnson brand baby products fulfill mothers' security needs better than a generic brand of baby products. In actuality, most of the time, there is nothing about Johnson & Johnson's product that is substantially different from its generic counterpart. The difference is in the feeling the customer gets. Through advertising and marketing, consumers feel that there is a substantive difference in the Johnson & Johnson product and have a higher confidence in their purchase.

This point of difference can also be functional, such as Dr. Pepper's unique flavor of soda. Functional points of difference tend to be product related, while emotional points of difference tend to be brand related. The brand is your company's name, logo, and equity.

People appreciate local businesses, so this locality can work to your advantage. This is especially true if your product or service benefits a uniquely local audience. The fact that your bricks-and-mortar storefront is around the corner can reassure them and make them more apt to use your services than the services of a company four states (or countries!) away.

Points of difference can also be based on price. Retailers have known this for years. Wal-Mart stores began their empire based on price. The Yugo automobile's point of difference is price. Interestingly, price as a point of difference works both ways—high end and low end. On the high end, a very high price for a certain item can confer a sense of pride in the buyer or a perception of quality (even if the same item is offered for less elsewhere).

Because companies can offer goods and services on the Web without incurring the overhead expenses of a sales team and retail shelf space, price discounts have been a big attraction for shoppers online. Examples of this low-price point of difference include Amazon.com and online brokerage services, which offer a minimal charge per trade. It is important to keep in mind that these are commodity products (we discussed the types of products you can sell online in Chapter 2). Commodity products sell well on the Web through price and added value. Some other types of products do not sell well based on price point. You do not want to market your considered purchase products at an unusually low price or they will probably be viewed as inferior quality!

Graphics Development

There are three basic styles of graphics. The first is illustration, which includes anything hand drawn such as sketches, cartoons, and hand-drawn typefaces. The second is the photographic style, and the third is a straightforward informational style which includes pure text with a logo and geometric, abstract shapes.

Online advertising and traditional advertising should marry. If you have decided to use a photographic style in an outdoor ad, follow it up with the same photo (or one using the same recognizable theme) on the Web. The style should be used to help accurately portray the personality of your company.

- *Illustrated style.* Examples include the cover page of the *New Yorker*, ads for the cartoon channel, and ads for Metropolitan Life Insurance (Snoopy). This style is hand sketched, personalized, and intimate. If you want to establish an intimate feel with your customer or your business provides a high level of service to clients, this may be a good option for you. For example, a day care center may develop an illustrated style for all of its literature, signage, ads, and Internet communications. A tutor, a dance instructor, or a personal trainer might do the same.
- *Photographic style.* Examples include Discovery.com, pet Web sites, and Web sites selling cars, motorcycles, or real estate. These employ photographs and use a photographic style in their advertising. Images can be straightforward or modified using a computer program to increase color saturation or create overlays and movement.

There is no mistake that these businesses are the planned purchase, high-risk purchase categories. In this case, pictures of the merchandise are part of the selling story. They help a customer decide whether to purchase or which one to purchase—without leaving home! This is a big advantage of the Web. If your ad photo-

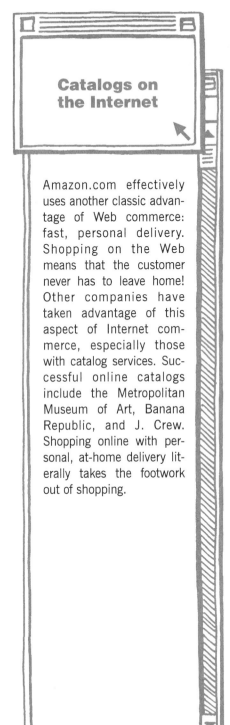

Catalogs on the Internet

Amazon.com effectively uses another classic advantage of Web commerce: fast, personal delivery. Shopping on the Web means that the customer never has to leave home! Other companies have taken advantage of this aspect of Internet commerce, especially those with catalog services. Successful online catalogs include the Metropolitan Museum of Art, Banana Republic, and J. Crew. Shopping online with personal, at-home delivery literally takes the footwork out of shopping.

graphs are cute, eye-catching, or just plain appealing, people who are looking for visual cues to make their purchases will be more likely to visit your site. After all, you have the best photos of kittens for sale, Mercedes-Benz cars, or vacation homes in the Adirondacks. These are people seeking visual information. Give it to them.

Photographic style also works well for gearheads, fashion junkies, and music lovers. High-end design, both industrial and fashion-based, are communicated very effectively with photographs. As always, think of your audience when deciding on your graphical style. People who love rock stars and celebrities will also love pictures of them. Photos can be hip, leading-edge, real world products, but do not make the mistake of using them just for the sake of having them. What customers really want to see is content and graphics that mirror the intent of the site. Make sure your content and graphics are appropriate to the product first and foremost! Then go for the image types you need.

- *Abstract type style.* Examples include libraries, news services, newspapers, and other services where the product is information. The abstract style uses geometric shapes, bright or pastel colors or degrees of contrast, texts and fonts, and layout to strategically bring attention to a text message. The placement, color, or font of an item in an abstract style ad or site can lend meaning to that message.

This style is generally used for informational services. It is less intimate than the hand-drawn, illustrative style and less explicit than the photographic style. Here the text often is the product.

Copy Development

Where is copy used? Use the same description of your business in different places—online Yellow Pages, search engines, directories, local newspapers, and traditional print. Be sure to take advantage of the signature at the end of your e-mail. This e-mail signature is a piece of text that is automatically inserted at the end of your e-mail. It usually contains your contact information such as your phone number and a hot link to your Web site. Use every opportunity to employ your logo and slogan.

What is "sell" copy?

- a description of your *business*
- a description of products or even a *description for each of your products*
- emotional benefits
- functional benefits
- points of difference, memorable and unique
- differentiating factors or attributes

You want copy points that intrigue. Use whatever concerns the customer the most—their fears, desires, hopes, and needs. How does your product fit into the rest of their life—with their family, society, and identity? The most inspirational and motivating messages address our drive to self-actualization. That is the highest aspiration of a person, to be the best self they can be (they get to define what that is!). The U.S. Army appeals to the drive of young people to self-actualize with its slogan, "Be all you can be."

Ads can also address lower level needs, such as the human need to belong or feel accepted. This is a "keeping up with the Joneses" approach, and it never gets tired. Examples of ads that address belonging needs include any product that addresses social standing. This includes everything from Clearasil to Pepsi.

Finally there are ads that address one's most basic needs, such as the need for safety or shelter. These ads often use scare tactics (a home security system, some insurance companies, or legal services). While the scare tactic approach is not for everyone, it works for those most basic human needs and is also tirelessly effective.

Humorous ads work well on the Web. The Web is a personal medium, it reaches a person intimately and not in the context of a crowd. Therefore, humor can work like an inside joke. (Ever see the jokes that get posted to a long e-mail list? They are jokes enjoyed alone.) The Web is intimate yet anonymous. That

DEFINITION PLEASE

The degree to which a consumer remembers an ad—any ad on any medium—is called **recall**. Some ads have high recall ("Where's the Beef?"), while others are quite low. The best ads have high recall and also high **persuasion**. Persuasion is the extent to which a message convinces a potential user to buy the product or change his behavior. In the 1960s there was a public service announcement featuring a Native American looking at trash on our nation's highways and letting a tear roll down his cheek. Throwing trash out of the window of the car became socially unacceptable largely due to that ad. The message had a high level of persuasion.

is why pornography is a popular subject. But personally embarrassing subjects are popular, too, such as health problems. Personal medical problems can be addressed in an anonymous and intimate way. We will be seeing more and more of this aspect of the Web used.

Media Planning

A media strategy sets forth *who* you want to reach, *where* you want to reach them, and *how many times* you wish to reach them. There are objectives in media planning that spring from the overall marketing strategy, such as building awareness for a new business, increasing repeat business among those who already use the business, or stealing customers from a competitor. These overall goals help to guide the placement, level, and emphasis of advertising and publicity spending.

Reach and Frequency

When it comes to notifying users and potential users about your business, two concepts from traditional media planning are helpful: reach and frequency. Reach is the breadth of audience your message contacts. Frequency is the number of times your message touches them.

Now is the time for the great Ping-Pong ball analogy, which helps describe reach and frequency. If I have 100 Ping-Pong balls, I can toss them out to 100 different people who would each hold one. Each Ping-Pong ball is a single message (ad) from my company. In this case I have reached as many people as I can with all of my available messages. That is maximum reach to a broad audience, also described as a broad reach.

A broad reach is good for general interest type products, not specialty items. For example, broad reach media goals are good for a new snack food, which everyone might like. But they are not so useful for say, pantyhose, which are worn only by a smaller segment of the audience. Broad reach media goals are also a priority for new product introductions where the maker wants to achieve a general awareness about a new item.

A *narrower reach* is desirable for an item that will appeal to a targeted group. This narrower group is the *target audience*. Using the Ping-Pong ball analogy, the pantyhose maker may not wish to distribute all of its messages to everyone. The company may choose to deliver its messages to only 50 percent of the audience, the other 50 percent would be "wasted" on the wrong target.

Secondly, there is the concept of frequency. If I threw my Ping-Pong balls (messages) to half of the audience, they could each hold two. I have reached my target audience twice. Many ad agencies claim that a target audience should be reached at least three times before they really remember the message. In this case, to be sure that I could reach a certain group at least three times, I would choose thirty-three people (perhaps adult working women who wear pantyhose) and toss them three Ping-Pong balls each. Even if I have missed some adult women pantyhose wearers, I am still better off than if I tossed a message to everyone in the audience.

Media Planning Wrap-Up

Once your media goals are outlined, you are in a better position to evaluate the merits of different vehicles for your message. The next chapter will cover the many kinds of vehicles on the Internet for your message, such as broadcast-type advertising, direct one-to-one advertising, banner ad placement on high-traffic spots, and more. Traditional advertising outlets should not be ignored. Using a local newspaper to drive traffic to your site is an effective tool. Traditional advertising should be used in conjunction with Web advertising for maximum impact. Understanding all of the media outlets available to you will help you make informed and effective choices.

Creating a Brand Image

Automobile manufacturers are the undisputed kings of creating brand images. Ford and Dodge have both done exceptional jobs in building a brand image of their truck lines as rugged and dependable. Jeep has done such a good job at building a brand image that for decades the name Jeep was synonymous with off-road vehicles. Think of the quality your product or service best conveys and use that to build a brand image, not only for the products but for your business as well.

Through the careful design of your site and the information on it you can present a brand image that will entice customers to take the extra step to contact you. Branding is even more important for people-selling services than it is for selling product because of the intangible nature of services.

Ten Truths of Web Marketing:

Take this ten-point quiz to check your Web marketing savvy. True or false?

1. If you build it, they will come.   *True*   *False*

2. Everyone needs a Web page.   *True*   *False*

3. The Web is a great leveler.   *True*   *False*

4. Web pages need as many graphics as will fit.   *True*   *False*

5. Getting a Web page up is the easy part; maintaining it is the hard part.   *True*   *False*

6. Everyone in the world is on the Web.   *True*   *False*

7. Once you have a Web page, sales will skyrocket.   *True*   *False*

8. Only big corporations can afford Web pages.   *True*   *False*

9. Web pages should be as simple as possible.   *True*   *False*

10. You should advertise your Web page by every means available.   *True*   *False*

Answers:
1. F, 2. F, 3. T, 4. F, 5. T, 6. F, 7. F, 8. F, 9. F, 10. T

Address
http://chapter_eleven.com

Link

Getting Your Message Out:

Traditional and Online Tactics

Getting Out the Message

Once you have designed your campaign, it's time to look at how you will implement it. There are dozens of ways to get your message out to your potential customers. In the following sections we will give you the lowdown on how to get your carefully constructed message out to the masses.

Traditional Marketing

One of the best ways to promote your Web site, as it is to promote anything, is through traditional mass media. E-mail marketing depends on getting names from your existing traffic, and affiliate marketing only works once you have people visiting your Web site. But how do you best utilize traditional forms of media like newspapers, radio, television, and traditional direct mail in a way that drives traffic to your site, without breaking your wallet?

It is a fact of life: traditional media is expensive. It is expensive to produce and expensive to run. The closer you live to a major city, the more it is going to cost you. The first rule of traditional advertising is, you have to spend money to make money.

If your Web site was built to supplement an existing business, you are probably very familiar with traditional advertising. If you do not have an advertising agency or an in-house marketing professional, you have probably hired freelancers, or at the very least done some media purchasing yourself. Once your Web site has gone through its launch, start making a big deal of it in your existing advertising efforts. Make sure every advertisement has the URL of your site in big, bold letters. Leave some room to tell your customers about the convenient online ordering or wealth of product information you have on your Web site.

If you are doing your business solely on the Internet, chances are you have not had much experience in traditional advertising. It still remains the fastest way to generate new traffic to your site, but you must make sure it is memorable. You want that person who is sitting in her car and hears your commercial to remember that URL when she is at home sitting in front of her computer.

Advertising agencies can be expensive, often charging a media placement fee on top of their creative fees and the cost of advertising with the radio station or newspaper, but they are the best equipped to come up with a marketing plan that will be creative, well placed, and memorable. Be sure to check around with different agencies. Ask to see samples of their work and ask them to generate samples of how they would promote your Web site. Do not be shy; if the agency wants your business, they will do a little work to show you just how much.

As e-mail marketing is to your Web site, direct mail is to traditional advertising. Direct mail, especially direct mail that is targeted to your existing customer base, is a good, cost-effective way to get the message out about your new Web site. For relatively small expense, you can design a simple flyer or self-mailed card that tells all about the features of the new site. Fortunately, with a direct-mail piece of this nature you can get very specific. Tell your customers about the searchable database or the personalization features you put into the site. You spent weeks planning it; now is not the time to be modest.

Newspapers and magazines can be very expensive to advertise in, and advertising agencies often get the best deals for their clients. But you, too, can negotiate with some of the smaller papers in your area. A good rule of thumb is the more advertising space you buy, and the more often you want your ad to appear, the less you'll pay for each ad. Let the newspaper representative help you come up with a plan that works for you and fits your budget. These sales representatives will also know of any special sections coming up that will help you reach a more targeted audience. Special sections often cost more, but they can truly help you reach a good range of potential customers.

The most expensive media to advertise in is television and radio. Not surprisingly, the closer you are to a major metropolitan area, the more expensive TV and radio airtime will be.

If you already run radio and television advertisements as a matter of course, that's great! Use those ads to showcase your new Web site. Make your URL as much a part of the commercial as your company name or phone number. If you have the money in

Connecting Direct Mail with the Web

A good way to drive traffic to your site from direct mail, and measure just how effective the mailing was, is to make an offer to your customers. Offer them free shipping or $5 off their first order if they do so before a certain date. Offers have the added benefit of letting you measure the results of your direct mail-campaign, by tracking how many orders come in using the offer, or at least inquiring about it.

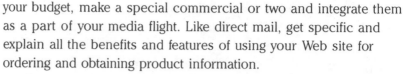

your budget, make a special commercial or two and integrate them as a part of your media flight. Like direct mail, get specific and explain all the benefits and features of using your Web site for ordering and obtaining product information.

Get creative. Remember that because your Web site is available for anyone in the world, at any time, do not limit yourself to advertising only in your area. Look for special events that will appeal to your customers. If you sell crafting supplies, look for local craft shows, or even craft shows that are not local. Often for a small fee you can sponsor events. In return you get an advertisement in the event brochure and sometimes the opportunity to hang a banner. If you sell bass fishing supplies, look for local fishing tournaments or even fishing publications that are created locally. Ask the local bait shop if you can put some flyers on his counter. Look for local fishing tournaments to sponsor, and make sure your Web site is prominently displayed at every opportunity. As always, be sure and target your sponsorships to focus on events that will interest your customers. Creative marketing opportunities are everywhere. Go grab them!

Nontraditional Marketing

There are a lot of opportunities for innovative and creative marketing if you know where to look. One simple, creative, nontraditional marketing strategy is sponsoring a little league team. For relatively little expense, your company name or Web site goes right on the back of the team jersey. You will often get advertising space in the little league program along with your sponsorship.

There are lots of low cost, creative marketing opportunities just like this if you take the time to search them out. Unless you are selling a product such as cars, which appeal to everyone, take the time to search out opportunities that match the interests of your customer base.

Charity events, too, are often great ways to market your new Web site. For a small donation that is often tax-deductible, the charity will give you advertising space in its event program and sometimes even mention your company or your Web site as a sponsor of the event. Charitable contributions are a good idea for any business, besides the obvious Good Samaritan benefits to giving money to charity, people like doing business with civic-minded companies. Your charitable contributions make you stand out from all the other companies out there that may still care about local issues but do not do anything to help. If you support charities, make sure to put a page on your Web site that says that. You should be proud of your charitable contributions. Let your customers know a portion of your profits goes out to help others. It generates a good feeling about your company, and customers will be more likely to continue to do business with you.

Tournaments and outings are great ways to promote your Web site if they are the kinds of things your customers are interested in. If you sell golf products or find that many of your customers like the sport, then contact your local golf courses and ask about upcoming tournaments. At major courses and country clubs, hardly a week goes by when you do not find some kind of tournament. Speak to the tournament coordinator. For a small fee, you can often sponsor the event, or even get your company name and Web site on golf towels, golf balls, even tees. The return on the relatively small investment can be outstanding if you target your efforts to attract potential customers.

Seek out associations in your community. Local animal shelters, after-school programs, and even religious organizations often have events that they need sponsors for. As with all the other events mentioned, a small donation not only gets you a lot of advertising exposure, but it gives you a way to tell your customers that you care about the same issues they care about. It makes your business more than just a large corporation and leaves them with a good feeling about where their money is going. The small amounts you spend (and often the money is tax-deductible as charitable giving anyway) earn you a lot of respect with your customers, and get you a lot of advertising play.

Any media campaign should include these nontraditional forms of advertising. Find some room in your budget and speak to your advertising agency (if you have one) about creating some generic advertisements promoting your Web site that you can use at these

Sponsor an Event

Local events are great ways to get your name out without spending a lot of money. Many towns sponsor carnivals and festivals, and often they are looking for sponsors. Contact your town chamber of commerce and check what events are planned for the near future and inquire as to sponsorship costs. If your chamber of commerce has never explored having local businesses fund their events through advertising-based sponsorships, tell them now is the time to start and make a sponsorship offer. Most organizations will jump at the chance to get some extra money.

Targeted Direct Mail

Sometimes, organizations will let you have access to their membership lists so you can send targeted direct mail. In that case, remember to be respectful and not abuse the privilege. Make the members an offer if they try your Web site and make sure they know how you support their organization. Only use the list once, unless you get permission to do otherwise. If you are careful and respectful, access to these member databases can be a wealth of information on new prospective clients.

kinds of events. Invest in a banner and ask if it can be displayed at the event, or if they can distribute flyers for your Web site.

Online Marketing Strategies

Banner Advertising

Now that you have created your Web site, it's time to get the word out and start building traffic. Building traffic simply means getting people to come to your Web site and take a look around. There are many ways to do that, one of which is banner advertising. A banner advertisement is a clickable graphic or image that is used for the purpose of advertising on the Internet.

Why should you utilize banner advertising instead of more traditional methods of advertising your Web site? Well, for one thing, you are advertising right where you want your customers to be! Advertising on the Internet makes it very easy for your customers to get to your Web site. Traditional advertising means they have to not only sit down at their computer and connect to the Internet, but they have to remember your URL once they are online. The careful creation and placement of banner advertising means that your customers can just click right to your site.

Nowadays it's very difficult to navigate around the Internet without running into banner ads. They appear at the top and sometimes the bottom of nearly every page. Chances are you do not even notice them anymore unless they have something that catches your eye. That first banner ad for AT&T had something that caught people's eye. The copy enticed them to click on the banner, which took them to the intended site. Early banner ads were static buttons, relying on clever copy to deliver an action. Now, many banner advertisements rely heavily on animation, with motion and sometimes even sound!

The key to success in banner advertising is not necessarily having the most flashy banner out there. True dynamic banners that catch the eye and imagination of the person looking at the ad are an absolute must. But the use of these new technologies must be balanced against the time they take to download. Web analysts are not convinced that animation is always a good thing. Much like your site itself, banner ads must download and resolve themselves on screen very quickly, in most cases, even quicker than your site. Whereas people have traveled to your site to see your information, banner advertisements are like commercials on the Internet. Many people have little patience for them. If your banner does not download fast, potential customers will be off the page and on to something else before they've even seen it! And that is a waste of money. Much like traditional advertising, you pay for each time your ad is shown (this is called an impression). If the ad does not download quickly, you will pay for an impression that your potential customer will never see.

Banners come in many sizes, defined by the number of pixels the banner takes up in width and length. As with traditional advertising, the larger your banner the more you can expect to pay for it.

Creating a banner ad is not difficult, but just like programming a Web site, it must be handled carefully. There are many ways to get a banner ad that reflects the graphic design of your site and is engaging enough to get people to want to click through to your site. Most Web site development firms can create banner advertisements for your site for an additional fee. While this may be an attractive alternative, remember that banner advertising is just that—advertising. If you have an advertising agency, you may want to consult them on the best way to lure your customers to the site. After all, your corporate advertising agency is in the business of writing copy that sells your product. They are well-equipped to write copy that will sell your Web site as well.

There are companies, like Web site developers, who specialize in designing banner advertisements. A simple search through any engine should produce a list of companies who can promise you outstanding banner ads. These professional developers know how best to design ads that are eye-catching, well written, and, most importantly, quick to download.

Banner Ads

The very first banner advertisement ever to appear on the Web was from AT&T. It showed up on a site called Hotwired in 1995. The ad was a simple rectangular button that read "Have you ever clicked your mouse right here? You will!" A lot of people did, and Internet advertising was born.

DEFINITION PLEASE

An **interstitial ad** appears in a separate, automatically opened browser window while a Web page loads. This type of advertisement tends to contain more graphics and higher technology presentations than your average banner ad. **Hyperstitial ads** are displayed on the same browser window while you wait for a World Wide Web page to load. Hyperstitials are more like television commercials and harder to ignore than interstitial and banner ads. Do interstitials work? Some studies find people are more likely to click on an interstitial ad than on a banner ad, but many people find them annoying and feel they slow access to the pages they really want to see.

As with anything on the Internet, you can create your own banner advertisement the same way you would a Web site. There are many online tools you can use to design your very own banner ad such as CoolBE.com, JalapenoSoftware.com, BannerCreationServices (www.total-harmony.com/promotion/banner_creation.html). These tools often have a series of stock backgrounds you can choose in a variety of sizes. You add your own copy (either written by you, or by your advertising agency) and the program acts much like the WYSIWYG site building tools, generating the code for your advertisement and providing you a finished product.

If you do not use a professional to design your banner, it may take you some trial and error to determine which banner works best for your site. Once you have one made, it's time to get it to go to work for you.

First you need to decide where you want to have your ad appear. You really need to weigh this decision carefully. Advertising on a site with high traffic will expose your Web site to the largest possible audience, but what is the benefit to advertising on a site that would attract very few people who would buy from *you*? If you sell vegetarian cookbooks, no matter how well trafficked a site like Meat Lovers Recipes is, it will never attract the kind of people who will take interest in your site and make a purchase.

Research sites used by your core constituencies. Your vendors and customers often make great places to place banner ads. Companies you already do business with will be amenable to placing your advertisement, and they will charge you less than the large, high-traffic sites. A few well-placed banner ads that are targeted to your target audience is more cost effective, and a better return on your advertising dollar, than lots of banner ads that are randomly scattered across the Internet.

Once you have thought carefully about where you would like to place your banner ad, you need to contact the administrators of the Web sites you've chosen. Sometimes a Web site has a page with information about exchanging links or advertising with them. Other times you'll have to send an e-mail to the administrator or use a contact phone number to reach him.

The cost for placing your banner ad is often called its CPM, or cost per thousand impressions. If the advertiser's CPM is $50, then you pay $50 for every one thousand people who see your ad. While a thousand impressions may seem like a lot, for high traffic sites, you may run out of impressions in just the first week. Multiply that by a few different sites and the amount of time you need to make an impression on potential customers, and the cost for banner advertising can be substantial. Remember, the more popular the site, the more money it can command for banner advertising.

There have been many studies to determine the best placement for banner advertisements. Some suggest that placing an ad in the lower corner nearest the right-hand scroll bar will result in more successful click-throughs (when people click to your site through your ad). Unfortunately, you will rarely get to decide where your advertisement goes on someone else's site. The ad size, the number of ads, and the overall design of the site you are advertising on will determine where they are able to place your ad.

Once you have planned and carefully executed a banner advertising campaign, how do you determine if that campaign is successful? One measure of a successful banner advertising campaign is the CTR, or click-through ratio. This is a method of rating how many times your banner has been clicked on, and it appears as a ratio. For example a CTR of 1% means that one out of every hundred people who saw your ad clicked on it. Of course, a high CTR is an example of a successful ad both in design and placement. Low CTRs mean you should probably reevaluate either your placement or your design.

Look carefully at CTRs for the same advertisement placed in different locations on different sites. A banner ad may be very successful on one site but not so much elsewhere. Go with what works, and change your ad placement strategy to move the ones that are less successful to better sites, or better locations.

Affiliate Marketing

Affiliate marketing is becoming one of the hottest and most lucrative ways to build business relationships and make some money on the Internet. Affiliate programs (sometimes also called

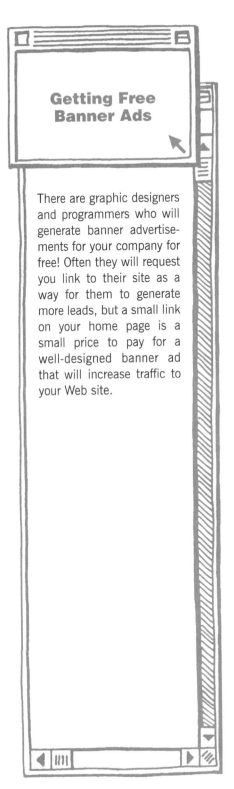

Getting Free Banner Ads

There are graphic designers and programmers who will generate banner advertisements for your company for free! Often they will request you link to their site as a way for them to generate more leads, but a small link on your home page is a small price to pay for a well-designed banner ad that will increase traffic to your Web site.

Banner Ad Effectiveness

Do banner advertisements actually work? A recent study by Andersen Consulting says that banner ads are actually more effective than other forms of traditional advertising. Of 1,500 highly experienced Web users surveyed by the company, one-fourth reported going to an online storefront to shop after seeing a banner advertisement. This 25 percent effectiveness compares with 14 percent for magazine advertisements, 11 percent for television commercials, and 4 percent for both radio and billboard advertising.

reseller, associate, or partnership programs) are systems of revenue sharing used by companies who market products and services online. The Web site you partner with has goods and services (for an example, Amazon.com, which has one of the very best affiliate programs available). You are paid referral fees, or commissions, by linking your Web site to these larger ones.

Let's say you sell bass fishing equipment. Working with Amazon.com, you customize a link to their site where your customers can browse and purchase books about bass fishing. As payment, you get either a flat rate or a percentage of the total order your customer places. This benefits your bottom line in a very real way, and it makes your customer feel good about your Web site. After all, you helped them find products that interest them. Amazon.com profits by the increased order, and everyone makes out well. Good affiliate marketing programs can help you build an online income even if your site has relatively low traffic.

Choosing an affiliate program that will work for you requires some research. You already know what your customers want. You've created your entire site, and even your e-zine, to give them the information they desire. Now you need to take the next step. Examine the demographics of your customers and try to think like them. What other products would they be interested in? Affiliate programs go beyond just books and CDs, although these are two of the most popular, and lucrative, affiliate programs. Even major search engines and informative sites like About.com are starting affiliate programs. Rather than pay you for orders, as About.com does not sell anything, they pay for click-throughs from your site to one of theirs. In this kind of affiliate marketing program you link to one of their guide sites. If you sell bass fishing products, you would link to their fishing pages where your customers can get more information about fishing. Every time your customers successfully click from your site to About.com, you get money. Of course you want to avoid a lot of this type of affiliate program for a very specific reason: Your customers are leaving your site. If they leave your site, they are not spending money on your products. So choose affiliates like this carefully.

There are many sites that rank affiliate programs for you. Taking a long look at their criteria and comments is a good way to get started researching which affiliate program you want to join. There are several Web marketing sites that have done some of this research for you such as:

AssociateCash.com
2-Tier.com
Affiliates-Directory.com
Top10Affiliates.com

Do not take their word for it and do not just join an affiliate program because they think it's the best. Make sure the programs they recommend fit in with the content and tone of your site. Do your homework; it will pay off in the end!

A lot of Web businesspeople look at affiliate programs as a quick way to make a lot of money. They join several affiliate programs, plaster their site with banner advertising promoting the affiliate partner, and expect the checks to roll in. And they are surprised when they do not. The key to success in affiliate marketing is selecting one or two high-quality programs that match the subject of your Web site. This is important. No good will be served by selecting affiliate programs with businesses that do not match the interests of people traveling to your

site. Once you have chosen your programs with care, promote your affiliations on your site, using search engines, e-mail, your e-zine, even newsgroups and discussion lists are good places to promote both your site and your new affiliations. If you choose relevant affiliates, and are careful with whom you choose to partner, you can expect to make some money and promote your site.

You can also start your own affiliate program to build traffic to your site. When you decide what things

Keep Your Reputation

Remember, you are entering into a partnership with your affiliate. You want to do some research into the business practices of any affiliate program you want to join. Company reputation goes a long way here. Make sure the affiliate program you join is run by a company who treats their affiliates honestly and fairly. The tracking of your sales or commissions is done by them, so make sure they offer 100 percent accountability and respond to your questions in a timely manner. Make sure you only link to sites with reputable business dealings, who offer products or services you would use yourself. All it takes is one of your customers to become unhappy with your affiliate program. You will never be able to earn this customer's trust again, and through no fault of your own, beyond poor research, you have lost this customer's business, probably for good.

Who Is Linking to Me?

Anyone can set up a link to your Web site. While asking permission to do so is the ethical thing to do, it is not mandatory. Finding out who is linking to your site is smart business for preventative customer service. There are a lot of sites on the Web with content your customers might deem negative. These same customers do not always realize that you have little or no control over who provides a link to your site.

You can use your referrer log to check referring sites. It is also the most difficult to decipher. You can also use search engines to make a quick check of sites that link to you. Because search engines index every page of a Web site, and follow all the links on that page, they keep track of who is linking to whom. Both AltaVista and HotBot allow you to search for links in their databases.

Unfortunately, you have little recourse if someone is linking to you from a site you feel is inappropriate. The best you can do is send a letter to the Webmaster of the referring site and ask him to remove the link.

would be of interest to your customers, seek out similar Web sites and ask if they would like to affiliate with you! Many Web site tracking programs, like Web Trends, can give you the name of the site that your customers were on just before they came to you. (This is called the referring site.) Based on this information, you can offer click-through bonuses. This can be a cheaper alternative to banner advertising as you are only paying for impressions that generate business for your Web site.

As with any other method of building traffic, you must be careful when undertaking an affiliate marketing plan. But with good planning and some hard work, you can use affiliate marketing to increase awareness of your site, give your customer more of the information and services you want, and even make a little money on the side.

Search Engine Listings

A Web site that nobody sees is useless in promoting and marketing your business. Search engines are the way most users find the information they want on the Internet, so it is key to make sure your site is not only listed on the major search engines, but listed well. Users are more likely to click through to sites that appear as one of the top ten results, but most sites appear poorly on searches, if at all. Knowing how search engines work will help you construct your site and target your marketing efforts to improve the chance you will be found by potential customers.

There is no special trick that will guarantee your site will appear on every applicable search, or even that it will appear in the top ten, but properly listing your site can help potential customers all over the world find your site.

How Search Engines Work

Web search engines operate in two ways. They are either a true search engine or a directory. A directory is compiled by humans and the sites are organized by category. It is more organized than the listings in a search engine, and rather than listing Web pages individually, it only lists Web sites. Yahoo! is a directory rather than a true search engine. Short descriptions of the Web site and its

Affiliate Marketing Scams

Affiliate programs are a great way to promote your Web site, give your customers added value within your site, and even make a few dollars for yourself if done right. As with all things, there are certain affiliate programs that are merely scams where your Web site does the work and you never get the reward. Here are some things to watch out for when looking at affiliate programs.

1. The old adage, If it sounds too good to be true it probably is, is truly advice to live by. Read the fine print and see what is actually being promised. For example, be wary if you're promised a percentage of profits, but have no way to verify what the profits are. Why would you participate in a percentage of zero, or even less than zero?

2. Unfortunately, in the advertising world people often pay late or not at all. Just because it's legitimate does not mean you'll get paid.

3. Finally, beware of strangers. Who is the company? Where are they? Are their phone numbers listed in the yellow pages? Do you really want to do business with someone you cannot sue? That is a significant concern. Out-of-state lawsuits are expensive. There are a number of overseas businesses that target those in the United States and go to great lengths to hide their location.

If you are careful and choose your programs wisely, you run less of a risk of running into one of these scams. If you are not sure about the company or the program, then do not join. There are plenty of affiliate programs out there.

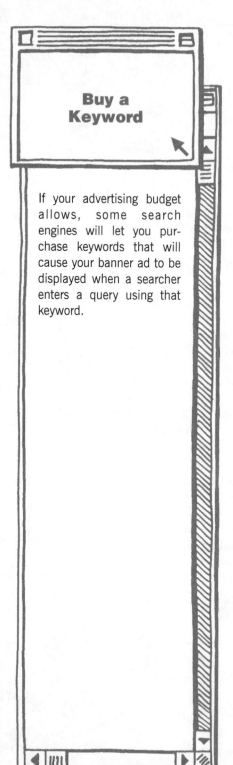

Buy a Keyword

If your advertising budget allows, some search engines will let you purchase keywords that will cause your banner ad to be displayed when a searcher enters a query using that keyword.

contents are written either by the submitter or an editor. A directory-type engine searches only the Web site descriptions, and only the descriptions that are submitted. Sites that did not submit to their directory will never show up.

Actual search engines, like HotBot, create their listings automatically. Using crawlers and spiders, search engines travel the World Wide Web, cataloging titles, body copy, and other into their database. If you change the content of your site, it will eventually affect how you appear on actual engines but not on directories, as they never look at the actual page.

Actual engines have three parts to them: the crawler, the index, and the search software. The crawler (sometimes called a spider) is an automated Web surfing program sent out to Web sites all over the Internet. The crawler reads every Web page, cataloging what it finds, and then follows the links on each site to other pages within the site. The crawler returns on a semi-regular basis, sometimes based on the frequency of your updating, sometimes on a monthly basis, to recatalog what it finds. If anything changes, those changes are cataloged and brought back to the index.

Everything a crawler catalogs then gets put into the index. The index is really just a copy of every Web page that a crawler has visited. Sometimes it can take a matter of days from the time a page has been "crawled" until it has been indexed. Sites that are not indexed will not appear as a search result, so even if you know your site has been crawled, be patient. It may take a few days until it appears as a search result.

Once the site is assimilated into the index, it is available to the search engine software. This software quickly reads all the pages in the database, looking for keywords and meta tags to find matches to a user's search. It then compiles a rank-ordered list of what it believes are the most relevant sites.

All search engines are not alike, and you cannot expect them all to catalog your site the same way. Some engines do not recognize image maps or frames, which means the crawler will not be able to find all the pages of your site. If it cannot find the page, a crawler cannot index it, and often the best and most relevant pages appear inside the site, not on the home page. When you constructed your Web site, hopefully you thought about customers with older browsers or slower computers. If you did, you probably included text links at the bottom of your pages. You can then rest assured that a crawler will index all the pages of your site. If you did not, it is a good idea to add text links. Do not rely on your frames or an image map. Having simple, text-based HTML links at the bottom of your page not only guarantees that a crawler will be able to get inside your site, but that customers whose browsers do not support frames or whose connections are too slow for image mapping can still get to all the information on the page.

Keywords

Each search engine ranks pages on a different scale, which means no site will come up in exactly the same position on two different engines. Search engines look for keywords in the title of a page and in the first few paragraphs of that page. A keyword is simply a word that would likely be used by someone searching for the content your site features. For example, if you sell copiers and fax machines, logical keywords would be "copier" and "fax machine." Selecting good keywords is a lot more subtle than it may seem at first. Even people who know their subject do not necessarily write good keywords because they do not think about all aspects of the topic. A good way to select keywords is to get help in generating them. Ask friends and customers how they would go about looking for your site on an engine or directory. Look at your competitors' Web sites and see what keywords they use. But whatever keywords you ultimately select, make sure you test them. If they do not work, there may be problems with your site that you're not aware of.

When placing keywords on your site, there are a few things to think about. If the keyword appears near the top of the page, most search engines will assume that it has a greater relevance in a particular search than a page where the keyword being searched on appears near the end. Some search engines also check for the number of times the keyword being searched on appears in a particular page. The more times the word appears in the title, headings, and body copy, the more relevant the page is assumed to be.

Search Engine Spamming

Because search engines sometimes rank their indexes on the number of times a keyword appears on the page, some people have begun a process called search engine spamming. Using the comment tags in HTML, they write the same keywords over and over, hundreds of times. This text is never seen by the user, but the spider picks it up. In the past this spamming technique has worked well, but now more and more engines are writing programs that not only allow their spider to ignore the spam, but then go so far as to penalize the site by assigning a negative weight to words that appear excessively.

Remember, search engines do not read text that appears in graphics. You could have a full-page graphic with every keyword known to man in it, but when the site is indexed by the crawler, it overlooks the entire image because it is an image and not text. So while graphical text is nice to look at, it will do nothing to help your chances of appearing in a site engine search.

Each page in your site may have different keywords associated with it. If you are selling golf supplies, you may have a page for woods, irons, putters, golf balls, and even apparel. How would you go about looking for a site that sells woods? Would you type in "woods"? If so, that is a good keyword for that page.

You should try to make your keywords two or more words long. Imagine how many sites will come up if you typed putters into a standard search engine. So many would appear that the odds of your site coming out near the top are astronomical. Instead, target your keywords so that a user doing a more specific search has a better chance of finding you. Quality putters, inexpensive putters, even golf putters has a better chance of coming up on a specific search than just putters. Target your site and your keywords not for the masses but for the specific shopper and you will have a better chance of appearing where they are looking.

Now that you know how search engines work, remember that making these keywords appear in good locations on your pages is important. The title is the most important place to have these keywords. One of the biggest reasons why Web sites are poorly ranked is a failure to utilize the title of the page to reflect keywords. So, for a page about putters, your title could read: "Quality golf putters at the lowest prices." By titling your page like this, not only do you get the benefit of having putters and golf in your title, but keywords like quality and lowest prices also appear. Someone searching on low-priced putters would have a great chance of hitting your page high in their search results.

Search engines also rank sites high when the keywords appear high up on the page. You can accomplish this by putting your keywords in headings and the first paragraph of your body copy. A good headline for the keywords "golf putters" would be "We carry the best quality golf putters at the lowest prices anywhere!" By using that headline, you fit all your best keywords high up on the page where they can be picked up and determined to be relevant by search crawlers and other software.

Keep in mind that graphics and tables can push your text further down the page. Search engines may mark keywords less relevant, even if they are in headline form and appear at the head of a block of body copy. To best optimize your chances of appearing favorably in a search, try to include some text high up on the page, ahead of tables and script information.

Meta Tags

Some experts on search engine submission swear by the use of meta tags. A meta tag is an HTML tag that appears at the top of an HTML document between the title and the head tags. It is used to convey all kinds of information about the document that cannot be seen by users but can be read by search engine crawlers. A meta tag that looks like this:

<META NAME="keywords" CONTENT="car parts, automobiles, classic cars">

would be read by search engines as keywords car parts, automobiles, and classic cars. This information, though, would never be visible to a visitor to your site.

Meta tags are often abused, though, containing hundreds of words or even the same word over and over again (under the assumption that search engines that rank by keyword frequency will think the particular site is very relevant). Most engine crawlers have figured out how to get around the tag, also penalizing sites that operate in this manner. More and more, engines are relying on keywords in the body of the page, and less on meta tags, so while including them in your site is important, you should not do it at the expense of the careful use of keywords.

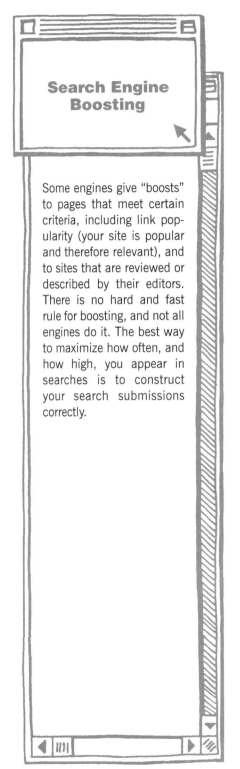

Search Engine Boosting

Some engines give "boosts" to pages that meet certain criteria, including link popularity (your site is popular and therefore relevant), and to sites that are reviewed or described by their editors. There is no hard and fast rule for boosting, and not all engines do it. The best way to maximize how often, and how high, you appear in searches is to construct your search submissions correctly.

Submitting Your Site

How can you get your Web site or pages listed in directories like Yahoo! and Look Smart or on search engines like AltaVista and Lycos? You can wait for engines to eventually find your page, but that's not the best approach. If the site is ready for the public, do not wait. Submit!

How do you submit to the search engines? Each one is slightly different. You should submit all your pages to InfoSeek and HotBot at once, using the information found on their pages. To remaining sites, only submit your key pages, your home page, and maybe two or three others of particular relevance.

There are literally hundreds of search engines on the Web, both large and small. AltaVista, Excite, HotBot, InfoSeek, WebCrawler, Lycos, and Yahoo! are the most important search tools on the Web. Most smaller engines are not really worth worrying about, but if you want to cover all the bases, you can register with each of the major players (use the submission information you can find on their sites). Use a multiple-registration service like Register It! to submit your page elsewhere.

Dos and Don'ts of Search Engine Submission

- Do not put a graphic at the top of a page, especially your home page. Search engines look at what's at the top of a page and they cannot read graphics. Put text at the top (especially your company name, description, and keywords). Move graphics down.
- Do not use your competitor's names, trademarks, or other identifying characteristics to try to trick their customers into going to your Web site.
- Do not use irrelevant words like "money" or "sex" to lure people to your site.
- Do not try to spam a search engine by repeating the same word or words over and over again on your pages. Engines know about this trick and will penalize you for it.
- Do not rely on meta tags. Several search engines ignore them.

Case Study:
Pacific Mailing & Shipping Systems

At Pacific Mailing & Shipping Systems in Seattle, Washington, the Web site has driven major increases in the bottom line. It's also responsible for major decreases in paper and mailing costs.

Malnory originally designed the Web site himself, but today he uses a Webmaster to keep it fresh and updated daily. "You can do a decent job of initial presentation (on the Web) for less than $2,000," he says. His monthly maintenance costs for the Web site run about $300 to $500 per month. "I pay the Webmaster's bill right away," says Malnory. "It's the best money I've ever spent." Malnory says that the business generated by the Web site has directly boosted the company's income by $75,000 to $100,000 per year.

Malnory also calculates that he saves about $2,500 per month on labor, paper, and mailing costs specifically because of the Web site. That's in addition to a savings of $1,000 to $1,500 per month in Yellow Pages advertising.

How has the Web site achieved such success, saved so much money, and generated such profits? It's due to the combination of methods Malnory has incorporated into the site.

First, the basics. "We use the Web site on every piece of literature we have, everything we mail out, and in every one of the numerous phone books we're in," explains Malnory. "We took the physical address out of the phone ads and replaced it with the Web address in boldface. This has saved a ton of money and brought in more business. The tag line on the end of our radio commercials is always a note to visit our Web site, along with the URL."

Another basic step that Malnory has covered is the registration of his site with all the major search engines. He uses an inexpensive (about $39) software tool called WebPromotion to register every single page of his site with multiple search engines at once. Not only does he register every page—and every new promotion—as they are created, but he also has made sure that the Web site includes all the important keywords related to mailing and shipping.

The result? "If you search on Alta Vista under postage meters and mailing machines," says Malnory, "we'll be the first 49 listings. With InfoSeek we are number one and with Excite we are number two. We get 7,000 hits per month from our Web site." That translates into about five or ten leads per day. However, says Malnory, "We do not have time to track the leads. We're too busy making money."

Once a new customer finds the Web site by any of the methods Malnory has used to publicize it, then Pacific Mailing & Shipping Systems either gets a phone call or an e-mail. About 80 percent of those who contact the company use the phone; the rest send an e-mail message. Those new customers routinely comment that either they found the company on the Web or looked it up in the Yellow Pages and then went to the Web site.

By the end of the year, customers will be able to order anything from supplies to high-end mailing equipment from the Web site in a secure environment. There are some exceptions. Malnory obviously will not sell high-end equipment to anyone outside of his region; instead he'll refer those customers to other dealers or to the manufacturer.

Customers are helped in discovering what's new by the extensive use of clickable dynamic banner ads on the front page of the site. They're not ads for other sites; they are ads for the company's own promotions. It's a clever and effective use of a standard Web advertising technique. "The banners get the most response," says Malnory. "To get customers excited, put something on the title page that's unique."

Malnory cites an interactive way the Web page saves him time and makes him money. "Suppose I'm talking on the phone to a customer," he says. "I send the customer to the product page (on the Web site). I can walk the customer through it in real time. Then I can print out a proposal and drop it in the mail." In this way, the customer does not have to wait for a brochure to be mailed—he can look at all the product information at the moment he places a call. And Malnory does not print or mail brochures anymore, he only prints proposals. Even there, some 10 percent of the proposals get e-mailed.

The company also utilizes advanced e-commerce methods to do business directly via the Web. "We have a major company here in Seattle with 400 locations in the country," says Malnory. "They're putting our Web site in their Web domain. So, their employees can order directly through their network to Pacific Mailing & Shipping System's Web site and the order is sent via the Internet."

Pacific Mailing set up online order forms specifically for this large customer. "It's a lot easier for them to order from us now," says Malnory, "and our orders from them have increased by about $5,000 per month."

What advice does Malnory have for business owners who want to make their Web site as successful as his? "Treat it like your only child," he says. "Nurture it every day; make sure it's informed, educate it. Register it with every search engine. Do not just register the domain name—register every page. Look at the meta tags, the HTML, what it says. Keep changing it. Stores change things to create excitement. Every time people visit your Web site, it needs to be new."

- Do make your page informative and helpful for your target audience.
- Do select relevant keywords and use them in your title and text.
- Do test your keywords.
- Do use multiword keyword phrases—they're very helpful to searchers.
- Do use graphics sparingly. Remember, a graphic is effectively invisible to a search engine.
- Do have alternative text links for graphics that both search engines and users with slow modems can read.
- Do offer a non-frames version of your site, if you use frames.
- Do update your site frequently. If you do not, your site gets stale (and you lose repeat traffic), and the search engine will figure out your update frequency and visit accordingly.
- Do try to get directories to review your site. Good reviews can increase rankings. (Several search engines have added directory services.)
- Do get your own domain name. It can improve your rankings.
- Do put your Web site address on all your advertising.

E-Mail Marketing

E-mail may be one of the oldest technologies on the Internet, but e-mail can still be very useful in soliciting new customers, as well as providing information and customer service to existing customers.

If you already have a business you know that direct mail can be one of the most successful ways to advertise. It brings your message directly to a wide range of potential customers and brings that message into their house in ways other media cannot. By targeting your direct mail on factors like age, interest, and spending habits, you can make sure your message reaches people most likely to buy your product or use your service. If you've never used direct mail yourself, you've seen it in use. Coupon packets like SuperCoups are an example of direct mail.

For Web-based businesses, or businesses expanding into e-commerce, there is a form of online direct mail called e-mail marketing. In just the past few years, e-mail use as a primary communication has exploded. Some analysts say that there are now 50 million e-mail users sending 15 billion messages per year! E-mail marketing takes advantage of this explosion, sending a direct-mail message to your customers through e-mail. By letting you send your advertising to thousands of potential customers without the high costs of printing and postage, e-mail marketing is an inexpensive and fast way to advertise your site. Also, like banner advertising, it is easy for customers to get to your site. Unlike more traditional forms of media, they do not need to remember your URL the next time they sit at their computer. The URL is right in front of them, making it easy for the customer to surf over to your site.

E-Mail Marketing Rules

But as with direct mail, there are some drawbacks to e-mail marketing and some rules you must follow in order to succeed.

Nobody likes getting bombarded with information they did not ask for or cannot use. I'm sure you get tons of junk mail at home that you just throw in the trash. Junk mail on the Internet has a name. It's called spam. Some people use the term spam to refer to any unsolicited e-mail, but in fact, spam is e-mail advertisements that people did not request and do not want.

So how can you best target your e-mail list to reach people who want to hear from you? The best method is through opt-in e-mail. Opt-in e-mail simply means people requested, or opted, that they join your mailing list. But remember, if people opt in you have to give them a way to opt out if they no longer want to be a part of your list.

The most rudimentary form of e-mail marketing is a simple e-mail sent to a customer in response to a question or to thank him or her for an order. The key to this kind of simple marketing is speed. After about forty-eight hours, your company name and message is forgotten. If they've sent you an e-mail, answer it quickly. If you do not have a form for it on your Web site already, ask your customer if they would like to receive offers and information by mail. Thank them for taking the time to purchase with you.

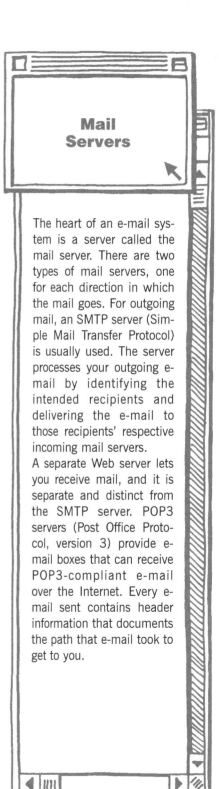

Mail Servers

The heart of an e-mail system is a server called the mail server. There are two types of mail servers, one for each direction in which the mail goes. For outgoing mail, an SMTP server (Simple Mail Transfer Protocol) is usually used. The server processes your outgoing e-mail by identifying the intended recipients and delivering the e-mail to those recipients' respective incoming mail servers.

A separate Web server lets you receive mail, and it is separate and distinct from the SMTP server. POP3 servers (Post Office Protocol, version 3) provide e-mail boxes that can receive POP3-compliant e-mail over the Internet. Every e-mail sent contains header information that documents the path that e-mail took to get to you.

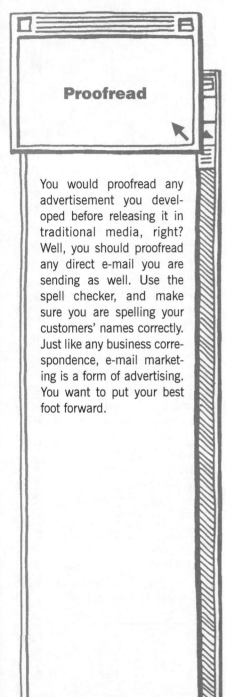

Proofread

You would proofread any advertisement you developed before releasing it in traditional media, right? Well, you should proofread any direct e-mail you are sending as well. Use the spell checker, and make sure you are spelling your customers' names correctly. Just like any business correspondence, e-mail marketing is a form of advertising. You want to put your best foot forward.

Personal touches like this go a long way toward making satisfied customers.

Any time you send a direct e-mail message, whether to a single person or your entire mailing list, remember to write succinctly. Get straight to the point. Remember, your customers are as busy as you are. They want to get whatever information they need and move on. Take some time to double-check your message, or ask someone else to do it for you. Direct e-mail with a lot of useless commentary will cause people to opt out your list, also called unsubscribing. Sending additional mail to people who unsubscribe is like beating your head against a brick wall; it will only alienate them further. So if someone decides to opt out, do not take it personally and let that person go. You never know, this person may come back.

You should periodically clean up your e-mail list. Check that the e-mail addresses are not getting bounced back to you. If so, look for common mistakes such as misspellings or 's in the wrong place. The more organized you are with your list, the better your results will be.

When sending direct e-mail, people often want to use HTML tags in the message. This might allow you to send one of your banner advertisements at the end of your message. Avoid this practice. Not all e-mail programs are HTML compatible, and these customers will receive a mess of useless characters in place of your well-designed message. A good rule of thumb is to always create for the lowest common denominator. Create your e-mail message for the lowest technology e-mail program and you will be guaranteed that everyone will be able to receive it.

Also, be careful about sending attached files. Besides increasing the file size, which can cause many e-mail programs to lag and even crash, virus-conscious customers will just delete the e-mail without reading it. Attached executable files, like documents, are the most common way to transmit computer viruses over the Internet. If your customer suggests something that you feel you must attach, be sure and confirm with them that they have the capability to download an attachment and that the program you used to create the file is compatible with theirs. There are many

versions of Microsoft Word, but not all documents created in Word will open on all versions.

Protect your customers. They are a valuable asset to your business. Take steps to keep their e-mail addresses private. Never sell your list. No matter the financial benefits in the short run, you will lose good repeat customers in the long run when your customers discover how their names got all over the Internet. Your customers are like gold, so treat their information that way. Also, when sending out simple e-mails to your list, never write the address of your recipients in the carbon copy or CC: field. If you do, everyone on your list will see the name of everyone else. While you may not sell the names, that does not stop someone else from doing it. If you put your corporate e-mail in the To: field, and use the BCC: or blind carbon copy field for the list, you can be rest assured that all the names on your list will be kept confidential.

List Rental

As your Web site grows, so will your mail list. There may come a time where sending out your e-mail to an entire list is tedious. There are some services like ListBot that will take care of subscriptions for you. These services manage your e-mail list. You simply generate the message and use their Web-based service to send your message to everyone on your list. Many of these services operate by putting a link on your page that prompts customers to enter their e-mail address to join the mailing list. These services also allow you to collect demographic information, which will be helpful in targeting your Web site even further.

So you've decided to build your own opt-in e-mail list, but you want to do some direct e-mail marketing now while you wait for the list to grow. There are companies that rent e-mail lists. Lists are priced by the thousand names and often are good for only one or two mailings, meaning you have to repurchase the list.

The cost of renting lists is an attractive feature. E-mail lists rent at about 10 to 20 cents per address. But unlike print lists, that price already includes not just the list but the merge/purge (which eliminates duplicate or bad names) and even the e-mail delivery. The cost per thousand runs between $150 and $200 compared to more than $500 for regular direct-mail lists alone.

DEFINITION PLEASE

A **signature file** is automatically inserted at the bottom of every e-mail you send, and it usually contains: Your name, your company name, the address, your e-mail address, and your Web site's URL (with a link to your Web site so a customer can visit again). Keep it short, no more than five lines: This way every message sent by you gives your customer ways to contact you again.

Legal E-Mail

Remember, any e-mail you send is as legal and binding as a document written on paper. It can be used against you in court, and e-mail is not as easily deleted as you might think. Take care when writing to your customers and using e-mail for business correspondence. If you are worried about something coming back to haunt, you should probably check with your lawyer.

There is a tremendous time savings too. Most list rental companies will send out your mailing from their server (to make sure that their lists are only used the number of times they are paid for). An order received by five in the afternoon can often be sent out to an entire list by midnight. The turnaround time is about one day, compared to over a month for traditional direct mail, which needs to be designed, printed, then mailed by traditional means.

The emphasis behind e-mail marketing is *direct* marketing, not mass marketing. The subscribers to e-mail lists do so voluntarily, and the companies that sell the lists use verification procedures to make sure that people really do want to be on a particular list. Most verification procedures require customers to reply to a query e-mail stating that they did in fact sign up for the list. Because list participants are voluntary, they can opt out of the list at any time.

There are some pitfalls to renting lists for your direct message. Not all companies are doing business ethically, and many have huge lists comprised of names of people who did not join voluntarily. Do not risk your good company name on sending this kind of unsolicited e-mail. People do not like spam, and there are channels they can go through to stop you from sending it. It is far better to target your e-mail marketing campaign to customers who want to hear from you than alienate thousands of people who are sick of getting information they consider useless and a nuisance.

But how do you know if a list you rent is a spam list? Lists take time to build. The average 70,000-person list takes more than three years to create. If you are being offered a database or list of 2 million names, ask the company how long it took to create. If the list came from big sites like Yahoo!, or Netscape you can probably rest assured that it is legitimate, but lists obtained from smaller sites without a lot of traffic should be eyed with suspicion.

E-Zines

Once you've generated a nice sized list, you will want to encourage these customers to come back to your site again and again. One great way to keep your company in the front of their minds is to develop an e-zine, or electronic magazine. An e-zine is really just a direct e-mail that is less business correspondence and more fun and informative. Deciding what your e-zine should be about is easy; it should mirror the content on your site. Do you sell classic car parts? Cookbooks? Create an e-zine with that in mind. You can build an e-zine about restoring classic cars, or finding new and exotic recipes. Change the topic every month, but keep it related to your site and your marketing goals.

E-zines are more labor intensive than regular targeted e-mail correspondence. They should read more like a magazine article, and that takes longer to write than a simple business letter. Your publishing frequency will depend on the time you have to devote to it. Monthly is good, but weekly is better. Think carefully about how much time you can afford to put into your e-zine, and then decide on a publication schedule.

Remember, people want your e-zine because of the information it contains. Do not bother going into current events unless they somehow impact your business. Your customers get their news from other sources, from you they want information they can use. Publish information about changes to your site. If you sell lumber, you can post short articles on building a birdhouse or repairing a fence. Think along specific lines when you come up with topics for your e-zine. Keep it interesting and informative. Keep your name where people will remember it.

Once you have your subscription process down and have decided what you are going to write about, give yourself a few weeks to get into a groove. Make sure the publication schedule you have set for yourself is not too grueling. After a while, your customers will expect to see your e-zine in their box. You do not want to disappoint them. If you are sure you have the e-zine under control, there are ways to promote it further, thereby promoting your site as well!

Sites like e-Journal, the Etext Archive, and ListCity all allow you to register your e-zine. By registering you are making the e-zine available to a wider audience, all of whom can then subscribe to

What Makes a Good Press Release

1. **Quality, newsworthy information:** Press releases should be written clearly and concisely, with interesting and newsworthy content. The idea behind the press release is to get someone to do a story on it, let the reporters know why that story is newsworthy.

2. **Accepted standard format:** You can find press release templates all over the Web. Press releases are not the time to get creative. Do not forget to make sure it has the dateline and the correct contact information. Too many ways to contact you are far better than too few.

3. **Include URLs that lead directly to the product information.** You want to make it clear to reporters and readers alike where they can find the product both on your Web site and in person should that be more to their liking.

your list. It is a great, inexpensive way to promote your e-zine, and your Web site.

PR on the Web

Press releases are used primarily to get the mass media like newspapers and TV news interested in your business. There are dozens of things your company does every day that are newsworthy, especially if you participate in a lot of nontraditional advertising opportunities and creative charity sponsorships. New products, promotions in your staff, even the launch of new online features should be written up in a press release.

Also, post your press release on your Web site. It's there to make your company look good. Besides, if a news service wants to do an article about your company or your product, your Web site is one of the first places a news service is going to look. If you do not have a PR page on your Web site, put one up. Make sure it is clear where PR information is located on the site.

This public relations page should have an e-mail link that goes right to your PR contact person, plus provide easy-to-find phone numbers and address information. You can also put a separate opt-in e-mail form on this page, allowing reporters to get on your mailing list for updates from your company.

If you have an opt-in list like this, send your press release out to reporters and PR agencies the same day it's ready to go. Do not wait. The key to press releases is timeliness and newsworthiness. Get it out, and make it interesting.

Once you've got the press release on your site, there are a few online ways to get it out in front of a lot of people very fast. There are companies that specialize in online distribution of press releases to journalists and news sites.

Press Promoter offers targeted lists for about $200 per release. They also have an online program that will help you write the release, or you can pay to have their staff write it for you.

NewsTarget is another service. It is less expensive than Press Promoter, but it only targets technology editors. If your site or product is not related to technology, you will not want to use their

service. Their distribution costs $100 for the first release and $50 for each subsequent release.

Internet Wire is a larger, more professional service that is also more expensive. Their service allows you to distribute your press release to technology editors, national newspapers, and TV. The cost is a lot higher than the smaller services, ranging from $225 to more than $5,000.

There are also PR wire services that distribute and store releases. The three major wire services are Business Wire, PR Newswire, and the Internet News Bureau. Each service offers fax or Internet distribution of press releases, but prices vary widely based on the type of release, its length, and the method of distribution you choose, so investigate them carefully.

Marketing to Newsgroups

There are other ways of marketing your business online without the expense of advertising and printing costs. One of these is through the judicious use of newsgroups. Newsgroups are like giant electronic bulletin boards where people of similar interests post and read messages from others who share the same pursuits.

The worldwide system of organizing these discussion groups on the Internet is called the Usenet. Usenet newsgroups have no rules or central organization, and they tend to come and go almost at random. You can find a Usenet newsgroup for almost anything.

Usenet newsgroups are subject based, that is, categorized by the subject of the discussion. We spoke a little about mailing lists earlier, and newsgroups have some of the same properties as mailing lists. But where you must subscribe to a mailing list, and anything you write to that list is only accessible by those who subscribe, anyone can visit newsgroups and anyone can respond.

Newsgroups are divided into distinct hierarchies. The first part of a newsgroup's name denotes one of nine categories. Those categories are:

ALT: Alt stands for alternative, and the newsgroups in this category are widely varied from alternative lifestyles and sexual topics

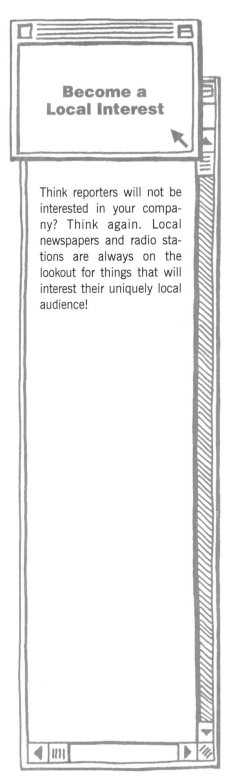

Become a Local Interest

Think reporters will not be interested in your company? Think again. Local newspapers and radio stations are always on the lookout for things that will interest their uniquely local audience!

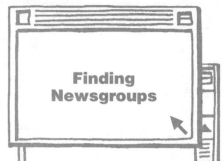

Finding Newsgroups

Searching through all the newsgroups that are available through your Internet service provider can be difficult and time-consuming, but there are ways to find newsgroups that will be of interest to your customers that may allow you to further your online marketing efforts. A Web site called Deja.com (www.deja.com) is an excellent source for finding the groups that will work best for you. Deja News acts just like an Internet search engine, but it searches only newsgroups, not Web sites. The Usenet Information Center (http://metalab.unc.edu/usenet-i/) is a good starting place to find the newsgroup you are looking for.

to more mundane discussions. Anyone can start an ALT group, but new groups in the other categories must be voted on.

REC: Newsgroups that fall under the .rec category deal with recreation. Sports, video games, hiking, and travel will often be found in rec. Even discussions on television and science fiction fall under this category.

SOC: Soc stands for social. Newsgroups in .soc talk about society and culture. Art, music, and even topics on religion will be found in the .soc category.

BIZ: Business newsgroups are found under .biz. Everything from stock tips and advice on day trading to e-commerce and advertising can be found in the .biz groups. Advertisements and promotions are often welcomed here, provided they contain truthful information. Advertisements are usually discouraged in other categories.

SCI: Newsgroups under .sci are related to science. Besides the major scientific genres like biology, chemistry, and zoology, you can find some technology-related items and medical newsgroups.

COMP: Computer-related newsgroups are found here. You can find discussions about hardware, software, and the Internet in this category.

NEWS: The .news category deals with the Usenet itself. It covers administrative topics, and announcements.

TALK: The .talk category is where you will find newsgroups about controversial issues. Abortion, gun control, and politics are popular newsgroups in this category.

MISC: This is for miscellaneous newsgroups that do not fit anywhere else.

You obviously do not want to make posts about your golf supplies Web site to a discussion group on football, so you need to find newsgroups that are of interest to your customers and appropriate to the subject matter. Simply posting a widespread advertisement can get you in a lot of trouble; Usenet users are notorious for being less than friendly with people who post out of topic and advertise where they are not wanted. They have been known to send large quantities of e-mail, and even e-mail bombs, to offenders with the intent of slowing down or crashing their mail program. So choose where and how you post wisely!

In order to read and respond to messages in newsgroups, you need to use a newsgroup reader. Both Netscape Communicator and Microsoft's Outlook Express have built-in news readers. You can use the help feature on both programs to access and subscribe to newsgroups. Both Communicator and Outlook Express also offer search features to help you find relevant newsgroups.

Once you get a list of newsgroups relevant to your company, take some time to read the posts first. Figure out the tolerance level of the people who participate in the group and what the current topics of discussion are. There are a wide range of topics, or threads, in any one newsgroup. After all, a group may simply be called golf, but cover a wide range of golf-related topics, from players and tournaments to strategy, equipment, and even the best courses.

If you are not posting an advertisement on one of the .biz groups (and if you are, it is advisable to spend some time watching what is acceptable there), you should really put up your newsgroup "advertisement" in a form similar to your e-zine. Make the information you post informative; tell the group about a new driver that is available or the newest technology in golf shoes. At the end of your post you can subtly suggest that if they want to see better specs or pricing information, they can go to your Web site. If your post is informative and genuine in its intent to convey information, you might also generate some sales. If your post looks like a thinly veiled advertisement for your site, you might anger a few people and turn off potential customers.

List of Search Engines and Directories:

AOL Search, http://search.aol.com/

AOL Search is primarily driven by members of the America Online service. This engine allows its members to search both the Web and AOL's own content from one place. AOL offers an external version for people using traditional dialup ISPs, but it does not list AOL content.

AltaVista, http://www.altavista.com/

AltaVista is one of the largest, most powerful, and most used search engines on the Web. It is a favorite among researchers for both the in-depth nature of its crawler and the different ways you can search. One of the ways that is most popular is a "real question" format where users can ask questions just as they would a research librarian and receive search-based results. This makes searching easier for people unfamiliar with the traditional Boolean method of conducting searches.

Ask Jeeves, http://www.askjeeves.com/

Ask Jeeves is unique hybrid of the human-powered search directory and a traditional search engine. Using "real question" searching, the site tries to direct you to an exact page within its cataloged database that will answer your question. In addition, it provides between five and ten matching Web pages from various other search engines. This is particularly useful if Ask Jeeves fails to find a match within its own database.

Excite, http://www.excite.com/

Excite is one of the most popular search services on the Web. Like Yahoo, it offers non-search material like sports scores and stock results to its user's personalized page. Excite is a crawler-type search engine that offers a good sized index, though it is not as comprehensive as AltaVista.

FAST Search, http://www.alltheweb.com/

Formerly called All The Web, FAST Search has lofty goals. The intention of FAST Search is to index the entire World Wide Web. It was the first search engine to break the 200 million Web page index milestone. This means it has in its index the text of over 200 million Web pages. When you search on FAST Search, you are searching these pages, making your results a more complete cross-section of what is available on the Web.

☒ HOTBOT
☐ YAHOO
☒ ALTAVISTA
☐ INFOSEEK
☒ LOOK SMART
☐ EXCITE

Go, http://www.go.com/

Go is a portal site originally produced by Infoseek and Disney. Like Yahoo! and MSN, it offers personalization features such as e-mail, weather, stocks, and sports scores, but it also offers the search capabilities of the former Infoseek search service, which has now been fully assimilated into Go. Go offers both search engine capability as well as a nicely sized human-compiled directory of sites.

GoTo, http://www.goto.com/

Different from most engines and directories, you must purchase listings on Go To. Where you appear on a search depends largely on how much you want to pay. The more you pay, the higher you appear on the engine. It is not a widely used vehicle for searching, and the money you spend for a listing here may well be served in your site marketing campaign.

HotBot, http://www.hotbot.com/

HotBot is a standard search engine with a huge index of Web pages. Its search features are above average, and because of that, sites that appear in results are typically more relevant than sites appearing in identical searches on other engines.

LookSmart, http://www.looksmart.com/

LookSmart is a directory-style engine. Its entire directory is compiled by descriptions provided by people. Much like Ask Jeeves, should a search fail to turn up a site from its directory, LookSmart will provide results from other engines like MSN search and Excite.

Lycos, http://www.lycos.com/

When Lycos first hit the Web it was a standard search engine, utilizing a crawler to index sites it used for searching. In 1999 it changed focus and became a directory model like its main competitor, Yahoo!.

Northern Light, http://www.northernlight.com/

Favored among researchers since its inception in 1997, Northern Light has one of the largest indexes of the Web, including a wide

degree of special collection documents that are not available to crawlers and therefore do not appear on other search engines. Searching the special collections is free, but it can cost up to $4 to actually view your results. That can get expensive, but these documents are invaluable for deep research and are worth the fees. Traditional searching of the Web is, of course, free.

Open Directory, http://dmoz.org/

Open Directory uses volunteer editors to catalog the Web. Many other Web sites get some of their search information from the Open Directory databases. Lycos and AOL's search engines rely very heavily on Open Directory data and categories.

Snap, http://www.snap.com/

Snap is a human-compiled directory of Web sites. Backed by CNET and NBC, it too has lofty goals and intends to be the champion of Internet directories.

WebCrawler, http://www.webcrawler.com/

Not the place to go when seeking avant garde or obscure material, WebCrawler has a decidedly small index of any major search engine. This is not always a bad thing, however. Having a small directory means that the results obtained from a search tend to be more targeted and less overwhelming.

Yahoo!, http://www.yahoo.com/

Yahoo! is the most popular search service on the World Wide Web. At this time, it is the largest personally compiled guide to the more than 1 million sites it has in its directory.

Add items to Cart

★★★ Ratings & Reviews

Compare Prices

Find Products

Buy Now!

Address http://chapter_twelve.com Link

Measuring the Success of Your Site:

Customer Retention and Tracking

Adding Value to Your Site

Some great technologies can add value to your site and help entice your customers to return. Brightware is a system that can automatically reply to customer questions. The company claims that with some preparation beforehand, the system can automatically reply to about 80 percent of common sales and service inquiries. The questions Brightware cannot answer automatically get routed to your customer service department.

There are several firms (like Firefly) that offer specialized merchandising technology that cross-sells items to customers based on their purchasing histories. The system looks at the purchasing histories of all your customers to correlate purchasing patterns with interests.

Now that you have designed and implemented a marketing strategy that is right for you, what next? You want to drive new visitors to your site and track just who is visiting your site, but you also want the folks who have visited you to come back. Why? Because repeat customers are the best customers. Once you have developed a rapport with your customer, he or she will rely on you for timely information and excellent service. This person will keep coming back to your Web site as both a visitor and a customer if you give him or her a reason to do so. In this chapter we'll talk about what brings people back, how to keep those precious customers coming to your site on a regular basis, and how to track the customers that visit your site.

Generating Repeat Traffic

The key to repeat traffic is fresh content. Web surfers expect their favorite sites to be updated often; they want to see something new and different every time they come back. If your Web site has the same old content every time they come, they will stop coming. If they stop coming, then they stop buying, and your site is nothing more than a glorified billboard. If possible, put something new and different on your site at least monthly.

In other markets it is not easy to come up with new content. A special feature updated monthly or weekly is a good way to keep people coming back. If you sell furniture on your Web site, a weekly design article or tip is something that people will return for. If they keep coming back, they will eventually buy.

Here are some ideas for monthly specials you can run to generate repeat traffic. Keep your content appropriate, though. Having a monthly special for the sake of it will not bring people back to your site.

- Special tip of the month (great for all kinds of sites)
- Special offer of the month
- This month in history (great if you can get a timeline in your industry)
- Project of the month

Running a contest or even a simulated game is always a good way to keep people interested. Weekly site-specific trivia games with a small prize will keep your customers coming back to your site. Contests are great, too. "Find a star on this Web page," "win a discount," or elaborate game show with prizes are fun ways to generate excitement. Whatever you choose, maintain a set schedule for new games and posting the winners from the old game. People will come back to play the new game if they're a winner.

Everyone loves a sale or a discount, and these are surefire ways to get people back to your site. Offer coupons on your page for members, or send a free offer with a customer's order. Customers will come back to your site to see what the new offers are. Giving free offers with orders builds good relationships and keeps customers buying from you, not your competition.

Some markets are perfect for adding chat capabilities to your site. People like to talk and they love to chat online. Nearly every business has some aspect that people will want to talk about. Adding a chat room to your site is not a difficult process, and the chat room alone will draw new visitors.

If you decide to put a chat system on your site, special moderated discussions will generate new visitors and keep your old customers returning for more. Moderated discussions help people get more information on specific topics. Find industry experts and sponsor a moderated discussion on your site. The moderator manages the discussion, fielding questions and typing the answers for the guest expert. Anyone can moderate a chat, and anything from new techniques in construction to doing business online can be the subject of a chat. Make it site specific, and promote it in your e-zine and through your direct e-mail efforts. If you have a specific schedule for moderated chats, your customers are sure to come back often and may even participate.

Another key driving repeat traffic to your site is through personalization. If you allow your customers to select the content that best suits them, you add value to your site. People stop coming just for your business and start coming for the information you provide.

Do not forget to use update notices in your direct e-mail campaigns. Let your opt-in customers know via e-mail every time your

Billboard Theory

If there is one mistake that businesses make more than any other it is treating their Web site like a billboard. They create it, launch it, and leave it alone, never to be updated again except in cases of new products or new pricing. This kind of static approach to your site will guarantee that people who visit your site once will never become the kind of long-lasting customers that are the foundation of good business.

site changes. The simple act of sending out a message is a good reminder to visit your site.

Customer Service

Customer service cannot and should not be ignored. Customers have more options than ever for finding information and purchasing products. Yes, they want low prices and they want the products fast. But what separates you from your competition is not going to be the lowest prices or the best selection. It is going to be how you treat your customers. Your competitive advantage is your ability to keep the customers you have.

Good customer service sounds simple. Provide what you promise, when you say you will, how you say you will, and throw in something extra to thank the customer for doing business with you. But in practice, too many companies do not follow these simple guidelines. A breakdown on any one of those promises will not only lose you a customer, but in this fast-paced communication world, may also lose you five or ten other customers as well.

Good customer service is even harder to provide in the world of e-commerce. There are very few chances for real interaction with your customers, and the people who shop online can be more capricious because of the anonymity of the Internet.

Customer service online strongly affects the perception of how you do business. Since you are rarely interacting directly with your customers, the key to getting off on the right foot is to show that you care about your customers. Do everything you can to make the shopping experience more personal for your customers. Putting pictures and biographies of your sales staff online reminds your customers that they are dealing with real people, too.

Give the customer as much information as you can on your site that lets them help themselves.

This concept of making your information available to your customers is known as customer self-help. If you answer questions with good, clear, comprehensive content, customers will be satisfied with your company because you have fully explained your promises.

Make sure your customers are able to contact you. In most cases, the only real contact you will have with your customers is

When to Update

Some markets, like music, lend themselves to more frequent updating as new artists come and old ones fall down the charts. If your market dictates more frequent updates to your site, then do it. You know your competition will.

when something has gone wrong. While you may have gotten the customer the product at the right price, if it is a day later than you promised, that constitutes something going wrong to the customer. When something goes wrong, a customer wants to deal with it NOW. If they cannot find your e-mail address or phone number, they are not going to place an order with you again.

E-mail links and corporate information should be prominently displayed on their own page at the least, but it is recommended they are put at the bottom of every page. It does not have to be anything fancy, just a telephone number and contact name. Do not make it difficult for your customers to find you. You would not do business with a vendor who provides poor contact information; do not force your customers to make that same decision.

When you get an e-mail from a customer, make sure to send some kind of response quickly. A good rule of thumb is to answer all e-mails within twenty-four hours on business days and within forty-eight hours on weekends. Even if you send out a form letter to let the customer know you received his or her message and thank the customer for taking the time to write, immediate response is important to e-mail communication. People like to know that their problems are being handled in a timely manner and that if they sent good feedback it was received. Answering e-mails quickly and in a way that makes someone feel like a valued customer is one key to good customer service and high repeat traffic.

Be careful who you put in charge of e-mail customer service. Your first instinct may be to have your resident tech expert field customer e-mails. This really is not wise. Remember that at the other end of that customer e-mail is a real person. You want someone who has the sales skills to make that person a customer or, if the e-mail is from an existing customer, to make that person a satisfied customer. The best people to do this are salespeople, marketing professionals, and those with specific training in customer service. This is not to say that your technology expert or IS manager will not do a good job in handling customer feedback sent by e-mail, but you will probably be better

Who Wants to Visit a Web Site?

When the ABC network launched its new game show "Who Wants to be a Millionaire?" it also made the game available on its Web site. While we do not know exactly how much traffic it generated, we do know how many people in our office played! The game show was incredibly popular, garnering record ratings, and that popularity translated to the Web site as well.

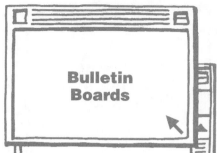

Bulletin Boards

If you are not ready to build a chat room on your Web site, then think about putting up a bulletin board. Bulletin boards are like chats but are not live or in real time. Customers and visitors can ask or answer questions from other visitors. In some markets, bulletin boards are very popular. Think of how many people have plumbing questions. If you sell plumbing supplies, putting up a bulletin board for plumbing and home improvement issues is a great way to keep people informed, and keep them coming back to your site.

If you decide to put up a bulletin board, make sure you keep close track of it. Not having a question answered is definitely a reason for a customer not to come back. If a customer's question is answered by another visitor, great! If not, or if that information is wrong, you need to make sure the customer has the right information in a timely fashion.

served in the long run by looking at e-mail feedback as a valuable opportunity to promote good customer service. Make the most of it!

The Need for Facts

Now that you have spent large amounts of time and money getting your business Web site running and functional, getting and retaining customers, how do you best measure its effectiveness? How do you know if your customers are utilizing all the features of your site?

You can measure your site's effectiveness by the number of sales it generates and the profit on those sales, but what if you've only developed an online business card, brochure, or presentation? What if the decision to put ordering capabilities on your site is dependent upon how well a more basic site is received?

All too often people forget about user tracking when designing a Web site. But once it is up and running, the need quickly arises for facts. How many people are visiting your site and how many pages are they actually looking at? If you do not know what your visitors like, how can you possibly know what to change and what to keep when the time comes to add fresh content to your Web site?

There are certain things to be aware of when the time comes to start measuring your site usage statistics. You can have the greatest analysis software on the market and hundreds of analysts to pore over every detail, but there are some things you can measure and some things you cannot.

Using Log Files and Page Views

The Web server records certain information about every user request it gets, and every page it downloads. This information goes into something called a log file. The information contained in the log file includes the date and time of the request, the name of the host that made the request, the page requested, the visitor login name (if your site requires a login), the site that referred the visitor to yours, that site's IP address, any cookie information from the visitor's computer, and any information your Web server sent out in a cookie. While this information is often inaccurate (and we'll explain why in a moment), it is not useless. You need to evaluate the data with an eye toward understanding how people use your site.

A good way to look at how often people have visited your Web site is through page views. A page view counts every page as its own entity, not as several different parts. So, every time someone looks at a page, it counts once, not once for each component file it contains. Some Web site statistic programs will calculate page views for you, some will not. If you do not have statistic software or have software that does not calculate page views, you can determine them based on hits counting only HTML files, not .gif, .wav files, or other files. You should also subtract the number of requests that failed (since a hit is counted for each *request*, not each completed request). Doing this will give you an accurate number of page views for your site.

It is a good idea to determine the number of page views each page of your site has received. Again, most commercially available site statistics packages will calculate this for you.

Many site statistics packages will allow you to graph your page views several different ways. Each way gives you a new insight into your visitors and what they are doing during the time they are at your Web site. One way to look at page views is over time. This feature allows you to determine when people are accessing your site. Are they looking at it during prime business hours? Late in the evening? Early in the morning? By having a good grasp on your customers and their habits you can look at this data in a new light, giving it more relevance to you. Do you sell business-to-business products? Are your customers searching you out during the course of their business day? At night?

One of the best ways to help you target your promotional efforts is by looking at page views based on the referring site. If a visitor clicks on a link or a banner to get to your site, your Web server will record the URL of the site he or she just left. This feature will tell you what site your customer was on immediately before he or she clicked to yours. By looking at these statistics you can measure the effectiveness of advertising methods like LinkExchange and banner advertising and get a good insight into

Web Site Stickiness

People use the term "stickiness" to describe not only repeat traffic, but keeping people on your Web site. While links to bulletin boards and chat rooms will enhance your repeat traffic, what keeps people interested in your Web site is their interest in your content. If you sell cooking supplies, sports scores may be interesting but not what your customers came for; If you offer personalization features that do not mirror your content, you are manufacturing reasons for your customers to visit. You are manufacturing stickiness.

The big portal sites like Yahoo!, Excite, and others utilize this kind of manufactured stickiness. You can get anything from free e-mail to your local weather forecast on their Web site. But more and more, this "all things to all people" mentality is starting to turn off visitors. People like sites where they get the information they want, the content that matters to them. Keep your personalization features in line with the content you offer on your Web site, and people will be happy to come back.

Customer Dissatisfaction Increasing

Two new surveys from Jupiter Communications and Socratic Technologies report that Web sites are doing a poorer job of answering customer e-mail in 1999 than they were in 1998. Of 836 shoppers studied in the Socratic Technologies report between October 6, 1999, and October 13, 1999, half of them left one Web site for a competitor's after a bad customer service experience. These experiences ranged from incorrect e-mail replies to a lack of customer support resolution.

the minds of your customers. Knowing the other sites your customers visit will help you determine their likes and dislikes, what interests them and what does not. Knowing this information will help you target your advertising campaigns and determine which sites you may want to partner with.

There are some problems with measuring your site solely based on page views. For one, the number of page views recorded in your Web server log is never going to reflect the true number of page views of your site. There are a lot of reasons for this, but the biggest is that a lot of requests made by browsers never actually reach your Web server.

Most browsers have caches that store the entire contents of the page for a limited amount of time. If a visitor requests a page from your site and then clicks the back button or comes back to the page later, the browser may not request the page from the Web server but bring it up out of the cached memory. You would never know that a visitor came back to your site, and the Web server will never register the page view. Even in cases where browsers are set not to cached pages, or you have designed your site with tags that prevent it from being cached, many Internet service providers use proxy servers, and proxy servers often cache pages just like browsers. If the ISP uses a proxy server, when the visitor's browser makes a request, the proxy server first checks its cache. If the page is there, either from this visitor's or from another user's session, it sends that page to the browser instead of making the request to your Web server. Caches are used to speed up the downloading of pages for the user, but if caches are being used, the page view will never be registered by your Web server.

Tracking Visitors to Your Site

Many people do not want to only look at page views but at the number of distinct visitors that may visit your Web site. After all, a visitor may look at several pages, and do so several times. But this must be said first off: there is absolutely no way to reliably count the number of visitors to your Web site. You can make a good attempt at determining the number of visitors to your site, but be forewarned, it will never be completely accurate.

There are three ways for you to definitively track visitors on your site: through their IP addresses, through cookies, or through member names.

IP Addresses

In a perfect world, you could use the IP address of your visitors to track their progress on your site. Every computer connected to the Internet must have a unique IP address. So you should be able to simply go into your Web server's log file and count the number of distinct IP addresses to come up with the number of visitors to your site, right? Wrong!

Although every computer connected to the Internet must have a distinct IP address, distinct does not mean static. While on the Internet, no two computers can have the same IP address, but that does not mean that the same computer always has the same IP address every time it logs on to the Internet.

This dynamic address assignment is a major stumbling block to using IP addresses to determine the number of visitors you've had. It is impossible to look at a log file for the week and gauge the number of visitors because if a customer visited you seven times, they would probably appear as seven different IP addresses. You can, however, look at IP addresses for a single day. Some customers may log off the Internet and visit you again later that afternoon, but most people will only visit you once a day. Counting the number of distinct IP addresses on a particular day would be the most accurate method of using IPs to determine your total number of visitors.

Cookies

Cookies are another way to help you determine the total number of visitors that have come to your site. If you create a cookie that has a unique value for each visitor, then you can count the number of unique identification numbers that have visited your site in a particular day, week, or month.

But this method is not infallible either. Many users turn off cookies in their browser, meaning their system will not accept them

Customer Appreciation

Do not underestimate how far a simple thank-you will go! Customers like to know that you know they have several alternatives to your company. Make sure you thank them often for sticking with you.

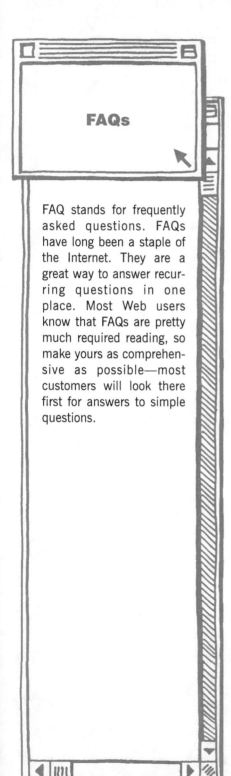

FAQs

FAQ stands for frequently asked questions. FAQs have long been a staple of the Internet. They are a great way to answer recurring questions in one place. Most Web users know that FAQs are pretty much required reading, so make yours as comprehensive as possible—most customers will look there first for answers to simple questions.

from your Web server. Also, some browsers delete old cookies. Old cookies can be user defined as weeks, months, or even hours old. Proxy servers create problems with cookies the same way they do with caching pages, and if more than one person uses a computer, it will only register as one visitor because cookies can only count machines that have requested information from your Web server, not individual people.

Membership

The third way to try and count visitors to your Web site is through membership. By asking your customers to log in when they visit your site, tracking how often they do so becomes much easier. You eliminate the problems of multiple users on the same computer by requiring a member login, as each user will log in with a unique user identification and password.

There is one major drawback to requiring a log-in procedure on your Web site. A lot of people feel that logging in is intrusive or annoying, and will not visit your site if you make logging in a requirement. Obviously you do not want to alienate your customers in this way. You can make logging in a more palatable experience by offering personalization options on your site and even offer financial incentives to logging in like added discounts or reduced-price shipping. But that will not make every potential customer happy, and you run the risk of losing customers if you force them to log in.

By combining all three of these options together and doing a little number crunching, you can come up with a good approximate number of visitors to your site.

Analyzing Site Visits

There are other things to look at when analyzing the effectiveness of your Web site. Some analysts prefer what is called the site visit. A visit is defined as a customer's stay at your Web site before going on to another site. Most Web site analysis software will calculate the average user visit, but as with all Web statistics, this is impossible to calculate with any real certainty.

The first reason for the fallibility of the visit is that customers can walk away from their computer. A customer can spend five minutes looking at your home page, then get up and go make a sandwich before coming back and clicking on a new page. This will make your customer's visit appear longer than it actually was. Even if they do not get up from the computer, they can be doing other things on their computer. There is absolutely no way to be sure that a customer is actually reading the pages on your Web site the entire time they are on the Web site.

Even trying to get a good handle on the URLs that refer customers to your site can be difficult. Because different browsers handle referral information differently, it is very difficult to know precisely what Web site sent you that customer. Frame-based navigation is the biggest culprit of false referral readings. When a customer clicks on a link contained in a frame, each browser handles the request differently. Some browsers will report that the main page URL was the referrer, others will report that the URL of the individual frame was the referrer, making accurate information cumbersome to decipher.

But, there is hope. Just because the statistics will never be 100 percent accurate does not mean you cannot use them. Through careful analysis of the reports your software develops, you can get a good average of how many people are actually visiting your site and what they are looking at while they're there.

Customer Feedback

Sometimes tracking your Web site statistics is just not enough. Web statistics reports will never tell you how much someone liked your site. It will never tell you what a customer thought of your interface design or order processing. For this kind of research, you have to rely on customer feedback or a survey of some kind.

E-Mail Feedback

Customer feedback most often comes in the form of an e-mail, sent by a customer to you, most often at the customer's

Answering Customer Service Questions

By phone: Clearly explain on your site what information they can get by phone. Consider the costs to your customer. Is an 800 number justified or will most of your customers bear the cost of a long-distance call?

E-mail: Do not rely on autoresponders. Use them only to let your customers know someone real will be addressing their question.

Regular mail or faxes: Quick turnaround is expected for regular US Postal Service mail, just as it is for e-mail. Do not make the mistake of letting questions and concerns that come in the old-fashioned way fall by the wayside. Take the time to answer the mail or staff someone to handle it if you receive a lot.

Why Use Page Views?

Looking at page views reveals how deep into the site your customers ventured and which pages are the most popular. Are they going straight to the page on new ways to build a doghouse? Or are they interested in the page where you sell the materials for that doghouse? Keeping track of which pages your customers enjoy will help you to make decisions regarding updating and changing the content of your site.

own initiative. These are customers who had such a strong feeling about your site that they sought out a way to contact you.

You can get better results from e-mail feedback by making it easy for your customers to tell you what they think. Putting a feedback link on every page makes it apparent to your customer that you value their opinions, and makes it easier for them to send you their thoughts.

While e-mail feedback is good, it lacks certain important aspects that make it particularly useful for measuring the popularity and success of your Web site. For one, you do not really get any information on who your customer is beyond a name. Are they male or female? What browser are they using? Do they buy other products like yours? Information like this gives you the context of the comments they are making. If you know that the customer is using an old browser, then a comment about not being able to view your catalog makes more sense. In order to get contextual information about your customers, you need to develop a form of some type.

Electronic forms are just like the paper kind. They ask specific questions for your customer to answer. What kinds of questions you ask really depends on the business you are in, but some basic things like age, hobbies and interests, computer hardware and software platforms, and even their profession can all give you information about your customers and what they are looking for. You always want to include a section for free-response comments. After all, it was a response comment that spurred your customer to contact you in the first place.

You may want to think about making all the questions except for name and return e-mail address optional. Some people do not like to divulge personal information, whether for fear of Internet security or any one of a number of other reasons. If you ask for too much and make it mandatory, some people will get turned off by the whole process and just click to somewhere else. Make sending feedback as easy as possible for your customers and they will respond with information you can use to help your business and your business Web site grow.

Electronic Surveying

But even an e-mail feedback link on every page and the best forms in the world will not always generate feedback from customers. Sometimes you need to go directly to them and ask what they thought. A good way to do this is through electronic surveying.

Rather than have a telemarketer call someone's home, electronic surveys randomly pick a certain percentage of visitors to your Web site and ask them if they would like to participate in a survey. Surveys should always be optional. Forcing someone to click through a multiple question survey only irritates people, and irritated people will never become good customers.

If the randomly selected visitor says yes, then the survey asks a series of predetermined questions such as where the visitor heard about your Web site, what his or her hobbies are, and what this person's Internet spending habits are. In a survey you can even ask for demographic information that you may not want to request via an e-mail form because people have opted to take part in a survey knowing they may be asked these types of questions. Any Web development firm can help you create the program that selects and queries your visitors for this valuable research.

Traditional Means of Contact

Do not just rely on electronic means for feedback. Some customers like to talk to a real person or feel that sending a good old-fashioned letter is more appropriate than an e-mail. Do not make it hard for them to do so. Make sure your corporate address, phone number, and other contact information is in easy-to-find places. Information like this can commonly be found on the very bottom of a Web page, and it's a good idea to stick with that trend as that is where people will first look. If possible, put your contact information at the bottom of every page. If that is impossible, then at least make sure that your traditional means of contact appear along with your electronic means. Give your customer every opportunity to tell you what they think, and they often will.

Garbage In, Garbage Out

There is an old axiom which states that the quality of data going in to a program determines the quality of the data that comes out. This is called the garbage in/garbage out theory and, unfortunately, applies very well to Web statistics. There is not a whole lot of data you can collect, and what you can is notoriously unreliable. Unreliable data going into an analysis means that the results you get are going to be just as bad. But should you just give up and not worry about how your site is used? Absolutely not. There is valuable information that can be obtained directly or inferred through analysis of Web site usage statistics.

True or False:

1. Once you build your Web site, you never need to look at it again. *True   False*

2. A special offer will help you drive repeat traffic. *True   False*

3. Any kind of personalization is good personalization. *True   False*

4. Customers are more satisfied with e-commerce in 1999 than they were in 1998. *True   False*

5. FAQ stands for Frequently Asked Questions. *True   False*

6. Customers expect that their e-mail queries will be responded to slowly. *True   False*

7. E-mail links should appear on every page. *True   False*

8. Moderated chats do nothing to help drive repeat traffic. *True   False*

9. Web site statistics programs can track every movement a user makes. *True   False*

10. Cookies are the only way to track a user's actions. *True   False*

11. Page views are the best measure of traffic on your Web site. *True   False*

Answers:
1. F. 2. T. 3. F. 4. T. 5. T. 6. F. 7. T. 8. F. 9. F. 10. F. 11. T

Managing for Success

Now you have a Web site for your business. It is online and generating both leads and sales for you. It is making your business easier, saving you time and money. Your marketing efforts are bringing new traffic to your site, and the customers who have visited have not only stayed to buy but have returned at a good rate.

Your online business is doing all this because you took the time to think and to plan when you developed it. You gave a lot of thought to what kind of Web site your business needed. You worked closely with your developer and hosting company to make sure you were building a good, functional site that would meet the requirements of your customers. You worked hard to implement a total Web solution for your business, and now it is proving successful.

You're not done yet.

One of the biggest mistakes people make is creating their Web site, launching it, and then never looking at it again. We already talked about the importance of updated content—giving your customers something new and different every time they come back—but there is more to good Web site management than just keeping your content new and exciting.

Managing for the Future

Your goals and success factors should, and will, change with time. Your online business is an evolutionary process and should grow as your business grows. If you ignore your site and its possibilities, you will miss out on a major opportunity to grow your business in the future. In the long run, you will probably also waste the money you spent on the initial investment.

In the following case study you will see how the band the Crusi-Fries initially built their Web site just as a way to generate awareness of who they were and when they played. Soon after they recognized how their Web site could do so much more for them and allowed it to evolve.

You can see from the case study that the Crusi-Fries had left their minds open when it came to what their Web site could do for them. Working closely with their development firm and lead developer they took advantage of new opportunities to expand their site

Crusi-Fries Case Study:

Crusi-Fries, a band local to the New York/New Jersey metropolitan area, was faced with the difficult task of how to attract more fans to their local shows, as well as to increase revenue obtained from merchandising like T-shirts, bumper stickers, and compact discs. They approached Bryan Phil of Manna Inc., a local Web developer and musician himself, for help.

"The first and most important issue with Crusi-Fries was getting the band's name out where it could be seen," Phil said. The band's main concern was getting more fans to their concerts and increasing their visibility. With little startup capital to deal with, Phil created a simple online presence consisting of not much more than an online business card.

"Our first hurdle was coming up with a domain name that would become a part of the band's brand image," Phil said. Luckily, the band had a unique name so the domain was easy to register. Crusi-Fries.com was born.

When Phil sat down with the band, they found that thinking from their customers' point of view was not difficult to do. The fans are mostly 18 to 35-year-old males, and lovers of independent music and musicians. Once the domain name was registered, building a small site to inform the public of show times and locations and other band news was easy.

Once the site went live, Phil and his marketing team backed up the launch with an intense mass media campaign. They put the URL for the band on every single flyer, bumper sticker, advertisement, and piece of literature the band had. The URL was even read off as a part of their radio advertisements. Their online campaign was just as intense. Phil submitted Crusi-Fries.com to every search engine he could find and contacted the Webmasters for local clubs and entertainment billboards to put small clickable banners on their sites.

Within weeks, the band was receiving a good number of page views that resulted in increased attendance at shows. Phil was pleased with the Web site's initial reception. "The increased attendance was really the first goal Crusi-Fries had for the site. We went live with the intention of boosting attendance at their shows and getting more show offers, and the Web site far exceeded expectations."

Once people started going to the site, it was clear they needed to do more than change the tour information to keep people coming back. Phil and his team suggested that the band take the site to the next level and start putting sound clips from some of their music on the site. The band was enthusiastic about the idea and Phil started to offer both MP3 and RealAudio files for download from the band's Web site. As a part of the next level of the marketing campaign, he went to music sites like RollingStone.com and submitted MP3 files on the band's behalf.

"MP3s are the new wave in music online. We figured that one of the best ways to grow awareness for the band was to treat them not like a local group, but like a big, national band. We submitted their clips to some of the biggest names in the MP3 business." When Phil and his team started submitting the clips to these large music sites, they were surprised to find how quickly visitors flocked to the band's Web site.

"We added an opt-in mailing list option," Phil said of the band's list. "The band thought it would be a good idea to be able to reach the fans directly." The list is generated off a simple form and managed by Phil's company. Information about the band is released to the list on a regular basis, including tour dates, information on the band members, and how they can get clips of new songs.

As people headed to the site, Phil and the band decided to expand, including a weekly diary of the band's tour written by the lead singer. People seemed to like hearing directly from the band and, to the surprise of the members, started to inquire about purchasing CDs and other band merchandise online.

The Crusi-Fries Web site is not for everyone. They truly have created their site for their audience, using language and graphics far more appropriate to the demographics of hardcore music lovers between the ages of 18 and 35 than any other demographic group. But that is the true key to building a Web site that will ultimately be successful. Like the band, you have to think of your customer; what they like and what they do not.

"Initially, the band was not sure how merchandise would go over, so before investing in a fully interactive e-commerce site, they opted for an e-mail to regular mail format," Phil said. In this method, customers fill out an e-mail detailing what products they would like to buy and then send a check via regular mail to the address on the Web site. Once the check is received, the merchandise is sent out.

to give their fans what they wanted. Those fans have now become customers, buying products and CDs online!

Once you have designed and developed your Web site you must be serious about *running* the site. The Web site is no more or less important than any other method you use to generate leads or sales, and you must commit the resources necessary to making it grow and expand to suit your business.

Success!

A survey conducted in the 1980s asked several heads of Fortune 500 companies if they felt successful. Less than a quarter of them actually said that they felt personally successful. The surveyors dove a little further and found that those who did say they felt successful had kept track of their goals, both short- and long-term goals. The executives who did not never felt like they had achieved any kind of real success! You must treat your Web site the same way those successful feeling executives did. If you do not have goals that you review and adjust as your Web site grows, you will never get a feeling that the site is successful.

Success should never be a static thing. The goals you develop for your Web site now should not be the same goals you have for the site in a month, in six months, or even in six years. Your goals should be reviewed and revamped as the Web site, your business, and the Internet grows. Amazon.com did not become the huge success it is by standing still. When they first hit the Web, they only sold books. Through time they have expanded into other commodity-based products like CDs. During the 1999 Christmas season, Amazon expanded again, introducing toys to their e-commerce site. Their Web site is constantly undergoing changes to accommodate new and revised goals and strategies. Your Web site should as well.

One of the ways you can help your Web site grow with your business is to evaluate constantly how your customers use the site. Do you have a customer who places large orders on your site? If so, how can you better accommodate this customer?

Some businesses have built customer-only areas on their Web site to handle special customers. Special customers can be anything from large corporate clients to the people whose purchasing habits meet a certain criteria. These areas are secured, requiring a password and user name to get in, but have special content that appeals to those customers. Customers can view previous orders and their payment history and place large scale, customized orders not possible through a form.

Think of Your Employees

Do not just think about your customers when looking to manage your Web site for the future. Think of how you can utilize your Web site for the benefit of your employees.

One company that has done an excellent job using the Web in this intranet (internal network) capacity is the Great Harvest Bread Company. Microsoft featured this franchised business in a recent advertising campaign because of the innovative ways they use the Net.

Great Harvest Bread Company is a network of individually franchised stores that sell whole wheat bread. Many customers are surprised to find out that the Great Harvest Bread stores are franchised because of the homey, mom-and-pop feeling they get when they come in. The franchise is based on a very unique principal. Rather than forcing stores to conform to a specific ideal, using the same ingredients in the same formulas, Great Harvest believes in basing their franchise on information and the sharing of knowledge.

Great Harvest has set up a secure Web site where franchise owners can share information. Through this information sharing, franchisees who are particularly good at marketing can help out those who are not. Franchisees who have a new method for scheduling or a new recipe are encouraged to share their knowledge and expertise with other owners. The technology of the Internet allows the franchise owners to tackle problems quickly and efficiently, making Great Harvest almost a new class of franchise and certainly one that will be copied in the future.

But how does this translate to your business? When the Great Harvest Bread Company began as a franchise, they did not immediately come up with this concept of information-sharing through the

Online Business Goals

- For a Web-only business, generate a profit in your third quarter of doing business.

- For an integrated Web/ real world business, generate 10% of revenue online.

- Reduce your customer service costs by 15%.

- Develop secure, real-time online ordering.

- Double your Web site traffic every three months.

Web. Instead, they allowed their Web site to grow and take on a form that would help the business as a whole. They were committed to making the Web site work for them and the franchise owners, and because of that commitment the Web site grew as the company did.

Once your site is in place, take a few months and evaluate where the site stands in comparison to your original objectives and goals. Have you met them? Exceeded them? Where have you fallen short of your objectives? Once you have a list of goals and how your site is doing, start thinking about what you can change. How do you change your site to meet the goals you have not met, and what new goals can you see in the future? It may be time to start using your Web site to cut down on printing costs or postage. Are your customers using the Web for e-mail and other correspondence?

There are just as many things to think about when re-evaluating your Web site as there are when you first build one. Your Web site is not a billboard and should not be treated as one. That is even more true in looking toward the future than it is in keeping customers happy. Business rules are ever changing, and with the high-tech, fast-response world of the Web, even the rules we take for granted now can change. Who knows what the Web will evolve into in the next five years. Make sure you and your business are ready to take advantage of everything it has to offer.

Top Five Mistakes of Web Management

1. *Not understanding why.* If you do not know why you built your Web site in the first place, you have no hope of ever managing it effectively. You need to know what you want the site to achieve. Have specific goals and review them often.

2. *Designing for yourself, not for your customer.* Your company and its organization is not what your customers come to your site for. Sure, they are going to want information on your company, and that's great for your About Us page. But it is your products that are going to get your customers to buy. Put the focus on your products and your customers' needs and save the self-promotion for the parts of the site where it's expected.

3. *Forgetting to budget for maintenance.* It costs money to maintain a Web site. How much varies, but it can be as much as half your original expenditure per year to keep the content fresh, add and change your products, and keep up with market trends. If you offer personalization that depend on daily updates, it can cost even more. Make sure you budget for redesigns, updates, and increased traffic in the coming months.

4. *Too much outsourcing.* One of the keys to good Web site design is consistency. When everything looks and functions the same, visitors and customers get a consistent, comfortable feeling from the site. If you give every new project to a new company, your site will never have a consistent feel. Pick your development firm well; you want to be able to give them all your projects and know that they'll be able to handle them.

5. *Treating the Web as you would your other marketing efforts.* The Web is different from all your other marketing efforts. It is not television. It is not print media. It is an entirely different medium, therefore, you cannot get good Web content out of recycling other things. Content for Web sites should be developed specifically for Web sites.

Measuring Your Goals

Your goals should fall into one of two categories: strategic or numeric. Numeric goals are easy to measure. These can be anything from an increase in sales to the numbers of new customers in a certain period of time. Your strategic goals are harder to quantify. These should be more subjective, with the strategic goals focusing on how you do your business. An example of a strategic goal would be having your salesmen do more of their business online, or the streamlining of your buying cycle. Both types of goals should be evaluated frequently and changed as your business and your Web site grow and evolve.

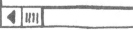

Add items to Cart

 Ratings & Reviews

 Compare Prices

 Find Products

 Buy Now!

Address http://appendix.com **Link**

Top Web Addresses You Need to Know

Not all of these Web sites sell things, but they are excellent examples of some high-end technologies and types of businesses on the Web. They illustrate all the principles we spoke of in the book, and some we did not. When the time comes to decide what features you would like to see in your site, visit some of these Web sites and see what they use and how they use it.

We've categorized them by subject.

Antiques and Collectibles
Art Louvre

http://mistral.culture.fr/louvre

View paintings, sculpture, and other masterpieces from the famous Paris museum.

Learn About Antiques and Collectibles

http://willow.internet-connections.net/web/antiques

Advice on how to pick and deal with antiques dealers plus information on a broad range of collectibles, from china, furniture, and quilts to dolls, can be found at this site.

National Gallery of Art

www.nga.gov

View 100,000 paintings and sculptures from the Washington, D.C. museum, searchable by artist or title.

Web Museum

http://sunsite/unc/edu/wm

Browse famous paintings, organized by artist and type of art—from Impressionism and medieval to contemporary—then click on the image to enlarge it screen-size. Biographies of artists and descriptions of types of art are at this 24-hour, free museum as well.

Auctions
OnSale
www.onsale.com

Bid on computers and equipment, sporting goods, and consumer electronics at the Web's biggest auction site.

Web Auction
www.webauction.com

Bid on a variety of products, starting at only $1.

Books
Amazon
www.amazon.com

This online bookstore, with over 2 million titles, is searchable by title, author, or topic and offers deep discounts. The site has reviews and recommendations, plus free e-mail reminders of books you may like.

Barnes & Noble
www.barnesandnoble.com

The big chain's online store is searchable by title, author, or topic and offers deep discounts on purchases, many live author chats, reviews and interviews from print, television, and radio outlets, and recommendations.

Books.com
www.books.com

Online store offers a huge selection of titles, easily searchable, at 20 to 80 percent discounts, and has reviews and book news.

BookSearch
www.booksearch.com

This site offers a free search service for out-of-print and rare books. It actually hunts for books instead of just checking its own database.

Bookwire

www.bookwire.com

A comprehensive resource about books and the publishing industry, with links to author Web sites, author appearances, reviews, and resources for writers.

The Independent Reader

www.independentreader.com

A guide to independent bookstores nationwide, this site offers monthly reviews of recommended books, with links to the stores' sites.

The Romance Reader

www.theromancereader.com

Hundreds of romance novel reviews, plus articles, author interviews, book signings calendar, and freebies (newsletters, bookmarks, even books) from the novelists.

Business and Finance

EDGAR Online

www.edgar-online.com

Corporate filings by public companies to the Securities and Exchange Commission are searchable by company name, filing type, or date. Full financial statements of companies are available to paid subscribers.

E*Trade

www.etrade.com

Buy stocks, mutual funds, and options online, plus track market indexes and favorite stocks.

Hoover's Online

www.hoovers.com

This site features company profiles, addresses and telephone numbers, key executives, statistics such as annual sales, number of employees, and recent stock price, and job openings. It is searchable by company name, industry, region, or amount of sales. Extra services are available to paid subscribers, such as archives of company news stories and historical financial details.

Idea Cafe

www.ideacafe.com

Information, quizzes, and resources for small business owners are provided with a light, humorous touch. Profiles, message boards, and handy tips are included as well.

The Motley Fool

www.fool.com/index.htm

David and Tom Gardner, authors of several investment guides, offer advice on investing in stocks, financial news, and analysis for the individual investor. The site also has bulletin boards and a searchable database by topic, and is also on America Online.

The Quote

www.quote.com

This site features stock quotes, breaking financial news, and overall performance for specific industries and cities; fee for real-time stock chart action.

Small Office

www.smalloffice.com

Articles and tips for small businesses, from sales and marketing, creating a Web site, saving money, and increasing efficiency, from *Home Office Computing* and *Small Office Computing* magazines.

The Street.com

www.thestreet.com

Stock quotes, breaking financial news, and commentary are included on this site. A fee is charged for stock and mutual fund tracking and other special features.

Cars
Auto-By-Tel

www.autobytel.com

Buy a new or used car, easily searchable by model type, with information on leases, reviews, and other resources.

Catalogs
CatalogLink

www.cataloglink.com

Browse offerings or order catalogs from many retailers, selling everything from clothing and home and gift items to sports, business, and computer equipment.

Catalog Mart

http://catalog.savvy.com

Browse or order from over 10,000 catalogs on over 800 subjects, from clothing to business and computer equipment.

The Gap

www.gap.com

The casual clothing chain's site has a mix-and-match feature to show how different styles, types, and colors go together with varying hair color and skin types, plus catalog listings, pictures, and a store locator.

J. Crew

www.jcrew.com

This site has catalog listings and pictures plus a store locator.

Lands' End

www.landsend.com

This site features catalog listings for clothing, luggage, and bed linens, plus an overstock section with discounts of up to 75 percent off.

Spiegel

www.spiegel.com

The Spiegel site has catalog listings for intimate apparel, electronics, and a deep discount section.

Children's Interest

Bedtime-Story

http://the-office.com/bedtime-story

Featured at this site are beautifully illustrated stories for children, searchable by topic—such as magical or humorous—and age group, plus plot summaries and estimated reading times.

Bonus.com

www.bonus.com

Over 1,000 activities for children, including quizzes, games, puzzles, educational material, and surfing to child-safe Web sites are included at this site.

Children's Express

www.ce.org

Monthly magazine with serious articles written by, and for, teenagers and preteens, largely on culture or politics.

Disney Books

www.disney.com/DisneyBooks

Read *Bambi*, *The Lion King*, and other beloved stories with colorful illustrations and sound clips.

Disney's Daily Blast

www.disneyblast.com

This site has daily games, activities, on-line crafts projects, and jokes for children. Read regular interactive stories and animated comics, and learn the alphabet and numbers with famous Disney characters.

Getting Real

www.gettingreal.com

A teenagers' site, this has weekly diary entries from teenagers, each focused on choosing a career, finding a college, arts, sports, or technology. Games, activities, message boards, and links to sites of teenage interest are included.

Kidnews

www.vsa.cape.com/~powens/Kidnews3.html

Articles written by children or classrooms include news, features, fiction, sports, and poetry.

Yahooligans!

www.yahooligans.com

From the search engine Yahoo!, articles and news on this site range from science, world geography, cultures, and history to art, entertainment, sports, plus games and bulletin boards.

City Guides

At Hand

www.athand.com

A guide to California, this site includes sightseeing, real estate, and arts, plus local guides for San Francisco, Los Angeles, Silicon Valley, and San Diego.

Boston.com

www.boston.com

From the *Boston Globe* and *Boston Magazine*, this site is a travel guide to New England, plus restaurants, arts, and nightlife for Boston.

CitySearch

www.citysearch.com

Extensive listings are included for nightlife, restaurants, music, art, talks, hotels, and shopping in about a dozen cities in the United States, including New York, San Francisco, Washington, D.C., Nashville, and Raleigh/Durham. Searchable by category, for example, restaurants can be searched by gardens, fireplaces, singles, and live music.

Lycos CityGuides

http://cityguide.lycos.com

Included are short guides to 400 cities in the United States, including maps, business listings, news, and description, plus Web links and descriptions for certain cities worldwide, especially Europe and North America.

New York Magazine

www.newyorkmag.com

This site has restaurant, movie, theater, music and art reviews, plus articles and personal ads.

Sidewalk

www.sidewalk.com

At this site you'll find extensive listings and many reviews for restaurants, movies, theater, nightlife, art, music, and shopping for nine cities in the United States, including New York, San Francisco, and Seattle; searchable by category.

Washington, DC City Pages

www.dcpages.com

Restaurant, music, theater, and art reviews, plus a DC top ten feature are included at this site.

Yahoo! Metros

www.yahoo.com/promotions/metros

Yahoo's city guide features Web links to resources and businesses in a dozen cities, including New York, Boston, Chicago, Miami, and Austin. You can also make your own local guide by typing in your zip code at local.yahoo.com.

Consumer Safety/Privacy

The Anonymizer

www.anonymizer.com

Surf Web sites without being tracked or send e-mail anonymously through this site.

Better Business Bureau

www.bbb.org

Learn how to recognize common scams, plus tips on buying safely and descriptions of the bureau's dispute resolution programs.

Computer Virus Hoaxes

www.kumite.com/myths

Learn to spot virus hoaxes on the Internet and read about well-known cases.

Cookie Central

www.cookiecentral.com

The last word on cookies, which allow Web sites to track your habits and preferences on the Web, this site also includes privacy protection tips and the pros and cons of cookies.

CyberPatrol

www.cyberpatrol.com

This site has child protection software to block objectionable online material.

CyberSitter

www.cybersitter.com

Child protection software to block objectionable online material is available at this site.

National Foundation for Consumer Credit

www.nfcc.org

Locate authorized budget counseling and debt management services—searchable by city—plus information on credit reports, bankruptcy, and a debt quiz from this network of nonprofit community budget counseling groups.

National Fraud Information Center

www.fraud.org

Learn how to recognize common scams, especially in telemarketing and against seniors, and know your rights under the law.

This site from the National Consumers League also provides tips on the safest ways to participate in online auctions.

NetNanny

www.netnanny.com

This site has child-protection software to block objectionable online material.

Pretty Good Privacy

www.pgp.com

Software to scramble your e-mail for privacy protection is available at this site.

Scambusters

www.scambusters.com

This site features a newsletter with tips on recognizing and preventing Internet scams, spam, and hoaxes.

SurfWatch

www.surfwatch.com

Child-protection software to block objectionable online material is available at this site.

Cosmetics
Cover Girl

www.covergirl.com

Makeup tips for face, eyes, lips, and nails, plus advice for quick makeovers can be found on this site.

Revlon

www.revlon.com

This site has information on cosmetics, hair, and fragrance products. A virtual face feature lets you pick a makeup look and offers detailed advice.

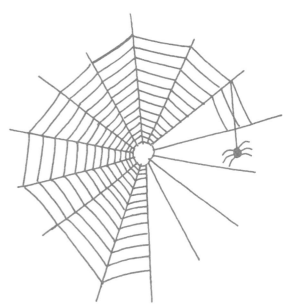

Crafts
Craftsearch

www.craftsearch.com

Search stores and suppliers for hobby, craft, sewing, and quilting by zip code. There are almost 5,000 links for these topics.

Dating
Love@1st Site

www.love@1st-site.com

This matchmaking service offers profiles and photographs, plus a privacy feature. It costs to join, but there is a free trial offer.

Match.com

www.match.com

Matchmaking service, with profiles and a privacy feature, charges a fee, but there is a free trial offer.

Education
American School Directory

www.asd.com

Basic facts on all public, private, and parochial grade and high schools in the United States, with links to their Web sites, can be found at this site.

FastWeb

www.fastweb.com

This site is a free college and graduate scholarship search service. Type in your profile and likely matches from the thousands in FastWeb's database will be sent by e-mail. Federal and local financial aid information, such as grants and loans, is also available.

Kids Web

www.npac.syr.edu/textbook/kidsweb

A library of information and links for children, from kindergarten through high school, is offered at this site. The site is searchable by subjects such as science (divided into biology, astronomy, chemistry, and so on), social studies, and the arts.

ScholarStuff

www.scholarstuff.com

This site is a directory of thousands of college and university Web sites in the United States and abroad.

Entertainment
ABC

www.abc.com

Look for plot summaries, cast biographies, and trivia quizzes of popular ABC shows such as *Ellen*, *NYPD Blue*, daytime soap operas, plus news shows at this site.

Ain't It Cool News

www.aint-it-cool-news.com

Gossip, advance news, and reviews (by amateurs) of test screenings of movies in production are featured at this site.

Blockbuster Video

www.blockbuster.com

Movie videos for sale or rental, music CDs and CD-ROM games for sale, plus some entertainment news can be found at this site.

CBS

http://marketing.cbs.com

Look for David Letterman's "Top 10 Lists," plus information on shows such as *60 Minutes*, *Murphy Brown*, daytime soap operas, and news shows.

Cinemachine

www.cinemachine.com

This site has movie reviews from print and online publications nationwide, searchable by title or keyword.

Dilbert

www.unitedmedia/comics/dilbert

This the official site of Dilbert, the famous comic strip by Scott Adams, which spoofs office life.

The Dominion

www.scifi.com

From the Sci-Fi cable television channel, this site offers science fiction galore, with movie clips and trailers, classic radio dramas (including Orson Welles), celebrity chats, games, and an online store.

Entertainment Asylum

www.asylum.com

This site has movie and television news, celebrity interviews, events coverage, and chat. Included are sound and video clips (requiring RealPlayer) in genres from science fiction to drama. Also accessible on America Online.

Entertainment News Daily

http://entertainmentnewsdaily.com

Featured on this site are book, theater, movie, music, and television news from major newspapers and trade publications distributed by the New York Times Syndicate.

E! Online

www.eonline.com

This site from the E! entertainment cable channel has movie and television news, gossip, sound and video clips of movie premieres, and chat.

Girls On Film

www.girlsonfilm.com

Offering movie reviews from four women in their twenties, this site also has movie news, celebrity interviews, gossip, and articles from readers.

GIST TV

www.gist.com

This site has local TV listings by zip code, which can be customized by time, channel, and show type; also included are articles, video previews of television programs, and chat forums.

Hollywood Online

www.hollywood.com

A guide to official movie Web sites and reviews, this site also has sound clips of celebrity interviews, entertainment news, and games.

Internet Movie Database

www.imdb.com

This vast resource has facts about over 100,000 movies, including cast, crew, plot summaries, reviews, film studios, running time, press releases, and more.

MovieLink

www.movielink.com

An online version of MovieFone, you can check movie times and buy tickets at local theaters. Search by title, star, time, type, and zip code.

MovieWeb

www.movieweb.com

Featured are video clips of trailers, photographs, plot summaries, and production notes from upcoming, current, and past movies, plus links to the movies' and studios' official sites.

Mr. Cranky's Guide to This Week at the Movies

http://internet-plaza.net/zone/mrcranky/thisweek.html

Unusually opinionated but often wildly amusing, this site has current movie reviews, with message boards for each film.

Mr. Showbiz

www.showbiz.com

Here you will find movie and television news, celebrity interviews, gossip, reviews, searchable database, games, and chat.

NBC TV Central

www.nbc.com/tvcentral/index.html

Look for plot summaries, cast biographies, trivia quizzes, and awards for favorite shows like *Seinfeld*, *ER*, *Frasier*, *Mad About You*, *Friends*, and daytime soap operas.

The Oscars

www.oscar.com

The official Academy Awards site, it has current winners, interviews and photographs, plus a searchable database of past winners.

PBS

www.pbs.org

Information and schedule dates for many public television programs on science, travel, nature, talk, mystery, children's shows (such as *Sesame Street*), and games.

Playbill

www.playbill.com

A comprehensive theater lovers site, you will find reviews, articles, theater listings nationwide, ticket purchases, plus tons of links to Web sites of Broadway shows, Tony Awards, musical comedy, history, etc.

Reel.com

www.reel.com

Rent or buy movie videos at this site, including thousands of classic, art house, foreign, and rare films. If you're having a tough time deciding, the delightful Movie Map feature lists movie categories with many subdivisions, such as Suspense/Thriller/Psychological/Mind Games, and suggests a long list of sleeper gems you may not have heard of.

Roger Ebert & the Movies

www.suntimes.com/ebert/ebert.html

Read movie reviews and learn about favorite movies from the *Chicago Sun-Times* critic of Siskel & Ebert fame.

Telerama

www.cinema.pgh.pa.us/movie/reviews

This movie review search engine has links to reviews in print and online publications (more extensive than Internet Movie Database's reviews) and is searchable by title or keyword.

Ticketmaster Online

www.ticketmaster.com

Buy concert or theater tickets, searchable by keyword or state.

Tony Awards Online

www.tonys.org

This official Tony Award site has articles, interviews, Tony Award nominations and winners from Broadway shows—past and present—a theater locator for shows, plus video and sound clips of the award ceremony.

TVgen

www.tvguide.com

TV Guide's site offers television listings by zip code, soap opera and science fiction sections, movie reviews and times, entertainment news, gossip, and games.

Food/Drink/Restaurants
Coffee Journal

www.tigeroak.com/coffeejournal

Articles and recipes about coffee and cafe culture worldwide are available at this site from the print magazine *Coffee Journal*.

Cuisinenet

www.cuisinenet.com

This site has thousands of restaurant reviews in a limited number of cities, but offers helpful price and opening hours facts.

CyberMeals

www.cybermeals.com

A free take-out and delivery service from thousands of restaurants in certain cities nationwide, menus are available in cuisines from Asian, European, and American.

Epicurious

http://food.epicurious.com

Recipes from great chefs worldwide, articles from *Gourmet* and *Bon Appetit* magazines, a limited number of restaurant reviews, and a searchable database of food articles from Conde Nast publications are all available at this site.

Fodor's Restaurant Index

www.fodors.com/ri.cgi

A thorough guide from the Fodor's travel guidebooks, this site has restaurant reviews for dozens of cities worldwide.

Food TV

www.foodtv.com

This site from the TV Food Network offers recipes from its many shows, from *Too Hot Tamales* to *Essence of Emeril*, answers to cooking questions, and a glossary of cooking terms and tips.

Godiva Chocolatier

www.godiva.com

Buy Godiva chocolates online, browse recipes, and find out where stores are located.

Good Cooking!

www.goodcooking.com

A gigantic collection of recipes, many submitted by readers, this site also has articles about types of food, ethnic cuisines, and facts; not especially well-organized.

Hot! Hot! Hot!

www.hothothot.com

Giant list of international spicy sauces for sale, this site is searchable by heat level, country of origin, ingredient, or name.

Meals for You

www.mealsforyou.com

Find many recipes, well-organized by type of food (seafood, meat, vegetarian), ingredients, diets, ethnic cuisines, and nutritional content.

NetGrocer

www.netgrocer.com

The first national online supermarket delivers nonperishables— from baby food and care items, beverages, canned goods, pet food, and pasta to staples like paper products—by Federal Express.

Once A Month Cooking

http://members.aol.com/OAMCLoop/index.html

Learn how to cook one month's worth of meals in one day, with tips on planning, buying in bulk, cooking and freezing, plus recipes.

Over the Coffee

www.cappuccino.com

A complete resource on coffee history, health, cyber and real world cafes, literature, health, and home roasting, this site also lists retailers for coffee beans and equipment.

Sally's Place

www.bpe.com

This site has restaurant reviews for several dozen cities plus detailed articles on specific foods, ethnic cuisines, and beverages.

Virtual Vineyards

www.virtualvin.com

Wines, food, and gourmet gifts are available at this online store.

Waiters on Wheels

www.waitersonwheels.com

This site offers a delivery service from restaurants in California, Washington, and Nevada. Various cuisines are available, with online menus. A fee is charged for each order.

The Webtender

www.webtender.com

This handy online bartending service offers instructions on mixing drinks and is searchable by drink name, ingredients, alcohol, and glass type.

Zagat Restaurant Survey

http://cgi.pathfinder.com:80/cgi-bin/zagat/homepage

From the *Zagat* print guides, this site offers reviews of top restaurants in several dozen cities in the United States that are compiled from reader comments.

Foreign Languages
Travlang Foreign Languages for Travelers

www.travlang.com/languages

This site offers common phrases in dozens of foreign languages, plus sound clips to hear correct pronunciations.

Free Stuff
Club FreeShop

www.freeshop.com

Free products and trial offers, from magazines and software to catalogs, are all available at this site.

Games
Gamespot

www.gamespot.com

Featured at this site are computer game reviews, downloads, and tips.

Happy Puppy

www.happypuppy.com

This site is a gathering place for computer game fans, with news, reviews, game downloads, and message boards.

Jeopardy!

www.station.sony.com/jeopardy

Play the famous television trivia game show here.

The Riddler

www.riddler.com

Many trivia quizzes and puzzles are available here, plus the chance to win prizes.

Suspect

www.electrastudios.com/suspect

Play detective and search for clues in this online murder mystery.

You Don't Know Jack

www.bezerk.com/netshow/index.html

Popular culture trivia quizzes are presented in a television game show-style, with sound clips and the chance to win prizes. Based on the popular CD-ROM.

Gardening
Gardening.com

www.gardening.com

An encyclopedia of over 1,500 plants, a plant problem-solver, and directory of related Web sites, searchable by subject, region, or keyword are found at this site.

Virtual Garden

http://vg.com

This gardener's best friend is on this Pathfinder site and features an encyclopedia of about 3,000 plants and trees, articles on gardening advice, seasonal tips and weather forecasts searchable by time zone, and answers to questions.

Genealogy
Ancestry.com

www.ancestry.com

This site offers free lessons on how to trace your family tree through birth, marriage, and death certificates and other records such as the Social Security Death Index. An online store sells genealogy software, books, and supplies.

Cyndi's List of Genealogy Sites

www.cyndislist.com

This site offers over 28,000 links in over 90 categories from different countries to libraries, publications, military sources, mailing lists, and newsgroups.

Gifts
1-800-FLOWERS

www.1800flowers.com

This online delivery service offers bouquets, plants, and food and gift baskets, which can be searched by item, price range, or special occasion.

Cybershop.com

www.cybershop.com

Gourmet cookware, foods, electronics, and home furnishings products purchased at this site are shipped gift-wrapped within 24 hours. The directory is easily searchable.

The Virtual Florist

www.virtualflorist.com

An online delivery service for bouquets and gift baskets, this site also offers free floral electronic greeting cards if your budget is tight.

Government

Census Bureau

www.census.gov

Oodles of statistics are available at this site on everything from population numbers, household income, age, ethnic group, housing starts, and businesses to computer ownership. Many reports as well.

Department of Education

www.ed.gov

Useful information at this site includes publications for parents on helping children learn various school subjects, using a library and preparing for tests, federal financial aid for college students, plus federal efforts to improve technology in schools.

Federal Trade Commission's Consumerline

www.ftc.gov/bcp/conline/conline.htm

This site from the commission's Bureau of Consumer Protection offers publications on all types of frauds including real estate, cars, credit, health and fitness, and the Internet. A separate section details how to report fraud.

Fedworld

www.fedworld.gov

A huge federal government site, you can find or buy reports or publications, find specific agency sites, browse databases with tax form information and federal jobs.

Food and Drug Administration

www.fda.gov

This site offers detailed descriptions of approved drugs for humans and animals, diet supplements, food, and cosmetics, plus drug news and consumer advice.

Healthfinder

www.healthfinder.gov

This encyclopedic site from the U.S. Department of Health and Human Services offers the latest government health news: choosing

quality care—health insurance plans, hospitals, long-term care, and medical treatment—hot topics like cancer, AIDS, and food safety; sections on seniors and children; support groups; and publications.

Internal Revenue Service

www.irs.ustreas.gov/prod/cover.html

This useful site has information on filing tax returns electronically, frequently asked tax preparation questions, regulations in plain English, downloadable forms and publications, and telephone/fax numbers for tax tips.

National Aeronautics & Space Administration

www.nasa.gov

At this site you will find the latest news, research findings, and history of the NASA space program. A multimedia gallery offers fascinating photographs and video of the Mars landing and space shuttle launches.

PubMed

www.ncbi.nlm.nih/gov/PubMed

This site gives you free access to MEDLINE with its nine million articles in medical journals from the National Institute of Health's National Library of Medicine database that feature the most recent research findings.

Small Business Administration

www.sbaonline.sba.gov

Featured on this site are extensive FAQs on starting, financing, and growing a business, plus a directory of offices and resource centers by state and a library of shareware for running a business.

Social Security Administration

www.ssa.gov

Find out your estimated retirement benefit based on your lifetime earnings, learn about retirement, survivors, disability and Supplemental Security Income benefits, and find the closest Social Security office by typing in your zip code.

White House

www.whitehouse.gov

Read presidential speeches, news releases, and achievements of the current Administration, plus learn how the federal government works and the history of the White House. There is also an easy-to-read children's section.

Health/Fitness
American Psychological Association

www.apa.org/pubinfo

This site has online booklets on mental health issues (from memories of childhood abuse and depression to sexual harassment) plus tips on how to choose a therapist.

CyberDiet

www.cyberdiet.com

Get tips on proper eating and exercise, with a database of calories and nutrients for common foods, nutritional profiles (based on age, sex, build, and activity level), and daily food planners.

The Doctor Directory

www.doctordirectory.com

Search this site for addresses, telephone numbers, specialties, medical school attended, and board memberships of physicians. You can search by state and city.

FitnessLink

www.fitnesslink.com

A comprehensive resource on fitness, this site has exercise, nutrition, diet and stress-busting tips, news, mailing lists and publications, plus message boards.

GriefNet

www.rivendell.org

This site offers support groups for the bereaved, from the widowed to parents whose children have died to women who have given up babies for adoption.

InteliHealth

www.intelihealth.com

From the Johns Hopkins Medical Center, this site has information on adult health by topic, medical journal article summaries, a nutrition database, and a nationwide doctor finder.

Internet Mental Health

www.mentalhealth.com

This site has descriptions and treatments for over fifty mental health problems, a directory of dozens of psychiatric drugs (with information and side effects), and medical journal articles.

KidsHealth.org

www.kidshealth.org

From pediatric experts at The Nemours Foundation, funded by the DuPont family, this site has resources on children's physical and mental health, first aid emergency tips, treatment, and support groups for parents. A children's section contains games, recipes, and animations on how the human body works.

Mayo Health Oasis

www.mayo.ivi.com

Extensive medical and health information from the world-famous Mayo Clinic includes drug and disease directories, and resources on women's and children's health, heart disease, cancer, allergies, and Alzheimer's. Medical and diet questions are answered by e-mail.

MedHelp

www.medhelp.org/index.htm

This nonprofit organization offers thousands of medical journal articles, support group listings, a patient network to find others with the same illness, and medical questions answered by e-mail.

Medscape

www.medscape.com

This comprehensive medical and health resource includes thousands of medical journal articles and daily medical news, searchable by topic, from surgery to women's health to managed care, drug name, or medical term.

Your Health Daily

www.nytsyn.com/med

Health and fitness articles from major newspapers and medical journals distributed by the New York Times Syndicate, plus message boards, are found at this site.

Home Decoration
Ask A Designer

www.askadesigner.com

Ask home design questions by e-mail, browse design tips and past questions, or locate an interior designer by zip code.

Home Ideas

www.homeideas.com

Extensive articles on decorating are searchable by room, plus there are free product catalogs and brochures and message boards.

HouseNet

www.housenet.com

Offering extensive resources for home and garden improvement and decorating, this site has articles, estimators for how much paint or wallpaper you'll need, and contractors by zip code.

Martha Stewart Living

www.marthastewart.com

Highlights of Martha Stewart's magazine, television program, radio show, and books provide decorating, entertaining, gardening, and home improvement tips plus recipes.

Insurance
Insuremarket

www.insuremarket.com

This site from Quicken, the maker of the personal finance software Intuit, offers competitive prices from different companies on

health, life, and auto insurance, plus advice on choosing a policy and figuring out how much coverage you need.

InsWeb

www.insweb.com

Receive competitive quotes from different companies on health, car, and life insurance online or by e-mail, plus articles and quizzes to help determine what kind and how much insurance you need.

Jobs/Careers
About Work

www.aboutwork.com

A community site on job hunting and career advancement, this site offers advice, weekly hot jobs profiles, bulletin boards, and sections for working at home, small business, and students.

Career Mosaic

www.careermosaic.com

Thousands of job listings, resume postings, and company profiles are included at this site. The extensive resource list includes professional organizations, salary and market trends data, career articles library, and news links.

CareerCity

www.careercity.com

Thousands of current job openings, hot links to 27,000 employers, free resume posting, salary surveys, directories, and hundreds of articles on careers; from the publishers of *JobBank* and *Knock 'em Dead* books.

Cool Jobs

www.cooljobs.com

Learn how to apply for various glamour and fun jobs including Club Med, Ben & Jerry's, television, movies, circus, F.B.I., and space jobs.

Internet Career Plaza

www.careerplaza.com

Job listings and placement agencies at this site are searchable by industry and region. Tools to write and post resumes are included.

Monster Board

www.monsterboard.com

Thousands of job listings, resume postings, company profiles and career tips can be found at this site. Build a desired job profile and a personal job search agent will e-mail likely job listings to you.

Legal
FindLaw

www.findlaw.com

An extensive directory of legal resources, this site has U.S. Supreme Court rulings, law firm listings nationwide, news, topics from labor to intellectual property, federal, state, and international laws; jobs; and message boards.

Maps
Mapquest

www.mapquest.com

Find a local map or get driving directions between two addresses by typing in any address in the United States, then zoom in for a closer look.

Music/Sound
Broadcast.com

www.broadcast.com

Sound clips available at this site range from concerts and CDs, live television and radio news, author interviews, business, sports, and public affairs. This is the biggest source of multimedia on the

Web due to partnerships with many television and radio interview networks and other companies.

CDnow

www.cdnow.com

Music CDs for sale—searchable by artist, album title, song title, or record label—are available at this online store. Articles and reviews cover all music genres from rock and jazz to classical.

CD Universe

www.cduniverse.com

Music CDs for sale—searchable by artist, album title, song title, and genre—with many sound clips, are available at this online store.

Classical Insites

www.classicalinsites.com

Biographies of famous performers and classical, romantic, and opera composers—from Beethoven and Chopin to Verdi—plus lists of recommended recordings. Also included is a music history section, sound clips of concerts, a music CD store, and message boards.

Country Spotlight

www.countryspotlight.com

Country music news, reviews, celebrity interviews from Loretta Lynn to LeAnn Rimes, and chat can be found at this site.

E Music

www.emusic.com

This site has music CDs for sale, including many hard-to-find items.

JAM TV

www.jamtv.com

Featured at this site are sound clips of concerts and interviews with rock musicians, plus biographies, list of recordings, news, chat, and CDs for sale.

Jazz Central Station

www.jazzcentralstation.com

Jazz news, articles about musicians, sound clips of recordings, music CDs for sale, and message boards are all included at this site.

MTV Online

www.mtv.com

Rock music news, video and sound clips, interviews with musicians, and celebrity chats can be found at this site from the MTV cable channel.

Music Boulevard

www.musicblvd.com

At this site you will find music CDs and cassettes for sale—searchable by artist, album title, or song title—plus special content for rock, jazz, and classical fans. Music news from MTV and VH1 is also available.

Opera America

www.operaam.org

Find out when and where specific operas are being performed, and by which opera company, from this nonprofit group's database of schedules.

Tower Records

www.towerrecords.com

The Tower site has music CDs for sale—searchable by artist, album title, song title, and genre—plus sound clips.

News
CNN Interactive

www.cnn.com

This site has late-breaking stories, with audio clips, from world, show business, and science/technology news.

C-SPAN

www.c-span.org

Video and sound clips of congressional hearings, Washington press conferences, speeches and court sessions, and book programs are available at this site from the C-SPAN cable channel.

Electronic Newsstand

www.enews.com

A magazine lover's site, featured are capsule summaries of stories from dozens of magazines, news about magazines, and "hype hell/hype heaven" features on who's getting bad and good press. Searchable by magazine name or category.

Los Angeles Times

www.latimes.com

The online version of this daily newspaper.

New York Times on the Web

www.nytimes.com

This online version of the paper has Book Review articles dating from 1980, author interviews and readings, real estate and job classified ads, plus online features such as CyberTimes—articles concerning online issues—and many message boards on a wide range of topics. Easily searchable.

NPR

www.npr.org

National Public Radio online has sound clips of complete *All Things Considered* and *Morning Edition* shows (with RealAudio) plus news story summaries.

Pathfinder

www.pathfinder.com

A huge site for Time-Warner publications, included are *People*, *Money*, *Time*, *Fortune*, and *Entertainment Weekly* magazines. The database is searchable by topic or publication.

Total News

www.totalnews.com

This site has links to dozens of news sites, including newspapers, television, radio, and magazines. It is searchable by category (national news, business, opinion) and topic.

Wall Street Journal Interactive

www.wsj.com

Featuring highlights from the print version, this site also includes original articles on small business and technology and a library with articles from over 3,000 publications (per-article fees). Membership fee is required.

USA Today

www.usatoday.com

An online version of the daily newspaper, this site also has articles on noteworthy Web sites and Internet issues.

Washington Post

www.washingtonpost.com

An online version of the daily newspaper.

Package Tracking
Federal Express

www.fedex.com

Track packages sent worldwide by Federal Express, arrange for pickups, fill out and print air bills, and find out addresses and hours of the nearest drop-off locations.

United Parcel Service

www.ups.com/tracking/tracking.html

Track packages sent worldwide by UPS, arrange for pickups, and find out addresses, hours, and maps of the nearest drop-off locations.

Parenting

Babies Online

www.babiesonline.com

This site has birth announcements with photographs and descriptions (searchable by baby's name and birthdate) plus free product samples and links to parenting sites.

BabyCenter

www.babycenter.com

This comprehensive reference site for new and expectant parents has pregnancy, baby care, health and nutrition information. Medical experts answer e-mail questions, and there is a store selling discount baby care products.

Family.com

www.family.com

At this site you'll find articles and message boards for parents on child rearing issues (from adoption, divorce, single parents, and discipline to family moves), planning activities, education—including helping with homework and gifted children—and games for children.

Parent Soup

www.parentsoup.com

A community site for parents with children of all ages, from teen-agers to babies. Features bulletin boards on topics such as discipline problems, education, and sibling rivalry, and news archives of interests ranging from product recalls to health and legislation issues. Experts offer advice to e-mail questions.

People Finders

Directories that list telephone numbers, addresses, and e-mail addresses of people nationwide include:

Bigfoot

www.bigfoot.com

555-1212.com
www.555-1212.com

Four11
www.Four11.com

Infospace
www.infospace.com

Internet Address Finder
www.iaf.net

Switchboard
www.switchboard.com

Pets
Animal Network

www.petchannel.com

At this site are breed descriptions and photographs of pets—dogs, cats, horses, fish—plus message boards on care, health, and behavior.

Cat Fancier's Home Page

www.fanciers.com

A comprehensive cat lover's site, you'll find breed descriptions and photographs, health care information, advice on raising a kitten, buying a purebred, resources on breeders and cat shows, and a bibliography.

Real Estate
Bank Rate Monitor

www.bankrate.com

Compare mortgage rates at specific banks in over 100 cities nationwide and consult step-by-step tips in choosing and applying

for a mortgage. A chart comparing credit card rates and tips on home equity loans and bank ATM rates is also offered.

Homebuyer's Fair

www.homefair.com/home

Compare schools, crime, demographics, and insurance rates in cities nationwide. Handy calculators figure out how big a mortgage you can afford, cost-of-living comparisons between domestic and foreign cities, monthly mortgage payments, renting versus buying a home, and the value of your home. Recent home sales in your city are also provided.

Reference
All-In-One Search Page

www.albany.net/allinone

A one-stop shopping for many reference sources, here you will find *Bartlett's Familiar Quotations*, Shakespeare's complete works, current U.S. legislation, people finders, and search engines.

Ask An Expert

www.askanexpert.com/askanexpert

Experts in many fields in a dozen broad categories—including career/industry, science/technology, and health—answer questions by e-mail or offer helpful Web sites.

Encarta

http://encarta.msn.com/Encarta/Home.asp

A smaller version of Microsoft's Encarta CD-ROM encyclopedia.

Encyclopedia Brittanica Online

www.eb.com

This site has thousands of articles from the print encyclopedia plus many online articles, including pictures, maps, a dictionary, and Web links. Fee for membership, but there is a free trial period.

Encyclopedia Mythica

www.pantheon.org/mythica

Here you can learn about thousands of myths and legends—from Greek and Roman to Celtic, Norse, Aztec, and Native American—with pictures.

Grolier Multimedia Encyclopedia

www.gme.grolier.com

This site has thousands of articles from the CD-ROM encyclopedia, with pictures, maps, Web links, and a children's section. Fee-based, but there is a free trial.

Learn2.com

www.learn2.com

An excellent reference for practical and fun tips, here you'll find useful information on home repair (fix a leaky faucet or toilet, defrost a freezer, clean a bathroom), personal care (get a close shave, repair pantyhose, tie a necktie), and parenting (childproof a home, burp a baby).

National Association of Investigative Specialists

www.pimall.com/nais

A comprehensive resource for Web sites plus books and articles on investigating people or businesses, this site is from a trade association for private detectives.

Reminder Service
E-Organizer

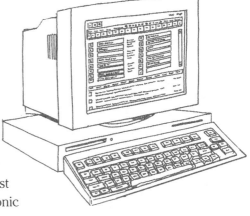

www.eorganizer.com

You'll never forget birthdays, anniversaries, parties, and other important days again: this service will e-mail you a reminder. Post your lists of chores and notes as well on this free online electronic organizer.

Science
Discovery Channel Online

www.discovery.com

This site from the Discovery cable channel features articles on nature, exploration, science, and technology, with a searchable database.

Seniors
Senior.com

www.senior.com

A money club site, here you'll find FAQs on personal and business finance, chats, information on classes and events, and news from national and local publications for seniors.

SeniorNet

www.seniornet.org

This site from a nonprofit group that educates older people about computers features over 200 message boards for people age fifty-five and older on topics from current events, health, religion, cooking, gardening, and computers to politics; you can also e-mail pen pals.

Sports
CBS Sportsline

www.sportsline.com

From CBS Sports, this site has articles on men's and women's sports, scores, sound and video clips, and chat.

ESPN

www.espn.go.com

This comprehensive resource for daily sports news from the ESPN cable channel covers sports worldwide.

GolfWeb

www.golfweb.com

Articles, golf courses worldwide searchable by country or name, message boards, even a partner locator can be found at this site.

Mountain Zone Skiing

www.mountainzone.com/ski/index.html

News from championship skiing worldwide, articles, product reviews and tips, interview sound clips, and message boards are found at this site.

SkiNet

www.skinet.com

This travel-oriented site has a resort finder that helps you pick a resort in the United States based on criteria such as lodging, value, snow quality, apres-ski nightlife, or vacation packages. A snow report for different areas, plus message boards about ski resorts worldwide, are also included.

Toys
Beanie Babies

www.ty.com

This site from the toy maker Ty has photographs and an official list of the tiny stuffed animals, from Mel the Koala and Fleece the Lamb to Bernie the St. Bernard. Many other stuffed toys, such as cat and dog collections, are included.

Dr. Toy

www.drtoy.com

Over 500 toys and children's products have been selected by a nonprofit organization for children's resources, based upon educational value and durability, and are described by age group, toy type, and cost.

Vermont Teddy Bear Company

www.vtbear.com

An online store for the handcrafted stuffed animals, you can order bears for special occasions, bears wearing outfits, or bears in the buff. Same-day shipping is possible with gift boxes and cards.

Special Occasions
American Greetings

www.americangreetings.com

Many electronic greeting cards are available at this site from the well-known card company. Searchable by special occasion, plus a reminder service. A fee is charged for animated cards only.

The Cyber Greeting Collection

http://home.stlnet.com/~binnie/cybrcard.htm

Many electronic greeting cards, with instructions on how to personalize, are available in a variety of different categories.

Hallmark

www.hallmark.com

Over 1,000 electronic greeting cards, plus a reminder service, are available at this site from the well-known card company. A fee is charged for animated cards only.

How Are You.com

www.howareyou.com/cards.shtml

Electronic greeting cards in many different categories are searchable by occasion or specialty.

Internet Card Central

www.cardcentral.net

Many different categories of electronic greeting cards are available at this site.

Travel
American Airlines Net SAAver Fares

www.americanair.com

Reduced airfares on last-minute domestic and international American Airlines flights, plus lower hotel and car rental rates, are available to subscribers of its weekly e-mail list.

Arthur Frommer's Outspoken Encyclopedia of Travel

www.frommers.com

This site from Frommer, the author of the original *Europe on $5 A Day* guidebooks, offers sightseeing guides, customs, and hotels for 200 top cities and islands worldwide; helpful articles on budget travel and travel tips; plus travel reservations.

CyberRentals

http://cyberrentals.com/homepage.html

Search for or post a short-term vacation rental for homes, chalets, and condominiums worldwide, with photographs, costs, and descriptions.

Expedia

www.expedia.com

Comprehensive travel resources, from making airline and hotel reservations to a huge travel guide organized by country, are available at this site. Helpful features include airfare comparisons, currency converters, and a low airfare finder by e-mail.

Fodor's Travel Service

www.fodors.com

The personal trip planner can customize trips to over eighty cities worldwide, allowing you to select hotels and restaurants based on price and location. A bed-and-breakfast finder lets you pick from over 2,000 in the United States, searchable by state, amenities (lakeside, romantic, etc.), and activities. Essential information and activities from Fodor's guidebooks, articles, plus a low airfare finder are included as well.

Preview Travel

www.previewtravel.com/index.html

Choose hotel rooms and make reservations worldwide; searchable by cost, amenities, and specific hotel chain.

Priceline

www.priceline.com

Pick the price you want and PriceLine will try to match unsold seats and reduced airfares on major airlines for domestic and international flights.

Rough Guides

www.hotwired.com/rough

With information from the print guidebooks, this site emphasizes offbeat destinations in Europe, the United States, and India.

Spa-Finders

www.spafinders.com

A worldwide spa locator, this site is searchable by category such as luxury, New Age, adventure, weight management, various sports, location, and cost. Online bookings and special offers are also available.

The Trip.com

www.thetrip.com

This site offers airline reservations, airport maps, hotel reviews, tips, and a low airfare finder by e-mail.

Travelocity

www.travelocity.com

A huge travel guide organized by country, this site features airline reservations, hotel bookings, and low airfare finder by e-mail, from SABRE, the airline reservation system.

Worldview Systems

www.wvs.com

Organized by country, this site provides a detailed guide to hotels, restaurants, arts, and going out in over 200 destinations worldwide.

Women
Cybergrrl

www.cybergrrl.com

Features include Femina—a search engine for women's resources on the Web—Bookgrrl—reviews and interviews for books by women—forums, plus articles on careers, love and friends, family and travel.

Femina

www.femina.com

A clearinghouse of information for women, this site includes topics such as arts, business, health, family/motherhood, education, activities, and clubs for girls.

HomeArts Network

http://homearts.com

This site provides articles on family, food, home design and money, including many from *Good Housekeeping*, *Redbook*, and *Town & Country*.

Women's Wire

www.women.com/guide

A lifestyle magazine, this site has articles on careers, health, money, style, business owner profiles, forums, and daily "good news" for women. Specific information for certain cities is also available.

Zip Codes

U.S. Postal Service Zip Code Lookup
www.usps.gov/ncsc

ROB LIFLANDER is a pioneer in the Internet business, having worked in the online world since 1992. He has an MBA from Columbia University. He is the president of Solvent Media, a Web development firm specializing in Internet business strategy, design, and production. He has built dozens of Web sites in all areas of business, from small storefronts to major manufacturers. The hallmark of Solvent Media's work is its focus on Web business strategy as a solid foundation for online success. Visit them at *http://www.solventmedia.com/*

Index

We Have
EVERYTHING!

Available wherever books are sold!

Everything **After College Book**
$12.95, 1-55850-847-3

Everything **Astrology Book**
$12.95, 1-58062-062-0

Everything **Baby Names Book**
$12.95, 1-55850-655-1

Everything **Baby Shower Book**
$12.95, 1-58062-305-0

Everything **Barbeque Cookbook**
$12.95, 1-58062-316-6

Everything® **Bartender's Book**
$9.95, 1-55850-536-9

Everything **Bedtime Story Book**
$12.95, 1-58062-147-3

Everything **Beer Book**
$12.95, 1-55850-843-0

Everything **Bicycle Book**
$12.95, 1-55850-706-X

Everything **Build Your Own Home Page**
$12.95, 1-58062-339-5

Everything **Casino Gambling Book**
$12.95, 1-55850-762-0

Everything **Cat Book**
$12.95, 1-55850-710-8

Everything® **Christmas Book**
$15.00, 1-55850-697-7

Everything **College Survival Book**
$12.95, 1-55850-720-5

Everything **Cover Letter Book**
$12.95, 1-58062-312-3

Everything **Crossword and Puzzle Book**
$12.95, 1-55850-764-7

Everything **Dating Book**
$12.95, 1-58062-185-6

Everything **Dessert Book**
$12.95, 1-55850-717-5

Everything **Dog Book**
$12.95, 1-58062-144-9

Everything **Dreams Book**
$12.95, 1-55850-806-6

Everything **Etiquette Book**
$12.95, 1-55850-807-4

Everything **Family Tree Book**
$12.95, 1-55850-763-9

Everything **Fly-Fishing Book**
$12.95, 1-58062-148-1

Everything **Games Book**
$12.95, 1-55850-643-8

Everything **Get-a-Job Book**
$12.95, 1-58062-223-2

The ultimate reference for couples planning their wedding!

- Scheduling, budgeting, etiquette, hiring caterers, florists, and photographers
- Ceremony & reception ideas
- Over 100 forms and checklists
- And much, much more!

$12.95, 384 pages, 8" x 9¼"

Personal finance made easy—and fun!

- Create a budget you can live with
- Manage your credit cards
- Set up investment plans
- Money-saving tax strategies
- And much, much more!

$12.95, 288 pages, 8" x 9¼"

For more information, or to order, call 800-872-5627
or visit www.adamsmedia.com/everything
Adams Media Corporation, 260 Center Street, Holbrook, MA 02343

FIND MORE ON THIS TOPIC BY VISITING
BusinessTown.com
The Web's big site for growing businesses!

- ☑ **Separate channels on all aspects of starting and running a business**
- ☑ **Lots of info of how to do business online**
- ☑ **1,000+ pages of savvy business advice**
- ☑ **Complete web guide to thousands of useful business sites**
- ☑ **Free e-mail newsletter**
- ☑ **Question and answer forums, and more!**

http://www.businesstown.com